PRIMATE FIELD STUDIES

Series Titles:

    Strategies of Sex and Survival in Hamadryas Baboons: Through a Female Lens
    Larissa Swedell, Queens College, The City University of New York

Forthcoming Titles:

    The Gibbons of Khao Yai
    Thad Q. Bartlett, The University of Texas at San Antonio

    The Spectral Tarsier
    Sharon L. Gursky, Texas A&M University

    The Ecology and Behavior of the Goeldi's Monkey
    Leila M. Porter, The University of Washington, Seattle

    The Socioecology of Vervet and Patas Monkeys
    Jill D. Pruetz, Iowa State University

PRIMATE FIELD STUDIES

Many of us who conduct field studies on wild primates have witnessed a decline in the venues available to publish monographic treatments of our work. As researchers we have few choices other than to publish short technical articles on discrete aspects of our work in professional journals. Also in vogue are popular expositions, often written by non-scientists. To counter this trend, we have begun this series. Primate Field Studies is a venue both for publishing the full complement of findings of long-term studies, and for making our work accessible to a wider readership. Interested readers need not wait for atomized parts of long-term studies to be published in widely scattered journals; students need not navigate the technical literature to bring together a body of scholarship better served by being offered as a cohesive whole. We are interested in developing monographs based on single or multi-species studies. If you wish to develop a monograph, we encourage you to contact one of the series editors.

About the Editors:

Robert W. Sussman (Ph.D. Duke University) is currently Professor of Anthropology and Environmental Science at Washington University, St. Louis, Missouri and past Editor-in-Chief of *American Anthropologist*, the flagship journal of the American Anthropological Association. His research focuses on the ecology, behavior, evolution and conservation of non-human and human primates, and he has worked in Costa Rica, Guyana, Panama, Madagascar and Mauritius. He is the author of numerous scientific publications, including *Biological Basis of Human Behavior*, Prentice Hall (1999), *Primate Ecology and Social Structure* (two volumes), Pearson Custom Publishing (2003), and *The Origin and Nature of Sociality*, Aldine de Gruyter (2004).

Natalie Vasey (Ph.D. Washington University) is currently Assistant Professor of Anthropology at Portland State University, Portland, Oregon. Her research explores the behavioral ecology, life history adaptations, and evolution of primates, with a focus on the endangered and recently extinct primates of Madagascar. Her work has been published in leading scientific journals and she is currently a guest editor for a forthcoming special issue of the *American Journal of Primatology*, "New Developments in the Behavioral Ecology and Conservation of Ruffed Lemurs (*Varecia*)." The Primate Field Studies monograph series serves her goal to educate students, researchers, and the public-at-large about the lifestyles and conservation status of our closest relatives in the Animal Kingdom.

Strategies of Sex
and Survival in
Hamadryas Baboons

Strategies of Sex and Survival in Hamadryas Baboons
Through a Female Lens

Larissa Swedell

Queens College
The City University of New York

Upper Saddle River, New Jersey 07458

Library of Congress Cataloging-in-Publication Data

Swedell, Larissa.
  Strategies of sex and survival in hamadryas baboons: through a female lens/Larissa Swedell.
    p. cm — (Primate field studies)
  Includes bibliographical references and index.
    ISBN 0-13-184548-9
  1. Hamadryas baboon—Sexual behavior. 2. Social behavior in animals. I. Title. II. Series.

QL737.P93S88 2006
599.8'65—dc22

                                                                            2004043189

Publisher: Nancy Roberts
Editorial Assistant: Lee Peterson
Full Service Production Liaison: Joanne Hakim
Senior Marketing Manager: Marissa Feliberty
Assistant Manufacturing Manager: Mary Ann Gloriande
Cover Art Director: Jayne Conte
Cover Design: Kiwi Design
Cover Photos: *Main image front cover and image on back cover:* courtesy
    of Larissa Swedell, *top images from left:* (1) Frans Lanting / Minden Pictures;
    (2) Nigel J. Dennis / Photo Researchers, Inc.; (3) Charles Krebs /CORBIS;
    (4) Brand X Pictures / Getty Images, Inc.
Manager, Cover Visual Research & Permissions: Karen Sanatar
Director, Image Resource Center: Melinda Reo
Manager, Rights and Permissions: Zina Arabia
Manager, Visual Research: Beth Brenzel
Photo Coordinator: Joanne Dippel
Full-Service Project Management: Dennis Troutman/Stratford Publishing Services
Composition: Integra Software Services Pvt. Ltd.
Printer/Binder: Phoenix Book Tech Park

Credits and acknowledgments borrowed from other sources and reproduced, with
permission, in this textbook appear on appropriate page within text.

Pearson Education LTD., London
Pearson Education Singapore, Pte. Ltd
Pearson Education, Canada, Ltd
Pearson Education—Japan
Pearson Education Australia PTY, Limited

Pearson Education North Asia Ltd
Pearson Educación de Mexico, S.A. de C.V.
Pearson Education Malaysia, Pte. Ltd
Pearson Education, Upper Saddle River,
    New Jersey

10 9 8 7 6 5 4 3 2 1
ISBN 0-13-184548-9

to J. R. S. for his
insight and inspiration

Contents

List of Figures

List of Tables

Acknowledgments

This book is based largely on my dissertation research, conducted between 1996 and 1998 in Ethiopia. None of it would have taken place without the invitation extended to me by Cliff Jolly and Jane Phillips-Conroy of the Awash National Park Baboon Research Project (ANPBRP) to visit Awash National Park during the summer of 1995. I am particularly grateful to Cliff Jolly, who originally suggested to me that there was still much to be learned about the behavior of female hamadryas baboons.

I am indebted to many other people and organizations for enabling me to conduct this research. In Ethiopia, Addis Ababa University (AAU) and the Ethiopian Wildlife Conservation Organization (EWCO) kindly granted me research permission and affiliation. At AAU, I thank Dr. Endashaw Bekele, Ato Hailu Zegwe, Dr. Seyoum Mengistou, Dr. Masreshe Fetene, and Dr. Solomon Yirga. At EWCO, I thank Ato Gebremarkos Woldeselassie, Ato Tesfaye Hundessa, Ato Tadesse Hailu, Dr. Fekadu Shifferraw, Weyzerit Almaz Tadesse, and Ato Getenet Wondimu Hailemeskel. Finally, a very special thanks to Ato Goitum Redda, who served as my translator and negotiator during those crucial first weeks at Filoha.

In the field, I have benefited from the use of the ANPBRP's field vehicle and equipment and for that I am grateful to Cliff Jolly and Jane Phillips-Conroy. Ato Minda Wordofa, Weyzerit Marta Minda, and Weyzero Radi Omar helped keep me healthy in the field between 1996 and 1998, and Ato Minda Wordofa was particularly valuable as my cook, carpenter, translator, negotiator, troubleshooter, and helper in all respects during my first field season. Several park scouts served as my guides and, most importantly, guards during my daily follows: these were Kebbede Yibelendes, Balai Chokol, and Regassa Akalu during my first field season and Kebbede Yibelendes, Ahamad Musa, and Kimfe Gezow during my second field season. Ato Kebbede Yibalendes in particular was a tremendous help. I am also grateful to the entire staff of the Awash National Park, who were accommodating and supportive in ensuring my safety and comfort at Filoha, especially Ato Kahasai Woldetensai, Messeret Mekuria, Fanuel Kebbede, and Abdi Weyiss. Thanks also to Thore Bergman and Jacinta Beehner for their help trapping baboons in December 1997 and January 1998, to Dana Whitelaw for her help collecting data and samples during the summer of 1998, to Andy Burrell and Pia Nystrom for their help trapping in July and August 2000, and to Teklu Tesfaye, Tariku Woldaregay, and Demekech Woldaregay for their help with fieldwork, camp logistics, and all else in 2000, 2001, 2002, and 2004. Teklu Tesfaye and Demekech Woldaregay have become a regular part of my research team over the past few field seasons and have proved invaluable.

Most recently, Ato Getenet Wondimu Hailemeskel has provided an endless amount of logistical help, smoothing out the bumps in the administrative road. Getenet has been part of my research team since 2001 and I thank him for his assistance in the field, not only with the fieldwork itself but also with logistics and the many negotiations that he carried off so flawlessly amid various local controversies. I am also grateful to Getenet for collecting the Afar tale about the origin of hamadryas baboons (in Chapter 1) from Hamedu Ture and transcribing it for me.

On May 28, 1997, a field accident disrupted my life and my research, and I would probably not be here today were it not for the help of friends, colleagues, and family after the accident. While following baboons up a cliff, a rock broke loose and hit me in the head, knocking me unconscious, fracturing my skull, and breaking several teeth. Balai Chokol resuscitated me and Kebbede Yibalendes walked eight kilometers to get help. The director of Awara Melka State Farm in Sabure; Atos Kahasai Woldetensai, Fanuel Kebbede, and Meseret Mekuria; and Cliff Jolly and Jane Phillips-Conroy all helped relay me to Addis Ababa for medical care. Thore Bergman called the U.S. Embassy for assistance; Dr. Richard Hodes arranged for emergency medical treatment and spent all night arranging and coordinating my medical evacuation to Israel; Drs. Elias Solomon and Milliard Derebew cleansed and stitched my head laceration; the staff at the Blue Nile Clinic in Addis Ababa treated me throughout that night; and Jane Phillips-Conroy was instrumental in contacting my family and making emergency arrangements. Scholastic Overseas Services (SOS) International Travel Insurance chartered a private plane, at great expense, to fly me to Hadassah Hospital in Israel for further treatment, and Ato Tekeste Bereket of the American Embassy obtained special permission on very short notice for the SOS plane to land in Addis. Barbara Swedell and Eric Sargis flew to Israel on only a day's notice, Eric cancelled his summer research plans to nurse me back to health at home in New York, and Ralph Swedell flew to New York for a week, breaking his vow to stay away from big cities. I am grateful to all of these individuals, as well as to the many others who, without my knowledge or recollection, also played a role in my postaccident care and evacuation. I offer my apologies to those whom I have not thanked by name.

I also owe thanks to those who were instrumental in helping to develop my ideas before, during, and after my dissertation research. Dr. Meredith Small at Cornell University originally inspired me to study primate female reproductive strategies and has been a great source of motivation and support over the years. Drs. Marina Cords, John Oates, Cliff Jolly, Fred Szalay, Terry Harrison, and Eric Delson, among others, all contributed to the development of my knowledge and ideas about primate behavior, ecology, and evolution during my graduate career. Drs. Cliff Jolly and John Oates have given me many valuable comments on my work at various stages and have been especially instrumental in helping me to see the forest through the trees. Drs. Fred Szalay, Eric Delson, John Oates, and Jill Shapiro have all been unfailingly supportive and encouraging. Finally, Marina Cords, my graduate advisor, was always there with advice, guidance, and constructive criticism, especially during the project design and analysis phases of my research, and has provided me with a standard of scientific excellence that has been difficult, if not impossible, to live up to.

The five members of my dissertation committee—Drs. Marina Cords, Don Melnick, Cliff Jolly, John Oates, and Colleen McCann—took the time to read my dissertation, attend my defense, and give me numerous suggestions for improvements and revisions. I am especially grateful to them for squeezing a second defense date into their busy schedules on very short notice after a bout with malaria necessitated the cancellation of the first defense.

Financial support at various stages of my graduate career (and beyond) came from many sources. A graduate fellowship from the New York Consortium in Evolutionary Primatology (NYCEP) supported four years of my graduate studies. A travel grant from the Sheldon Scheps family helped to fund my preliminary trip to Awash in the summer of 1995. The National Science Foundation (SBR-9629658), the Wenner-Gren Foundation for Anthropological Research (6034), the L. S. B. Leakey Foundation, and the National Geographic Society (6468-99) have all granted funding to support my dissertation and postdoctoral research. Additional financial support throughout my graduate career has been provided by Helen Melton and Barbara Swedell, to whom I am enormously grateful.

More recently, I am grateful to those who have facilitated the writing of this book. I thank Bob Sussman and Natalie Vasey for inviting me to contribute to this series, Jane Phillips-Conroy and Bob Sussman for their many comments and suggestions for improvement, Leslie Connor for copy editing the manuscript, and Nancy Roberts and Dennis Troutman for their assistance during the submission and production process. I also thank Tim Pugh and Julian Sanders for their help translating my maps to a digital vector-based format for the purposes of this book, rendering them far more visually appealing than the dissertation versions. Finally, I am grateful to the PSC-CUNY Research Award Program and the American Association for the Advancement of Science (AAAS) Women's International Science Collaboration (WISC) Program for supporting my ongoing research during 2002, 2003, and 2004.

Permission was granted to me by several publishers to use published material for the purposes of this book. I thank Kluwer Academic/Plenum Publishers for permission to use material from my article entitled "Affiliation Among Females in Wild Hamadryas Baboons (*Papio hamadryas hamadryas*)," published in the *International Journal of Primatology* (volume 23, issue 6) in 2002. I also thank Karger AG Publishers for permission to use material from two articles published in *Folia Primatologica*: "Two Takeovers in Wild Hamadryas Baboons" (volume 71, pages 169–172, 2000) and "Ranging Behavior, Group Size and Behavioral Flexibility in Ethiopian Hamadryas Baboons (*Papio hamadryas hamadryas*)" (volume 73, pages 95–103, 2002). Finally, I thank Barbara Swedell and Julian Saunders for permission to use their photos in Chapter 1 and Chapter 3.

My greatest thanks go to my family and close friends. From back home during 1996–1998, I received support and sustenance from many friends and family members, and am especially grateful to Helen Melton, Barbara Swedell, Ralph Swedell, Gloria Potocki, and particularly Eric Sargis for their many trips to the post office, their faith in my many endeavors, and their endless patience. For support, friendship, and encouragement during the writing of this book, I am grateful to my colleagues at Queens College and the City University of New York graduate program, to Lisa Vaia, and especially to Julian Saunders.

Strategies of Sex and Survival in Hamadryas Baboons

1

Hamadryas Baboons: The Male as Leader and Icon

Since the days of the ancient Egyptians, hamadryas baboons have intrigued scientists and laypersons alike. The majestic lion-like mane of the hamadryas male is the first thing one notices upon observing a group of hamadryas baboons, and it is thus no surprise that males have occupied the primary position in both cultural and scientific representations of the species. The role of the more unassuming hamadryas baboon female, on the other hand, has been relatively neglected, both by the ancient Egyptians and by twentieth-century scientists.

HAMADRYAS BABOONS IN ANCIENT EGYPT

King Tut's tomb is surrounded by a painted wall mosaic of hamadryas baboons. As such a prominent location in a tomb implies, hamadryas baboons occupied a prominent position in ancient Egyptian society. Although not native to Egypt, baboons were brought there in predynastic times from the Horn of Africa. Like many other animals, hamadryas baboons were often kept as pets and were highly regarded by the ancient Egyptians, in both secular and sacred ways (Germond & Livet 2001). It is due to this association with ancient Egyptian mythology that the hamadryas are often called "sacred baboons" in northeastern Africa.

In ancient Egypt, the hamadryas baboon was considered to be one of the mortal incarnations—in addition to the ibis, an elegant bird—of Thoth, the god of wisdom and scholars (Ions 1982). It was Thoth who was

1

responsible for weighing and judging the souls of the dead, and this role is reflected in Egyptian illustrations in which a hamadryas baboon is often depicted sitting on the edge of a scale.

One ancient Egyptian myth shows an interesting parallel to the natural behavior of hamadryas males. Apparently Tefnut, the sister and wife of Shu, once escaped into the Nubian desert in the shape of a lioness. Shu and Thoth were then sent by Ra, the sun god, to retrieve Tefnut. After transforming themselves into baboons, Shu and Thoth tracked down Tefnut in the desert and Thoth then won her over with his magical powers. Although Tefnut ultimately married Shu, in some versions of the story it is said that she instead married Thoth on their return trip from Nubia (Ions 1982).

Akin to Thoth's role in the retrieval of Tefnut, hamadryas baboon males are talented at finding and retrieving females. As discussed in more detail later, male hamadryas aggressively herd females out of their natal family units into new family units and, in many ways, can be seen as controlling female behavior. It has even been suggested that one of the primary mechanisms leading to the formation of the hamadryas-anubis hybrid zone in Awash National Park was repeated kidnapping of anubis baboon females by hamadryas males (Nagel 1973; Kummer 1995), a behavior that may have been observed by the ancient Egyptians as well. (It is actually unlikely that such abductions have contributed significantly to the formation of hybrid groups; rather, migration by hamadryas males appears to have played a larger role; see Phillips-Conroy et al., 1992.)

HAMADRYAS BABOONS AND THE AFAR PEOPLE

Also found in the semidesert regions of eastern Ethiopia and northern Somalia are the Afar people, nomadic pastoralists who subsist largely on the milk and meat of their livestock (Getachew 2001). Frequently at war with other nomadic tribes in the area, the Afar are reputed for their traditional rite of passage to manhood whereby a male member of an enemy tribe is killed and his testicles are worn on a string around the neck. Fortunately for the baboons, Afar hunting does not usually extend to wild animals, nor do the Afar take much notice of the baboons in general except during droughts or other times when they use the same resources, such as doum palm nuts and water holes. The Afar do have their myths about the baboons, though, one of which was told to Getenet Wondimu Hailemeskel by an elderly Afar man named Hamedu Ture who lived in Doho, a small village north of Filoha.

As the story goes, hamadryas baboons used to be human beings who lived much like the Afar do today. They lived in a beautiful area surrounded by trees, open grassland, and a river. Each family, inhabiting a separate hut in the village, consisted of a husband, his several wives,

Afar nomads, such as this young girl, frequent the Filoha area. *(Photo by Barbara Swedell)*

and their children. They had no knowledge of or belief in a higher being or God, but instead worshipped elements of nature such as large trees and rocks.

The hamadryas people subsisted mainly on fish, which they would catch each day at the nearby river. One Sunday at the river, an odd-looking man came to them, introduced himself as Sheik Hussein, and asked them why they were fishing on Sunday. He explained to them that God had ordered all human beings not to work on Sundays, and that by doing so the hamadryas were deliberately violating God's orders. The hamadryas wondered why this was the case, and Sheik Hussein explained further that God was their lord and that they were the slaves of God. He created everything in six days and rested on Sunday, so they must, in return, celebrate God on this day. Sheik Hussein added that the hamadryas must obey these orders in the future and cease to fish on Sundays. The hamadryas agreed.

Unfortunately, none of the hamadryas kept their promise. Several Sundays later, Sheik Hussein appeared again and reprimanded them for disobeying his orders. He told them that they had broken their promise and must now be punished. He then declared his punishment, which was that the hamadryas must leave their villages and walk on four limbs in the wild, spending their nights on cliffs and in the trees instead of in their huts. They would no longer be human beings, but would be one of the social animals that lives in the wild, fighting with one another in groups. And so it was that the hamadryas became baboons and henceforth inhabited the forests and open grasslands, feeding on grass and fruits from trees and drinking at the river.

HAMADRYAS DISTRIBUTION AND TAXONOMY

Today, hamadryas baboons inhabit only the Horn of Africa (Ethiopia, Sudan, Somalia, Djibouti, and Eritrea) and the southwestern corner of the Arabian peninsula in Yemen and southwestern Saudi Arabia (Kummer 1968a; Kummer et al. 1981; Wolfheim 1983; Biquand et al. 1992a; Al-Safadi 1994; Kamal et al. 1994; Zinner et al. 2001a). Much of their distribution consists of semiarid, desert-like regions, and it is for this reason that hamadryas have yet a third common name, "desert baboon." This label distinguishes the hamadryas ecologically from other baboons: the "savanna baboons" of the grasslands in east and southern Africa and the "mountain baboons" of the Drakensberg in South Africa.

Distributed across the African continent are five main forms of baboons, commonly known as olive (or anubis), yellow, chacma, Guinea, and hamadryas. While they are commonly referred to as separate species and are often classified as either five species (e.g., Hill 1967; Napier & Napier 1967, 1985; Hayes et al. 1990) or two species (Thorington & Groves 1970; Kingdon 1974; Smuts et al. 1987) by behavioral ecologists and others, they in fact hybridize at the borders between their respective distributions (Jolly 1993). This lack of reproductive isolation, and in particular the well-documented hybrid zone between hamadryas and anubis baboons in Ethiopia (e.g., Phillips-Conroy & Jolly 1986)—coupled with genetic evidence suggesting a lack of differentiation among (sub)species (Williams-Blangero et al. 1990; Hapke et al. 2001)—suggests that a single-species classification may be most appropriate (Jolly 1993; Disotell 2000). Most taxonomists, therefore, today agree that all baboons should be placed within a single species—which, according to the rules of nomenclature, must be called *Papio hamadryas* as that was the first name used—with five or more phenotypically and geographically distinct subspecies (e.g., Szalay & Delson 1979; Groves 1993; Jolly 1993). While baboon taxonomy is still controversial and no one classification is universally accepted, I will follow Groves (1993) and Jolly (1993) in adopting the single-species classification in this book.

HAMADRYAS SOCIAL ORGANIZATION

Hamadryas baboons are unique among primates with regard to their complex, multilevel social system and their extreme male-dominated society, both of which have been viewed as adaptations to the harsh, semi-desert environment in which they evolved and in which most live today (Kummer 1968a, 1968b; 1971b). Three main levels of organization have been described as characterizing hamadryas baboon society (Kummer & Kurt 1963; Kummer 1968a, 1968b; Abegglen 1984), as follows: *Troops* are large aggregations (usually over 100 individuals) that assemble at sleeping sites but do not otherwise function as cohesive social groups. Each troop includes one or more *bands*, whose members travel together during the day and coordinate their movements. The band is probably the social grouping analogous to the "group" or "troop" of other monkeys such as macaques, mangabeys, or olive baboons. Adult members of different bands rarely interact, and when they do interact, they usually do so agonistically. Even when two or more bands share a sleeping cliff, each band travels and forages separately from other bands during the day.

Within each band are a number of *one-male units* (OMUs). Each OMU consists of one adult "leader" male, one or more adult females, their offspring (to about the age of two to three years, at which point juvenile males no longer associate regularly with their natal OMU and juvenile females have been incorporated into another OMU), and sometimes one or more "follower" males. Also within bands are "solitary" males, males who are

Bands of hamadryas baboons typically travel and forage as a coordinated unit. *(Photo by the author)*

neither leaders of OMUs nor are attached to an OMU as a follower male. Solitary males, as well as older juvenile males, move freely within the band, do not associate regularly with any one OMU, and interact mainly with other solitary males and juveniles.

Cohesion of hamadryas one-male units is maintained by aggressive herding behavior of leader males, who threaten and bite females that become spatially or socially separated from the rest of the unit. A leader male appears to have nearly exclusive sexual access to the females of his unit, whereas follower males copulate relatively rarely and appear to be awaiting future reproductive opportunities (Kummer 1968a; Abegglen 1984; Stammbach 1987). Unlike in other baboons, males rarely interact aggressively over estrous females or attempt to copulate with another male's females, but instead appear to "respect" other males' "possession" of females and do not typically interact with females when they already "belong to" another male of the same band—regardless of the relative dominance rank between the two males (Kummer 1968b, 1971a; Kummer et al. 1974). When a leader male loses his females, the recipient is often a younger follower male of his own unit (Kummer et al. 1978; Abegglen 1984). In fact, older leader males have been reported to voluntarily relinquish their females to younger followers, with whom they have developed a friendly relationship and to whom they might be related (Kummer 1968a; Abegglen 1984).

Four one-male units sitting at the top of the Wasaro cliff just after dawn, responding to a scream nearby.

Abegglen (1984) observed a fourth level of social organization between that of bands and one-male units. In Band I near Erer Gota, Abegglen noticed that certain males, both solitary and with females, associated more frequently with one another than they did with other males. Abegglen saw obvious physical resemblances among these males, proposed that they were close kin, and called their associations *clans*. (Unfortunately, Abegglen's proposition was never confirmed with genetic data because samples were never obtained from these males.) Abegglen reported that OMUs within each of these clans were spatially distinct from OMUs in other clans, both during daily travel and on the sleeping cliffs. Males tended not to transfer out of their natal clan, and males of the same clan tended to have affiliative social relationships with one another, characterized by grooming among solitary males and formalized, stereotypical "notifying" behavior (whereby one male quickly approaches, looks at, presents to, and then leaves another male) among leader males and between leader males and their followers (Kummer 1968a; Stolba 1979; Abegglen 1984). The clan structure has also been observed by Stolba (1979) in other bands near Erer Gota.

PREVIOUS RESEARCH ON HAMADRYAS BABOONS

Some of the earliest research on hamadryas baboons was conducted by Sir Solly Zuckerman in the 1920s and 1930s on a group of captive hamadryas baboons at the London Zoo (Zuckerman & Parkes 1930, 1939; Zuckerman 1932). Zuckerman saw social behavior, sexuality, and aggression as being intrinsically linked. He drew these conclusions from his observations of frequent and persistent fighting among the hamadryas males over access to females and the resulting high incidence of injury and death. Zuckerman believed that animal behavior was in no way modified by captivity, and that the high levels of aggression he observed among hamadryas in captivity were no different from patterns of behavior in the wild. We now know, of course, that such high levels of aggression are unusual, both among hamadryas and among other wild primates, and were more likely attributable to the fact that over a hundred baboons were confined to a 100×60 ft. enclosure, rather than the 300×300 ft. area that a band normally occupies in the wild (see Chapter 4).

A more accurate view of hamadryas behavior came from the pioneering work of Hans Kummer and Fred Kurt in 1960 near Erer Gota, Ethiopia, about 180 km northeast of the Awash National Park (see Figure 1–1). Kummer and Kurt spent 12 months surveying baboon troops and collecting behavioral data on several bands in the Erer Gota area. It was this research that first documented the multilevel social structure of wild hamadryas and illustrated the differences and similarities between hamadryas in the wild and in captivity (Kummer & Kurt 1963, 1965; Kummer 1968a).

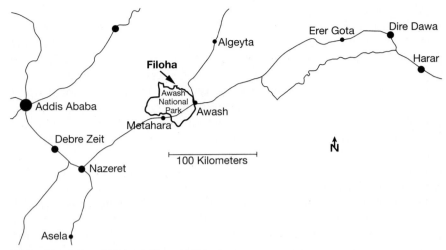

Figure 1–1 Road Map of Central Ethiopia

Then, in 1967, Kummer and his colleagues Walter Götz and Walter Angst carried out a series of experiments in the Awash area in which they captured and moved individual baboons between hamadryas and anubis (*P. h. anubis*) groups. These experiments demonstrated important details about hamadryas male herding behavior and its power to condition both hamadryas and anubis females. These experiments also revealed the apparent "respect" that hamadryas males have for each other's "possession" of females, a concept that was further investigated by Kummer and his colleagues in their captive colony in Zurich (Kummer et al. 1970, 1974, 1978; Bachmann & Kummer 1980; Sigg & Falett 1985).

In 1968, Ueli Nagel studied several groups of wild baboons, including hamadryas, as part of an ecological comparison of hamadryas baboons, anubis baboons, and hybrid baboons in the anubis-hamadryas hybrid zone along the Awash River (Nagel 1971, 1973). Anubis-hamadryas hybrid and mixed groups within this hybrid zone have subsequently been studied by Hansueli Müller (1980), Kazuyoshi Sugawara (1979, 1982, 1988) and members of the Awash National Park Baboon Research Project (Jolly & Brett 1973; Brett et al. 1977, 1982; Phillips-Conroy & Jolly 1981, 1986, 1988; Phillips-Conroy et al. 1986, 1992, 1993, 2000; Nystrom 1992; Beyene 1993, 1998; Bergman 1999; Jolly & Phillips-Conroy 1999, 2003). Much of this research has shown that behavioral patterns that distinguish hamadryas males from anubis males, especially male herding behavior, are found in various intermediate forms in hamadryas-anubis hybrids, and that the degree to which a hybrid male is more hamadryas-like or more anubis-like (and the correlated intermediate behavioral patterns that he shows) can profoundly affect his mating success in hybrid and mixed groups.

The only multiyear study of wild hamadryas baboons was carried out near Erer Gota by a series of investigators on one of the bands first observed by Kummer and Kurt in 1960, "Band I" of Cone Rock. Kummer's students Jean-Jacques Abegglen, Alex Stolba, and Hans Sigg conducted observational research on this band over a period of five and a half years between 1971 and 1977. This research has produced valuable longitudinal data on life histories and reproductive parameters as well as information on ranging patterns and ecological differentiation of female roles during foraging (Abegglen & Abegglen 1976; Abegglen 1984; Stolba 1979; Sigg 1980, 1986; Sigg & Stolba 1981; Sigg et al. 1982). The demographic and reproductive data from Band I, reported in Sigg et al. (1982), are particularly informative because all 67 members of the group were individually identifiable due to trapping and ear-tagging of juveniles and adult females. Unfortunately, this research had to be aborted in 1977 because of the escalating political turmoil in the Horn of Africa, and subsequent research on Ethiopian hamadryas baboons was limited to those that had been captured and brought into captivity in Europe.

THE NEGLECTED ROLE OF THE FEMALE

Most of this early research on wild hamadryas suggested that female mating strategies and social relationships among females played a negligible role in hamadryas society. Female behavior was generally assumed to be relatively unimportant in determining patterns of association and interaction, and the control that hamadryas males exerted over females seemed to leave little opportunity for the expression of female mating strategies, should they even exist. With the exception of Sigg (1980), however, none of this early research focused specifically on females, and even Sigg did not focus his observations on individual females but instead conducted "focal group sampling" of entire one-male units.

More recent research on captive hamadryas, much of which has focused specifically on females, has shown that female mating preferences, female affiliative relationships, and competition among females do play a role in hamadryas social organization, at least in captivity. In contrast to earlier reports from studies of wild populations, captive hamadryas females have been shown to exhibit both competitive and grooming relationships with one another (Stammbach 1978; Stammbach & Kummer 1982; Coelho et al. 1983; Chalyan et al. 1991; Gore 1991, 1994; Vervaecke et al. 1992; Colmenares et al. 1994; Zaragoza et al. 1996; Leinfelder et al. 2001) and also to express preference for some males over others in the context of unit takeovers (Bachmann & Kummer 1980). Given that other aspects of hamadryas social behavior, specifically the one-male unit social structure and the herding behavior of males, are little modified by captivity (Kummer & Kurt 1965), the same is likely true of female behavior. Given

Verena grooming Darth's foot on the edge of a cliff 2 km west of Wasaro. This image depicts the subservient, submissive role of the female in hamadryas society that has pervaded the literature for decades.

that mate preferences, female social relationships, and female competition occur so widely in female primates, and in baboons in particular, it would be surprising if they were entirely absent from hamadryas society, even if male vigilance and aggression limited their expression to subtle or even surreptitious interactions. Because both the behavior and pelage of male hamadryas make them more visible and obvious to observers, and because most previous studies of wild hamadryas have focused specifically on males rather than on females, details of hamadryas female behavior may have been easily overlooked in previous field studies.

The state of knowledge of hamadryas social behavior prior to this study clearly left many unanswered questions regarding the social and mating strategies of hamadryas females in the wild. I therefore set out to address some of these questions with this study: Do females have social or sexual relationships with non-leader males? Do females form affiliative relationships with one another as well as with their leader male? Do females compete with one another and experience differential access to food or mates, conception, or offspring survival? By focusing exclusively on female social behavior in a population of wild hamadryas baboons in Ethiopia, this study aimed to answer these questions as well as to generally elucidate the role of female behavior in hamadryas society.

2

Reproductive Strategies in Primates: Conflicts between the Sexes

Why should we expect hamadryas females to have reproductive strategies of their own? Why should the interests of hamadryas females differ from those of hamadryas males? To answer these questions, we must first look at the differences between male and female reproductive strategies in animals as a whole and why they should—and often do—differ.

SEXUAL SELECTION AND PARENTAL INVESTMENT

Charles Darwin (1871) noticed an apparent difference between the reproductive strategies of males and females as well as sex differences in conspicuous morphological traits. To explain these differences, he developed the theory of sexual selection, which, he proposed, operates by two mechanisms: (1) selection resulting from competition between members of one sex for members of the opposite sex, or mate competition, and (2) selection resulting from differential choice by members of one sex for members of the opposite sex, or mate choice. These processes could potentially be manifested as male-male competition, female-female competition, male mate choice, or female mate choice. Darwin pointed out, however, that the most common pathways by which sexual selection operates are male-male competition and female choice.

One hundred years later, Robert Trivers (1972) pointed out that the apparent prevalence of male-male competition and female choice compared to female competition and male choice could be explained by a fundamental asymmetry in parental investment by males and females. Males produce vast numbers of sperm cells almost continuously and thus have a virtually limitless number of potential offspring while investing very little energy in each one. Females, on the other hand, produce many fewer egg cells, invest far more energy in each one, and release them at long intervals. Females also typically invest far more energy in their offspring after birth than do males, at least in mammals, and this is especially true for primates. Females thus have an inherent limit on their number of potential offspring and invest far more in each than do males.

When maternal investment is greater than paternal investment, females are the limiting resource and the reproductive success of each male depends on the number of females to whom he can gain access. In such a scenario, we expect selection to favor morphological traits or behavioral strategies that enhance a male's ability to compete for access to females or that increase a male's chance of being chosen as a mate. Conspicuous traits that distinguish one sex from the other but that do not pertain directly to reproduction, or secondary sexual characteristics, are often called sexually selected traits because they are presumably the result of sexual selection by either male-male competition or female choice. Theoretically, sexual selection should favor such traits in males but not in females.

Females, on the other hand, have a limited number of potential offspring and invest heavily in each one. We therefore expect them to employ strategies to maximize offspring quality rather than quantity. The importance of offspring quality is especially true for "K-selected" animals, such as primates, who mature late compared to most other mammals and have longer reproductive and life history parameters, including long gestation periods, long periods of lactational amenorrhea, and long interbirth intervals. These lengthened reproductive periods are beneficial to the production of high-quality offspring because they allow enough time for healthy development and socialization of offspring. They also, however, increase the relative importance of each individual offspring for a female's lifetime reproductive success.

MALE REPRODUCTIVE STRATEGIES

The reproductive success of a male primate is limited primarily by the number of females he can inseminate. We therefore expect selection to have favored both morphological traits and behavioral strategies of males that maximize their number of fertilizations.

A male's ability to compete with other males may be enhanced by secondary sexual characteristics such as large body size, large canine size, and, in nonprimates, horns or tusks. Such conspicuous traits that occur in males but not females—or sexually dimorphic traits—are generally associated with social systems in which males aggressively compete for access to females, that is, those with multi-male groups or one-male groups in which male takeovers are common (Clutton-Brock 1984; Plavcan & van Schaik 1992). The large size of bodies and canines in male but not female primates is most likely selected for when it has a greater effect on the differential reproductive success of males than of females in a given species (Clutton-Brock 1984).

Rather than aiding in male competition, conspicuous morphological traits may also benefit a male through their attractiveness to females. In nonprimates, such traits include the familiar peacock's tail and the elaborate plumage of many other birds. In primates, the majestic manes of both gelada and hamadryas baboons have been suggested to have evolved via sexual selection by female choice (Jolly 1963). It is also possible that manes aid in male-male competition, as a large, fluffy mane makes a male appear to be bigger and stronger—and better able to defeat rival males—without the associated energetic costs.

Males may also employ *behavioral* strategies to maximize their number of fertilizations. A male might simply try to maximize the number of females with whom he mates, or he may attempt to maximize both the

It has been suggested that the majestic mane of the hamadryas adult male is a trait that has evolved through sexual selection, either because females prefer males with larger, fluffier manes or because having a large mane aids a male in defeating his rivals. *(Photo by the author)*

number of females with whom he mates *and* his number of copulations with each female. A variety of behavioral strategies may aid in achieving these goals.

Male-Male Competition for Mates

In order to attain the most fertilizations, males must compete with one another for access to females. Male-male competition occurs in various ways, depending on the social system.

One strategy that males use to maximize their number of fertilizations is the physical exclusion of all other males from a group of females. Exclusion strategies lead to a one-male or age-graded male social structure. Within such a social system, males are relatively intolerant of one another and aggressively prevent other males from being a member of the group; if other males are allowed in the group, then they are simply prevented from mating by the dominant male. In such a system, males are generally intolerant of one another in the presence of females, but may tolerate one another when no females are present, as exemplified by the existence of all-male bands in many species with one-male social systems (Cords 1987; Rowell 1988; Newton & Dunbar 1994; Robbins 1995). A similar phenomenon exists in hamadryas baboons, in which adult males interact affiliatively far more with one another when they are *not* in association with females. An exclusion strategy necessitates a high degree of aggressive competition among males either within or between groups (Popp 1983). Furthermore, because there are many more males than defendable groups of females in the population, group takeovers may be common and the duration of any one male's exclusive access to a group of females (and thus his reproductive life) may be extremely short.

Many primates live in multi-male–multi-female groups. Unlike in one-male groups, in which males attempt to maintain exclusive access to females at all times, males in multi-male groups typically compete for females only when they are most fertile, or in estrus (see p. 20 for a discussion of the estrus concept). In multi-male groups, males are usually ordered into a dominance hierarchy, and rank often correlates with priority of access to females (although not as often as is generally presumed). In many multi-male group-living species, males often try to maintain consort relationships with estrous females to the exclusion of other males. These consortships are only temporary, however; a male will allow another male to take over his consort partner after a few minutes, hours, or days, depending on the species and the individual involved. Male-male competition within multi-male multi-female groups characterizes a great number of primate taxa, including non-hamadryas baboons.

Males may also compete via *sperm competition*. In species in which females mate with multiple males over short periods of time (i.e., within

Hamadryas males have smaller testes than other baboons, suggesting that, unlike other baboons, they do not undergo sperm competition. This is consistent with the rarity of observations of hamadryas females copulating with males other than their leader male. *(Photo by the author)*

a single estrus period or a single day), the sperm of several males may compete for fertilization (Harcourt et al., 1981; Bercovitch 1989; Manson 1995b). Such competition should result in selection for higher quantity and quality of sperm as well as genital morphology that aids in producing more or better quality sperm or depositing it further into the female reproductive tract. That sperm competition occurs in primates is supported by a general association between multi-male breeding systems and traits such as larger testes, longer sperm, and larger penises (Harcourt et al., 1981; Verrell 1992; Dixson 1993).

Infanticide by Males

Male infanticide—or infant-killing—occurs in many mammals, including wild felids, brown bears, and rodents (Brooks 1984; Packer & Pusey 1984; van Schaik 2000b; Blumstein 2000). Circumstantial and/or observational evidence of infanticide by males has also been reported for many populations of wild primates, most notably Hanuman langurs, *Semnopithecus entellus* (Hrdy 1974, 1977; Vogel & Loch 1984; Sommer 1994; Borries & Koenig 2000) but also Thomas's langurs, *Presbytis thomasi* (Steenbeek et al., 1999; Steenbeek 2000), howler monkeys, *Alouatta* spp. (Clarke 1983; Sekulic 1983; Crockett &

Sekulic 1984; Crockett & Janson 2000), capuchins, *Cebus olivaceus* (Valderrama et al., 1990), red colobus monkeys, *Procolobus badius* (Leland et al., 1984; Struhsaker & Leland 1987), black and white colobus monkeys, *Colobus guereza* (Onderdonk 2000), redtail monkeys, *Cercopithecus ascanius* (Leland et al., 1984), blue monkeys, *C. mitis* (Butynski 1982; Leland et al., 1984; Fairgrieve 1995), lemurs *Eulemur, Lemur, & Lepilemur* (Jolly et al., 2000; Rasoloharijaona et al., 2000), *Papio* baboons (Shopland 1982; Collins et al., 1984; Smuts 1985; Palombit et al., 1997; 2000; Weingrill 2000; Swedell & Tesfaye 2003), chimpanzees, *Pan troglodytes* (Goodall 1977), and mountain gorillas, *Gorilla gorilla* (Fossey 1984; Watts 1989).

The most widely accepted hypothesis to explain the occurrence of infanticide in nonhuman primates is the sexual selection hypothesis (Hrdy 1974, 1977; Hausfater & Hrdy 1984; van Schaik & Janson 2000). According to this explanatory hypothesis, infanticide is a male competitive strategy in which, by killing the infant of another male, a male increases his own relative fitness and brings the infant's mother into reproductive condition sooner than she would have had her infant survived. This hypothesis predicts that a male will not kill his own infants, but only those of his competitors, and that, after the infanticide, he will then gain an opportunity to sire offspring with the mother of the killed infant sooner than he would have otherwise. Indeed, infanticide by males often occurs during group takeovers in one-male group-living species, in which case most infants in the group at the time of the takeover have presumably been sired by a competitor and most future infants will be sired by the new, infanticidal, male. In theory, a genetically based tendency to commit infanticide upon taking over a new group would be selected for if it results in higher reproductive success among the males who do it.

In many primates (howler monkeys, langurs, blue monkeys, redtail monkeys, anubis baboons, and gorillas), infanticide appears to be associated with (1) male takeovers, male immigration, or changes in group leadership, in which the infanticidal male is a new or newly dominant male (Hrdy 1974, 1977; Butynski 1982; Collins et al., 1984; Crockett & Sekulic 1984; Leland et al., 1984; Vogel & Loch 1984; Sommer 1994; Fairgrieve 1995); or (2) aggressive intergroup encounters, after which the victim's mother may transfer into the group of the infanticidal male (Fossey 1984). In such cases, infanticide may be an adaptive male strategy. Not only do males in these cases appear to be killing infants of other males, but the infants killed are of a sufficiently young age that their death may cause their mother to return to reproductive condition sooner than she would have if the infant had survived. In many of these cases, females do copulate with infanticidal males during and after male takeovers and infanticidal events (Hrdy 1977; Crockett & Sekulic 1984; Vogel & Loch 1984; Newton 1986; van Schaik 2000a) and, in hanuman langurs at least, the infanticidal males sire those females' offspring (Borries et al., 1999).

Many authors suggest, however, that sexual selection may not be a very useful explanatory hypothesis in many of the documented cases of infanticide (Boggess 1984; Bartlett et al., 1993; Sussman et al., 1995; Dolhinow 1999). These authors point out that infanticide may simply be interpreted as a pathological, sometimes maladaptive, behavior attributable to abnormal conditions such as high population densities or human disturbance. In this sense, infanticide may be viewed as an epiphenomenon of periods of intense aggression, such as those during group takeovers and intergroup encounters (Bartlett et al., 1993; Sussman et al., 1995). This explanation could account for the cases of infanticide that do not appear to support the sexual selection hypothesis, such as males killing their own infants, infanticide that is not followed by mating with the infant's mother, and infanticide that appears to be random and is not associated with male takeovers of one-male groups (Sussman et al., 1995). Angst and Thommen (1977) suggest that infanticide is correlated with unstable social relationships and that this may explain its occurrence during group takeovers. Proponents of the generalized aggression and social disturbance explanations for infanticide note that most of the reported evidence for infanticide, even that attributed to the sexual selection hypothesis, is highly circumstantial and few infanticides have actually been witnessed (Boggess 1984; Bartlett et al., 1993; Sussman et al., 1995). In addition, it has never been shown that males who commit infanticide achieve higher reproductive success than males who do not, or that a tendency to commit infanticide is to any degree heritable (Sussman et al., 1995).

Despite these criticisms, there is a general pattern to the occurrence of infanticide in primates: It occurs in undisturbed as well as disturbed populations (Newton 1986; Newton & Dunbar 1994), it is usually associated with male takeovers, and in most cases it is either very likely or has actually been shown with genetic data that infanticidal males kill the infants of *other* males rather than their own (Struhsaker & Leland 1987; Hrdy 1984, Hrdy et al., 1995; Borries et al., 1999; van Schaik 2000a). Cases of infanticide in contexts other than those predicted by sexual selection may simply be maladaptive side effects of a behavioral pattern that is otherwise adaptive. It is possible that infanticide represents a sexually selected male competitive strategy in some species and not others, and that some species exhibit this behavior for other reasons, whether they be adaptive or not.

Sexual Coercion by Males

Given that males should, in theory, be selected to maximize their number of matings, one might expect them to attempt to force females to copulate with them in the event that females are unwilling sexual partners. Sexual coercion of females by males occurs in many other mammals, such as bighorn sheep (Hogg 1984), elephant seals (Le Boeuf & Mesnick 1991), and wild horses (Berger 1983). Such aggression has the potential to seriously injure females and can even be lethal in some cases (Le Boeuf & Mesnick 1991). In species in which sexual coercion occurs, females appear to employ strategies to avoid serious injuries inflicted by males (Mesnick & Le Boeuf 1991).

Sexual coercion of females by males also occurs in primates (Smuts & Smuts 1993; Clutton-Brock & Parker 1995). In chimpanzees, macaques, and baboons, males are often aggressive toward females who consort with or attempt to copulate with other males (Berenstain & Wade 1983; Lindburg 1983; Goodall 1986; Manson 1994). In gorillas, chimpanzees, and orangutans, males sometimes attack females who reject their mating attempts (Nadler & Miller 1982; Galdikas 1985a, 1985b; Mitani 1985; Nadler 1988).

Male Mate Choice

Based on the theoretical frameworks of sexual selection and parental investment outlined earlier in this chapter, one would not expect males to be selective in their choice of mates. In general, males should simply attempt to copulate with as many females as possible. Males might, however, show selectivity in choice of mates in situations in which they are unable to monopolize all of the females that are locally available, such as when there are many females in a group, when females are widely dispersed, or when breeding seasonality and/or estrus synchrony among females is pronounced. Selectivity of mates may also be advantageous in species in which lengthy consortships necessarily accompany copulation, as substantial time and energy may be expended in such a consortship (Anderson 1986). Furthermore, the number of ejaculates a male can produce may be limited, at least over a short time frame (Nakatsuru & Kramer 1982; Robinson 1982; Small 1988); if this is the case, then males should prefer to mate first with the highest quality females of those available.

While primate males do not generally appear to be very selective in their mating behavior, male vervet monkeys and macaques sometimes prefer higher-ranking over lower-ranking females (Keddy 1986; Samuels et al., 1984) and males of numerous primate species prefer adult multiparous females (i.e., those who have given birth to multiple offspring) over younger nulliparous or primiparous females (Berenstain & Wade 1983; Anderson 1986). Such a preference makes sense in light of the fact that older, multiparous females have demonstrated an ability to survive, to reproduce successfully, and to raise multiple surviving offspring. In addition, male chimpanzees appear to prefer newer, more unfamiliar females (Morin 1993), and recent evidence suggests that male anubis baboons prefer females with larger sexual swellings (Domb & Pagel 2001).

FEMALE REPRODUCTIVE STRATEGIES

Unlike males, females have a finite number of potential offspring. A female primate, therefore, can best improve her lifetime reproductive success by maximizing the *quality* of each individual offspring. Offspring quality may be increased in various ways, including reproducing at the most appropriate time (with regard to maximizing food resources and minimizing energy expenditure during gestation and lactation), choosing the best mates (either for genetic quality of offspring or to promote offspring survival), competing effectively against other females (for food, mates, or offspring survival), or inciting male-male competition (either agonistic or sperm competition).

Female primates not only mature late compared to most other mammals, but have long gestation periods, long lactation periods, and long interbirth intervals. These lengthened reproductive periods are beneficial to the production of high-quality offspring because they allow enough time for healthy development and socialization of offspring. Several reproductive parameters, though, such as reproductive seasonality and birth synchrony, do vary among primate species and may be advantageous in some, but not all, ecological and/or social situations.

Timing of Reproduction

Reproductive Seasonality and Synchrony. Seasonal variation in mating behavior and births occurs in many primates. Functionally, reproductive seasonality makes sense in habitats where there is a great variance in food supply from one season to another, in which case females may be expected to time their reproduction so that offspring are born or weaned when food resources are most abundant. There also may be advantages to having many infants in the group at the same time, such as a reduced likelihood of predation or infanticide (Chism et al., 1983; Boinski 1987; Lindburg 1987).

As do many nonprimate mammals, many female primates synchronize their reproduction even more so than on a seasonal basis. Such reproductive synchrony has been interpreted functionally in many ways. Some authors have suggested that it is a female strategy to reduce the likelihood of male desertion (and thus increase paternal care), because it reduces the probability of a male finding another mate before his original mate comes into reproductive condition again (Emlen & Oring 1977; Knowlton 1979). Synchrony of mating may also be a mate choice strategy, in that it reduces the ability of a single male (or the highest-ranking male) to monopolize all estrous females. Often, synchrony of reproduction is not explained by the value of synchrony of mating, but rather by the value of synchrony of *births*. It may be advantageous for females to all give birth at the same time, either because a very specific time of the year is seasonally best for nutrient acquisition for their developing offspring and/or because the presence of many same-aged infants in the group at one time reduces the likelihood of any one female's infant being harassed and/or killed, either by conspecifics or by predators (Chism et al., 1983; Clarke & Glander 1984; Boinski 1987; Izard 1990). Synchronous births might also promote better social development of offspring, in that they allow each female's infant to grow up and associate with same-aged peers, as well as with other adult females who are mothers (Clarke & Glander 1984; Izard 1990).

Nonfertile/Post-Conception Estrus.   Typically, female mammals are sexually receptive only during a short period of estrus that occurs cyclically until a female gets pregnant and then resumes after her infant is weaned (Heape 1900). In most mammals, this period of estrus correlates well with the secretion of ovarian hormones leading up to ovulation and thus corresponds with a female's most fertile period (Dixson 1998). Behaviorally, estrus is characterized by heightened attractivity, receptivity, and proceptivity of females (Beach 1976) and is generally assumed to be a good indicator to males of a female's likelihood of conception. Many species, including baboons, also have morphological signs of estrus, such as sexual swellings and face color changes, that correspond with behavioral estrus.

Among anthropoid primates, behavioral estrus is often decoupled from ovulation in that mating activity also occurs during nonfertile phases of a female's cycle (Dixson 1998). Although a female's *motivation* to copulate, and thus her "proceptivity" (Beach 1976), does vary across her cycle and is usually most pronounced around ovulation, many female primates, unlike most other mammals, are always physically *capable* of engaging in sexual activity and often do so when they are not actually fertile, especially in captivity (Wallen 1990).

Estrus behavior that occurs outside of a female's most fertile periods is called nonfertile estrus, situation-dependent estrus, or pseudoestrus. Estrus behavior after conception, called post-conception estrus, occurs in many primate species and may benefit females in several ways. First, it may function to develop and maintain male-female social relationships (Wallis 1982; Small 1983; Andelman 1987; Cords 1988), including inhibiting male-female aggression, which may be less likely to occur when a female is in estrus than when she is anestrus (Wallis 1982). Second, it may temporarily increase a female's dominance rank and access to resources, at least in species, such as chimpanzees, in which a female's reproductive state has an effect on these factors (Wallis 1982). It may also confuse paternity and thus facilitate paternal care of offspring in species in which paternal care contributes to offspring survival, or inhibit infanticide in species in which infanticide occurs. Post-conception estrus as a strategy to prevent infanticide might be especially beneficial when new males enter or take over a group; if a female is pregnant when a new male arrives but solicits copulations with the new male, he may be less likely to kill the female's offspring due to the possibility that he might be the father. Females of many primate species show post-conception estrus when new males enter or take over a group (geladas: Mori 1979b; hanuman langurs: Hrdy 1977; redtail monkeys: Cords 1984), suggesting that prevention of infanticide may be a possible functional explanation for post-conception estrus in many primates.

Female Mate Choice

What Is Female Choice? Mate choice is defined by Halliday (1983) as "any pattern of behavior, shown by members of one sex, that leads to their being more likely to mate with certain members of the opposite sex than with others." Evidence of female choice in the evolutionary sense, that is, as a selective force, must be provided through a demonstration of nonrandom mating by females leading to differential male reproductive success. Due to limited knowledge of paternity and long life spans, determining lifetime reproductive success in male primates is logistically difficult. Evidence for nonrandom mate choice by females, however, is easier to attain.

First, though, it is important to note that nonrandom mate choice in an evolutionary sense, which may or may not occur, is not the same as the exertion of female preference in the context of mating, which clearly does occur. With the exception of orangutans and chimpanzees, forced copulation does not generally occur in primates. Although patterns of mating behavior are always compromises between the preferences of and competition among both males and females, female primates do appear to be able to exert choice in mating. Females may initiate copulations by approaching, maintaining proximity to, looking at, or sexually soliciting males (e.g., Janson 1984; Olson 1985; Cords et al., 1986; Bercovitch 1991a). They may also refuse to mate with males, and may do so by simply walking away or sitting down or by chasing and biting males that attempt copulations (Lindburg 1983; Cords et al., 1986; Andelman 1987; Huffman 1987; Manson 1991; Pereira & Weiss 1991). Females may also circumvent male competition and aggression from males to a certain degree by engaging in surreptitious copulations (e.g., Imanishi 1957; Huffman 1992; Gygax 1995).

Another important distinction is that between female *choice* and female *preference*. The two terms have often been used synonymously in the primate literature, but they are quite distinct. Female choice, as just described, is an *action* with a potential evolutionary effect. Female preference, on the other hand, is an underlying *motivation* that may or may not be expressed (Heisler et al., 1987; Small 1989). A female may prefer one male, but may be prevented from gaining access to that male by the preferences of and competition among other individuals, and may thus "choose" (or settle for) another male instead. One way to assess underlying mate preferences is to look at an accumulation of choices over a long period of time that show a consistent pattern. This pattern is the underlying preference, which may not always be expressed (O'Donald 1983). In theory, if male choice, male-male competition, and female-female competition could be controlled for, then successful copulations would be a good indicator of female preference. However, these factors are always present, at least in a nonexperimental situation. Thus, behavioral indicators on the part of females, such as frequency of approaches, proximity maintenance, and sexual solicitations, must be used instead. These sorts of behavioral patterns may indicate which males females prefer; they do not necessarily, however, reflect female choice, because choices are always constrained by the preferences of and competition among other individuals.

Evidence of Female Preference and Choice in Primates.   Based on sexual selection and parental investment theory, one might expect female primates to be particularly concerned about maximizing the quality of each offspring by being selective in their choice of mates. Selectivity, however, does not appear to generally characterize female primate mating strategies. In many nonmammalian taxa, especially birds, females appear to choose males as mates on the basis of specific male traits that have evolved by sexual selection (Andersson 1982, 1994; Searcy 1982; Kirkpatrick 1987; Møller 1988; Petrie & Halliday 1994). Such highly sexually dimorphic morphological traits generally do not exist in primates; where they do (e.g., large body size, large canines, manes), *intra*sexual selection (Phillips-Conroy & Jolly 1981, Clutton-Brock 1984) is believed to have played a greater role in their evolution than *inter*sexual selection. Thus, when female primates are selective in their choice of mates, it is usually not morphological but *behavioral* qualities of individuals for which they have preferences.

Female primates have been reported to choose mates based on diverse attributes, including dominance rank, familiarity, novelty, parenting ability, and access to resources (Janson 1984; Keddy 1986; Price 1990; Bercovitch 1991a, 1992; Pereira & Weiss 1991; Huffman 1992; Manson & Perry 1993). In many primate species, females choose to mate with unfamiliar or extra-group males, even in the face of opposition by the resident male(s) (Cords 1984, 1988; Wolfe 1984, 1986; Cords et al., 1986; Richard 1985; Small 1989; Bercovitch 1991a, 1992; Pereira & Weiss 1991; Sprague 1991; Manson 1993, 1995a; Manson & Perry 1993). Even female gibbons (*Hylobates lar*) and siamangs (*Hylobates syndactylus*), who develop monogamous pair-bonds, sometimes seek extra-pair copulations (Palombit 1994; Reichard 1995).

Female preference for unfamiliar or extragroup males may be related to an avoidance of inbreeding. Due to their large investment in each offspring, primate females should be selected to be particularly careful about each one, and the harmful effects of inheriting two copies of a deleterious recessive allele—heightened by mating among relatives—could select for inbreeding avoidance. Thus, females may prefer unfamiliar males—immigrant, peripheral, or extragroup males—because those are the males to whom they are least likely to be related.

Mating with extragroup males may also be a way in which females influence the structure of groups by encouraging male migration between them (Huffman 1992; Small 1993). This would be an indirect way of avoiding inbreeding, by giving males a proximate motivation for leaving a group (due to lack of mates) or entering a group (due to solicitations by females in that group). Alternatively, females may prefer newly immigrated males (or males that are in the process of immigrating) because these males are most likely to remain in the group for a long period of time, providing the potential benefits of a long-term relationship with the female and/or her offspring (Bercovitch 1991a).

On the other hand, female primates may be attracted to unfamiliar males because they are simply trying to mate with as many males as possible (Small 1989). Female primates, including baboons, often mate with multiple males within a single estrus cycle or even within a single day (Tutin 1979; Taub 1980; Hrdy 1981; Wilson et al., 1982; Goodall 1986; Wolfe 1986; Small 1990; Bercovitch 1995). Polyandrous mating could benefit a female in several ways. First, it may increase the probability of offspring survival: it may confuse paternity and thus inhibit male infanticide, elicit paternal care, or simply promote tolerance of infants by all males (Hrdy 1974, 1977, 1979; Hausfater & Hrdy 1984; Small 1993; Bercovitch 1991a, 1995). Second, in multi-male groups, polyandry could promote social bonding and the establishment of many allies, which might be important to the female's (and her infant's) survival and reproduction within the social group (Smuts 1985; Small 1993). Third, it could be a way to produce genetically diverse offspring, which may be advantageous to the evolutionary survival of one's genes (i.e., offspring) in a changing environment (Wolfe 1986; Bercovitch 1991a). Fourth, it could be a strategy to ensure conception by keeping the reproductive tract full of sperm and to safeguard against potential poor-quality sperm (Small 1988). Females might also be inciting sperm competition among males (Haig & Bergstrom 1995; Keller & Reeve 1995; Manson 1995b) or depleting the sperm supply as a competitive strategy against other females (Nakatsuru & Kramer 1982; Small 1988; Sommer 1989b; Sommer et al., 1992).

Unlike much evidence of female choice from nonprimate taxa, female primates do not seem to prefer specific traits, but rather abstract qualities that may not even be heritable. No primate study has conclusively shown that females are choosing for males with heritable traits. Thus, although female primates may have preferences for some mates over others and are able to exercise these preferences, sexual selection by female choice does not appear to be operating among primates to any significant degree, especially compared to many nonmammalian species.

Female Reproductive Competition

Traditionally, competition has been studied in male rather than female primates. Variance in male reproductive success has usually been assumed to be greater than variance in female reproductive success, and innumerable studies have examined factors contributing to differential reproductive success among males. Over the past two decades, however, researchers have begun to concentrate on female competition and factors that affect differential reproductive success among females, and many have concluded that variance in female reproductive success is indeed higher than was previously thought (Hrdy 1981, 1986; Fedigan 1982, 1983; Wasser 1983b; Small 1984, 1993; Harcourt 1987).

Female primates compete in many ways, all of which may lead to differential reproductive success. They may compete over access to food resources, mates, social partners, or advantageous spatial positions in a group (e.g., Seyfarth 1976; Whitten 1983a, 1984; Barton 1993). They may use strategies to lower one another's fertility, such as harassment at specific times during the reproductive cycle (e.g., Dunbar & Dunbar 1977; Keverne 1979; Wasser 1983a). Females may also compete by attempting to harm one another's offspring (e.g., Silk 1980; Hiraiwa 1981; Sommer 1989a; Maestripieri 1994a). That success in female-female competition enhances fitness is usually inferred from correlations between dominance rank and access to resources, nutritional status, fertility, access to mates, or other measures of reproductive success (e.g., Silk et al., 1980, 1981; Small 1981; Whitten 1983; Fairbanks & McGuire 1984; Wallen & Winston 1984; Altmann et al., 1988; Abbott et al., 1990; Linn et al., 1991).

The effect of dominance rank on factors that lead to differential reproductive success seems to be most prevalent in cases in which resources are restricted, such as during periods of drought, or at least when resources are clumped in distribution (Harcourt 1987; Bercovitch & Strum 1993). Food availability is likely the main constraint on female reproductive success, and differential access to food resources may thus be the main factor behind correlations between female dominance rank and measures of reproductive success in many species. In some primates, however, such as marmosets (*Callithrix* spp.: Abbott 1984; Abbott et al., 1990), tamarins (*Saguinus* spp.: Epple & Katz 1980, 1984; Ziegler et al., 1987), geladas (*Theropithecus gelada*: Dunbar & Dunbar 1977; Dunbar 1980; McCann 1995), and talapoin monkeys (*Miopithecus talapoin*: Keverne 1979; Abbott et al., 1986), female competition appears to be prevalent whether or not the food supply is limited; in these cases, differential female reproductive success appears to be related to differential levels of aggression-, stress-, and/or pheromone-induced suppression of reproduction.

Whereas reproductive competition in males occurs mainly around the time of mating, female reproductive competition can occur at any stage of reproduction and at any stage of their lives. For females, competition begins at birth, in the form of physical harassment and competition for priority of access to food resources, and continues until well after parturition, in the form of aggression, kidnapping, and differential offspring survival.

Female Transfer

In the majority of primate species, it is the males who transfer between groups. In some species, however, females transfer between groups in addition to or in place of males (Moore 1984). In the latter case, female transfer may be a female strategy to avoid inbreeding (Pusey 1980; Pusey & Packer 1987; Stewart & Harcourt 1987). For example, as a female gorilla matures, it is likely that the one reproductively active male in the group is her father, as silverbacks have very long tenures—longer than the time it takes for a female to reach maturity and even as long as two or more female generations (Stewart & Harcourt 1987; Robbins 1995). Likewise, in chimpanzees, males are philopatric and mating appears to be inhibited between maternally related individuals in a group, supporting the notion that female chimpanzees emigrate to avoid mating with their close relatives (Pusey 1980).

Another benefit of female transfer may be a reduction in feeding and/or mating competition among females (Moore 1984). Female mountain gorillas appear to prefer groups with fewer females and tend to transfer from larger to smaller groups and from groups to lone males (Stewart & Harcourt 1987; Watts 1990), suggesting that female competition may play a role in gorilla female transfer decisions. Similarly, female red howler monkeys appear to experience competition for group membership and may often be forced to transfer due to competition from other females (Crockett 1984).

Females may also transfer between groups to avoid infanticidal males (Stewart & Harcourt 1987; Smuts & Smuts 1993). Females might transfer *out* of a group to avoid a potentially infanticidal immigrant male or transfer *into* a group to gain protection from infanticide from a particular male that has somehow demonstrated such a capacity (Wrangham 1982; Watts 1989; Smuts & Smuts 1993).

Female Incitement of Male Competition

One way for females to ensure that they mate with the highest-quality males is by inciting male-male competition. Females may incite *agonistic competition* among males, after which the females mate with the "winners" of the fights. By mating with many males within a short period of time, females may also incite *sperm competition*, which would result in fertilization by the male with the most motile sperm, leading to selection for larger testes and a higher quality and quantity of sperm (Short 1979;

Harcourt et al., 1981; Bercovitch 1989). It has been suggested that the function of female copulation calls (loud vocalizations given during mating) is to incite agonistic and/or sperm competition among males (Cox & Le Boeuf 1977; Oda & Masataka 1992; O'Connell & Cowlishaw 1994). Such calls may function to alert other males that a copulation is occurring, thus bringing them into proximity so that the female will not only have access to several mates but will be able to assess mate quality and choose the best quality male(s).

Female Strategies to Counteract Infanticide

As discussed earlier, infanticide by males occurs in many primates, including baboons, and females in species in which it occurs with regularity appear to have evolved strategies to counteract it. These strategies fall into two general categories: (1) preventing infanticide from occurring in the first place or (2) minimizing losses when it does occur (Hrdy 1977, 1979; Packer & Pusey 1983; Struhsaker & Leland 1987; van Schaik & Dunbar 1990; Hrdy et al., 1995; van Schaik et al., 2000).

Active Defense. One option for female primates is to attempt to actively defend their infants from infanticidal males. This has been sometimes observed but is usually not very effective, probably because in most species in which infanticide has been reported, males are substantially larger than females and are individually dominant to them (Hrdy 1977; Crockett & Sekulic 1984; Watts 1989; Pereira & Weiss 1991; Newton 1986).

Minimizing Losses. Sometimes female primates appear simply to be trying to minimize their losses during a potentially infanticidal situation. Females often not only refrain from trying to prevent males from killing their infants, but have even been reported to abort or otherwise return to reproductive condition sooner than normal in the presence of or following immigration by an unfamiliar male (Pereira 1983; Mori & Dunbar 1985; Colmenares & Gomendio 1988; Alberts et al., 1992). In captive hamadryas, takeovers have been causally related to a reduced postpartum amenorrhea, abortion, and premature birth (Colmenares & Gomendio 1988; Zinner & Deschner 2000). As we shall see in Chapters 5 and 6, takeovers of hamadryas females in this study were followed by sexual swellings and estrus behavior within two weeks, though whether these swellings actually occurred earlier than they would have otherwise is not known because the prior history of these females was not known at the time.

Abortion, premature birth, and an early resumption of estrus may be examples of the "Bruce effect," known to occur in rodents, whereby a female exposed to a strange male (or even simply his odor) reabsorbs her fetus and returns to reproductive condition earlier than normal. The Bruce effect, as well as the termination of parental investment that occurs in similar situations among primates, may represent a female strategy to forego further investment in an offspring that is likely to be killed anyway (Labov 1981; Huck 1984). By aborting a fetus or letting an infant be killed by an immigrant male, a female will begin ovulating again sooner than if she had tried to keep her offspring, and she will then be able to mate with the immigrant male and begin investing in offspring that will gain the male's protection.

Pseudoestrus and Post-Conception Estrus.   As discussed earlier in this chapter, many female primates engage in sexual activity during periods when they are not fertile. The most obviously nonfertile period during which female primates display pseudoestrus is after conception. Post-conception estrus occurs in many primate species, including vervet monkeys, *Cercopithecus aethiops* (Whitten 1982; Andelman 1987); rhesus and bonnet macaques, *Macaca* spp. (Conaway & Koford 1964; Glick 1980; Lindburg 1983; Small 1983); redtail monkeys, *Cercopithecus ascanius* (Cords 1984); blue monkeys, *Cercopithecus mitis* (Cords et al., 1986); gelada baboons, *Theropithecus gelada* (Mori 1979b); Hanuman langurs, *Semnopithecus entellus* (Hrdy 1977); tamarins, *Saguinus* spp. (Dixson 1992); marmosets, *Callithrix jacchus* (Hearn 1978); bonobos, *Pan paniscus* (Manson et al., 1997); and chimpanzees, *Pan troglodytes* (Wallis 1982).

As mentioned previously, post-conception estrus may be a means of manipulating a male's assessment of his own paternity, which might facilitate paternal care in species in which paternal care contributes to offspring survival or inhibit infanticide in species in which infanticide occurs (Hrdy 1977, 1979; Hausfater 1984). Post-conception estrus occurs in many primate species that live in one-male groups and often occurs specifically when new males enter or take over a group, suggesting that it may have evolved as a strategy to prevent infanticide in these species (Hrdy 1977; Mori 1979; Cords 1984; Struhsaker & Leland 1987; Watts 1989).

Proximately, post-conception sexual swellings and estrus behavior may be stimulated by the presence of a new or unfamiliar male. This may occur via pheromones (e.g., the Bruce effect) or through a general attraction to novel males (see the earlier discussion of female choice) that elicits mating activity when new males enter a group.

Other Manipulations of a Male's Paternity Assessment.   In addition to post-conception behavioral estrus, sexual swellings that occur shortly after a takeover (described in the previous section as a way to minimize a female's losses after a takeover) may also function to manipulate a male's paternity assessment. Zinner and Deschner (2000) reported that females showed reduced postpartum amenorrhea after being taken over by a new leader male compared to periods of stable group membership. These females, however, did not correspondingly reduce their interbirth interval, but simply underwent more estrus cycles before conceiving again. It thus appeared as if these females were using sexual swellings as a situation-dependent strategy to lower their risk of infanticide by (falsely) advertising to their new leader male that they were fertile again (and showing that they were not pregnant with another male's offspring).

Females may also try to prevent infanticide *before* group takeovers occur, by mating with extragroup males who are likely to take over the group. By doing so, a female may confuse paternity and thus decrease the likelihood of an extragroup male killing her offspring, both as an outsider and if/when he takes over the group of which she is a member (Hrdy 1977; Dunbar 1984b; O'Connell & Cowlishaw 1994). A similar strategy could be useful in multi-male groups: Females often mate with multiple males during a single estrus period, which may inhibit infanticide due to paternity confusion (Hrdy 1977, 1981, 1986; Hausfater & Hrdy 1984; Struhsaker & Leland 1987; Soltis 2002). Also in multi-male groups, females may forge long-term associations with males; these male "friends" might then help protect a female's infant from infanticide by other males (Smuts 1985; Palombit et al., 1997; Weingrill 2000).

Broader Implications of Infanticide and Male Coercion

Many authors have suggested that infanticide and aggression toward infants is a primary selective force leading to many aspects of sociality among female primates, including bonds between females and males (Wrangham 1979a, 1982; Fossey 1984; Watts 1989; van Schaik & Dunbar 1990; Sterck et al., 1997; Palombit 1999; van Schaik et al., 1999; van Schaik & Janson 2000). Treves (1998) proposes the conspecific-threat hypothesis for the evolution of primate social systems, an extension of Brereton's (1995) coercion-defense hypothesis, in which females are always at risk of aggression (to themselves or their infants) from unrelated males and so must adopt one or more defensive strategies, one of which is the association with a male for protection (Brereton 1995; Treves 1998). Palombit (1999) discusses infanticide avoidance as a primary reason for close bonds between female chacma baboons and adult males. He argues that in both chacma baboons and gorillas, sexually selected infanticide accounts for a large portion of infant mortality *and* females develop and maintain bonds with males (it is the females who are most responsible for proximity maintenance and do most of the grooming in both of these species).

REPRODUCTIVE STRATEGIES IN PRIMATES

Based on fundamental biological sex differences, male and female primates should use different reproductive strategies. Males should try to inseminate as many females as possible, whereas females should try to maximize offspring quality. Evidence of reproductive strategies in male and female primates generally supports these expectations.

Females may employ numerous strategies to ensure offspring quality. They may choose healthy, genetically compatible, or otherwise high-quality mates to maximize the genetic quality of their offspring. Alternatively, they may choose mates that are likely to promote offspring survival through care or protection of infants or simply by tolerance of infants (i.e., inhibition of infanticide). Females could also incite males to compete with one another, either by agonistic competition or sperm competition, so as to be able to mate with the best competitor (and pass on the genes for competitive abilities to their male offspring). Females may also compete among themselves, as effective competition against other females may increase a female's access to food resources and improve the health of both herself and her offspring. Finally, females may increase offspring quality by reproducing at the most appropriate time so as to maximize food resources and minimize energy expenditure during gestation and lactation.

Male primates, on the other hand, aggressively compete for mates, either by trying to monopolize sexual access to a group of females or by tolerating other males in a group and competing for access to estrous females. It is not clear whether higher ranking males have priority of access to mates; even if they do, lower-ranking males may use alternative strategies to achieve comparable reproductive success.

It is unclear, however, whether competition among males or females leads to differential lifetime reproductive success. There are always many factors contributing to reproductive success, and any one particular effect may be outweighed by something else, so that reproductive success evens out over a lifetime or even over the short term. For example, higher-ranking females may undergo more rapid reproductive maturation than lower-ranking females, but earlier age at first birth does not increase lifetime reproductive success if it also delays subsequent pregnancies, increases the risk of infant mortality, or decreases one's life span (Bercovitch & Berard 1993). Alternative life history and reproductive strategies may result in equivalent lifetime reproductive success over the long term (Dunbar 1988; Bercovitch 1991b; Brereton 1992). Overall, longevity may be the one factor that is most tightly correlated with lifetime reproductive success (Bercovitch & Berard 1993). Longevity, which may be independent of rank (Bercovitch 1991b) and may vary significantly between individuals, may outweigh any short-term advantages in reproductive success conferred by dominance rank or other factors.

CONFLICTS BETWEEN MALE AND FEMALE STRATEGIES

Although both male and female primates appear to pursue their own reproductive strategies independent of one another, these strategies often conflict. Individual behavior is inevitably constrained by the behavior of

Hamadryas females are essentially conditioned to stay near their leader males and do not appear to be free to pursue their own social or reproductive interests. This female is "kecking" at her leader male, a sign of submission. *(Photo by the author)*

others, and this is especially true for animals that live in social groups such as primates. The outcome of choice or competition for mates, therefore, will always be constrained by competition from (and among) other individuals and the mate preferences of other individuals. Reproductive behavior is ultimately a compromise between male and female interests.

This conflict between male and female strategies is particularly relevant to hamadryas baboons, in which female strategies appear to be obscured by those of males. From previous field studies of wild hamadryas, one might come to the conclusion that female strategies are either not expressed or simply do not exist at all. Like all female primates, however, hamadryas baboons would benefit from selecting high-quality mates and choosing mates in a way that promotes offspring survival. Like other females that live in one-male groups, hamadryas females may be at risk of infanticide when male membership changes and might therefore employ reproductive strategies to minimize this risk. Whether hamadryas females have any reproductive strategies of their own, however, was unknown and had remained relatively unexplored prior to this study. It was to explore and elucidate the perspective of hamadryas females that I began my field study in 1996.

3

Study Site, Subjects and Methods

THE FILOHA STUDY SITE

Awash National Park is located in the semiarid lowlands of the northern Rift Valley of Africa, about 150 kilometers east of Addis Ababa, Ethiopia (see Figures 1–1 and 3–1). The park is bordered on the south by the Awash River, along which there is a zone of hybridization between hamadryas (*Papio hamadryas hamadryas*) and anubis (*P. h. anubis*) baboons that has been the subject of long-term investigation by the Awash National Park Baboon Research Project (ANPBRP) (Jolly & Brett 1973; Brett et al. 1977, 1982; Phillips-Conroy & Jolly 1981, 1986, 1988; Phillips-Conroy et al. 1991, 1992, 1993; Jolly & Phillips-Conroy 1998, 1999, 2003). To the north, the park is bordered by the Kesem River (a tributary of the Awash), the Awara Melka State Farm and the accompanying village of Sabure, and an area of hot springs known as Filoha (*fil wuha* means "hot water" in Amharic) (Figure 3–2). At Filoha lies the northernmost outpost of Awash National Park and a cliff commonly used as a sleeping site by hamadryas baboons.

The Awash region has two periods of seasonal rainfall: the long rains, occurring for two to three months between late June and September, and the short rains, occurring sporadically and intermittently between February and May. Of the 500–600 mm of annual rainfall reported by the park headquarters (Nagel 1973; Yalden et al. 1996), the vast majority falls during the long rains, or wet season, of July and August.

View of Filoha outpost from top of sleeping cliff, with baboons in the foreground. *(Photo by the author)*

RESEARCH SCHEDULE

Most of the data reported in this book were collected for my dissertation research between October 1996 and September 1998, broken into two "seasons" of 8 months and 10 months, respectively. After my arrival in Ethiopia in early September 1996, I spent three weeks in Addis Ababa taking care of administrative details and the following four months at Filoha habituating baboons, learning to distinguish individuals, and collecting limited observational data at the sleeping cliff. I then began all-day follows and systematic data collection in mid-February 1997. Unfortunately, my research was interrupted by a field accident on May 28, 1997. After six months of medical treatment and recuperation, I returned to Filoha to resume data collection in December 1997 and continued through September 1998.

Between November 1996 and September 1998 I spent 986 hours, over 262 days, following and observing hamadryas baboons. Observation days and data collected were not, however, evenly distributed throughout the study period. Few observation days were possible between late June and September 1998 because this period coincided with the annual long rains in Awash. Rainfall at Filoha not only hinders observations, but the associated flooding limits one's ability to drive to other sleeping sites besides Filoha. In 1998, the rainfall also appeared to cause the baboons to travel

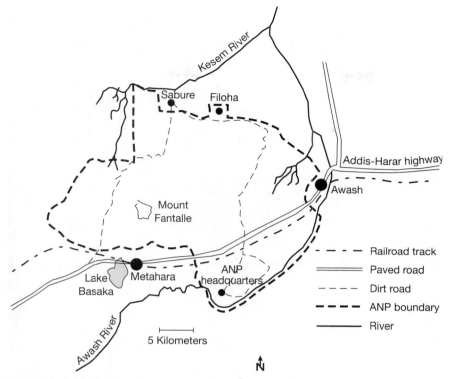

Figure 3–1 Map of Awash National Park

farther each day and to spend more time away from Filoha than during the drier months of the year (see Chapter 4 for further discussion of seasonal influences on behavior).

In addition to the data collected during my dissertation research, some of the observations discussed in this book have been made since 1998, during my summer field seasons in 2000, 2001, and 2002 and my winter field seasons in 2003 and 2004. Although the primary focus of these shorter field seasons was the collection of samples for genetic analysis, some behavioral observations from these periods also contribute to the results discussed in this book, totaling 234 hours over 99 days in July and August 2000 and 2001; June, July, and August 2002; and January 2003 and 2004.

THE BABOONS AT FILOHA

At least five groups, called "bands" by Kummer (1968a), of hamadryas baboons range in the Filoha area, both in and outside the park, and sleep on the numerous cliffs, each 5–10 km apart, that are scattered throughout

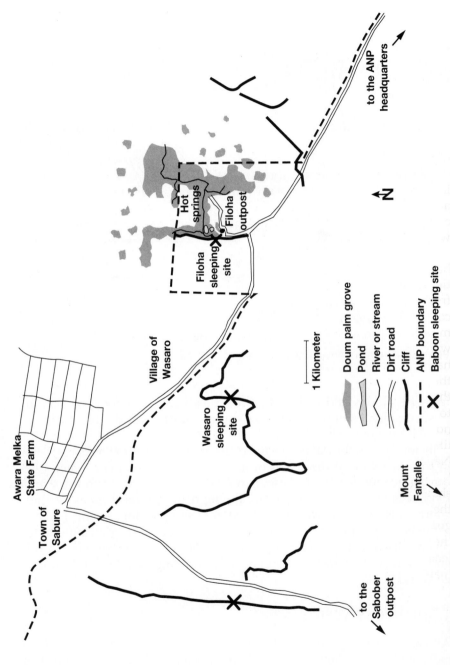

Figure 3–2 Map of the Filoha-Sabure Area

Awara Melka State Farm

Town of Sabure

Village of Wasaro

Hot springs

Filoha outpost

Filoha sleeping site

Wasaro sleeping site

Mount Fantalle

to the Sabober outpost

to the ANP headquarters

N

1 Kilometer

Doum palm grove
Pond
River or stream
Dirt road
Cliff
ANP boundary
Baboon sleeping site

the area (see Chapter 4 for details). One of these cliffs is about 200 meters from the Filoha outpost. A second cliff used by baboons, which I discovered in May 1997, is near the village of Wasaro, about 4.3 km from Filoha (see Figure 3–2).

My primary study group, "Group 1," numbered about 150 individuals in November 1996 and about 170 individuals in September 1998. The number of reproductively cycling (i.e., adult or subadult/adolescent) females ranged from 45 to 55 and the number of one-male units (and leader males) ranged from 22 to 25 over the course of the study period. Table 3–1 shows the composition of Group 1 during the 1997–1998 observation season (see Chapter 5 for more details on social structure and social organization).

I observed two other groups, "Group 2" and "Group 3," each numbering over 200 individuals, for periods of about three weeks each in April and May 1997. I used qualitative observations and data from Groups 2 and 3 to confirm that the broad patterns of behavior observed in Group 1 were typical for this population of hamadryas baboons.

All of the individuals in the Filoha population were phenotypically hamadryas and appeared to show no anubis admixture, with two exceptions. One adult male anubis baboon (*Papio hamadryas anubis*), a migrant from an anubis group along the Awash River (as shown by palm prints collected by the ANPBRP at both locations several years apart), was a member of Group 3 during 1997 and again in 2002 (and still was as of the writing of this book). Also, an adult male that appeared to be an anubis-hamadryas hybrid was a member of Group 1 until December 1997 and then either transferred to another group or died. I never observed either of these males with any females, and I assume that they did not gain access to any while they resided in hamadryas groups. Because anubis males do not attempt to maintain exclusive access to anestrous females, they are likely incapable of obtaining mates in hamadryas society (Kummer 1968b; Nagel 1973; Nystrom 1992).

Table 3–2 lists all females from both observation seasons, along with the shortened version of their name (for use in subsequent figures and tables), the number of scan samples I obtained for them, their estimated age category, whether they had a black infant during the study period, whether they underwent sexual cycles during the study period, the name of their leader male, the number of females in their unit, the number of follower males usually associated with their unit, the number of juveniles associated with their unit, their resulting number of potential social partners, and their number of adult or subadult potential social partners. Although there were no more than 55 adult and subadult females in Group 1 at any one time, I collected data from a total of 86 females over the two observation seasons. This discrepancy is due to the fact that these baboons were

Table 3–1 Group 1 Composition* (1997–1998)

Name of Leader Male of OMU	Number of Adult Females in OMU	Number of Subadult or Adolescent Females in OMU	Names of Females in OMU	Number of Infants in OMU	Number of Juveniles in OMU	Number of Follower Males in OMU	Total Members of OMU
Alexander	3	1	Fanny, Judy, Netty, Katy	1	2	0	8
Boris	2–3	0	Katrina, Natalie	0–1	2–3	1	6–8
Bruce	5	0	Janice, Carolyn, Ralaine	1–2	2	0	8–9
Casper	1	0	Wendy	0–1	0	0	2–3
Darth	2	0	Audrey, Verena	0–1	2	0–1	5–7
Emilio	2	0	Antonia, Lina	0–2	2	0	5–7
Fred	1	0	Wilma	0	1	1	4
Gus	1	0	Lorena	0	0	1	3
Hank	1	0	Ursula	0–1	0	0	2–3
Ike	3	1	Whoopie, Raquel, Belinda, Patsy	0–1	1	0	6–7
Jack	3	1	Talia, Holly, Meryl, Mira	1	1	0	6
Jerry	1	0	Delores	0	0	0	2
Jupiter	2–3	0	Venus, Serena, Luna	0–1	0	1	4–6
Ken	2	0	Barbie, Midge	0	0	1	4
Leonardo	5	0	Chiara, Roma, Gina, Anabella, Isabella	1–3	2	0	9–12
Max	3	2	Sylvia, Elena, Anja, Kaja, Tonja	0–2	0	0	6–8
Nick	1	0	Cassie	0–1	0	0	2–3
Orion	1	0	Virgo	0	1	0	3
Pete	0	1–3	Angie, Lizzy, Ollie	0	0	0	2–4
Rudy	1	0	Julie	0–1	1	0	3–4
Sebastian	2	0	Mara, Clea	0–1	1	0	4–5
Sting	1	2	Cher, Jewel, Tiffany	1–2	0	0	5–6
Ximeno	1	0	Juana	0	0	0	2
Zeus	2	0	Athena, Hera	0–1	1	1	5–6

*Not including solitary males and juveniles that were not consistently associated with an OMU (for definitions of age classes, see Table 5–1).

Table 3-2 Group 1 Females* over Both Observation Seasons

OMU—Name of Leader Male & Observation Season	Name of Female	Shortened Name (for subsequent tables)	Number of Scan Samples	Estimated Age	Had Infant during Study Period[1]	Cycling during Study Period[2]	Number of Females in OMU	Number of Follower Males Associated with OMU	Number of Juveniles Associated with OMU	Total Number of Potential Social Partners[3]	Potential Adult or Subadult Social Partners[4]
Pete 97–98 (1)	Angie (1)	ANG	4	Subadult (4–5 yrs)			1	0	0	1	1
Nick 97–98	Cassie	CAS	9	Young adult (5–6 yrs)	√		1	0	0	1	1
Jerry 97–98	Delores	DEL	1	Fully adult		√	1	0	0	1	1
George 96–97	Demi	DEM	4	Young adult (5–6 yrs)			1	0	0	1	1
Sylvester 96–97	Dorothy (3)	DOR3	19	Old (wrinkles)	√		1	0	1	2	1
Alexander 96–97	Fanny (1)	FAN	34	Old (wrinkles)		√	1	0	1	3	1
Pluto 97–98	Gloria (2)	GLO2	1	Old (wrinkles)			1	0	1	2	1
Ozzie 96–97	Harriet	HAR	14	Young adult (5–6 yrs)		√	1	0	0	1	1
Ximeno 97–98	Juana	JUA	31	Young adult (5–6 yrs)			1	0	0	1	1
Rudy 97–98	Julie	JUL	69	Fully adult	√	√	1	0	1	4	1
Eddie 96–97	Lolita	LOL	4	Young adult (5–6 yrs)		√	1	0	0	1	1
Gus 97–98	Lorena	LOR	10	Fully adult		√	1	1	0	2	2
Hank 97–98	Ursula (2)	URS2	83	Young adult (5–6 yrs)	√	√	1	0	0	1	1
Ralph 96–97	Ute	UTE	9	Fully adult		√	1	0	0	1	1
Orion 97–98	Virgo	VIR	81	Fully adult		√	1	0	1	2	1

(Continued)

Table 3–2 Continued

OMU—Name of Leader Male & Observation Season	Name of Female	Shortened Name (for subsequent tables)	Number of Scan Samples	Estimated Age	Had Infant during Study Period[1]	Cycling during Study Period[2]	Number of Females in OMU	Number of Follower Males Associated with OMU	Number of Juveniles Associated with OMU	Total Number of Potential Social Partners[3]	Potential Adult or Subadult Social Partners[4]
Casper 97–98	Wendy	WEN	0	Young adult (5–6 yrs)	✓		1	0	0	2	1
Ike 96–97	Whoopie (2)	WHO2	18	Fully adult		✓	1	0	1	2	1
Fred 97–98	Wilma	WIL	7	Fully adult		✓	1	1	1	3	2
Roberto 96–97	Ximena	XIM	2	Fully adult			1	0	0	1	1
Boris 97–98	Katrina (2)	KAT2	24	Fully adult		✓	2	0	1	2	2
	Natalie (2)	NAT2	24	Older adult	✓		2	0	0	2	2
Darth 96–97	Audrey (1)	AUD	29	Fully adult		✓	2	1	1	4	3
	Ursula (1)	URS	29	Young adult (5–6 yrs)			2	1	0	3	3
Darth 97–98 (1)	Audrey (2)	AUD2	218	Fully adult	✓	✓	2	0	1	3	2
	Verena (2)	VER2	218	Older adult		✓	2	0	1	3	2
Emilio 97–98 (1)	Antonia (1)	ANT	72	Fully adult	✓		2	0	1	3	2
	Lina (1)	LIN	72	Fully adult	✓	✓	2	0	1	3	2
Jupiter 97–98 (1)	Serena (1)	SER	108	Fully adult	✓	✓	2	1	0	3	3
	Venus (1)	VEN	118	Fully adult			2	1	0	3	3
Ken 97–98	Barbie	BAR	11	Fully adult		✓	2	1	0	3	3
	Midge	MID	11	Fully adult		✓	2	1	0	3	3
Pete 97–98 (2)	Angie (2)	ANG2	9	Subadult (4–5 yrs)			2	0	0	2	2
	Lizzy (1)	LIZ	9	Juvenile (3–4 yrs)			2	0	0	2	2

Sebastian 97–98	Clea	CLE	123	Fully adult		√	2	0	1	3	2
	Mara	MAR	123	Fully adult	√		2	0	0	2	2
Zeus 97–98	Athena	ATH	13	Fully adult			2	1	1	4	3
	Hera	HER	13	Fully adult	√		2	1	0	3	3
Boris 96–97	Katrina (1)	KAT	50	Fully adult	√		3	1	0	4	4
	Natalie (1)	NAT	50	Older adult	√		3	1	0	4	4
	Ophelia	OPH	50	Fully adult	√		3	1	0	4	4
Pete 97–98 (3)	Angie (3)	ANG3	3	Subadult (4–5 yrs)			3	0	0	3	3
	Lizzy (2)	LIZ2	3	Juvenile (3–4 yrs)			3	0	0	3	3
	Ollie	OLL	2	Juvenile (3–4 yrs)		√	3	0	0	3	3
Darth 97–98 (2)	Audrey (3)	AUD3	1	Fully adult			3	0	1	4	3
	Verena (3)	VER3	1	Older adult			3	0	1	4	3
	Carolyn	CAR	1	Fully adult	√		3	0	0	3	3
Emilio 97–98 (2)	Antonia (2)	ANT2	1	Fully adult	√		3	0	1	4	3
	Lina (2)	LIN2	1	Fully adult	√		3	0	1	4	3
	Linda	LID	1	Fully adult		√	3	0	0	3	3
Jupiter 97–98 (2)	Serena (2)	SER2	39	Fully adult		√	3	1	0	4	4
	Venus (2)	VEN2	39	Fully adult	√		3	1	0	4	4
	Luna	LUN	39	Fully adult			3	1	0	4	4
Jupiter 97–98 (3)	Serena (3)	SER3	6	Fully adult			3	2	0	5	5
	Venus (3)	VEN3	6	Fully adult	√		3	2	0	5	5
	Ralaine	RAL	6	Fully adult	√		3	2	0	5	5
Sting 97–98	Cher	CHE	9	Older adult	√	√	3	0	0	3	3
	Jewel	JEW	9	Subadult (4–5 yrs)	√	√	3	0	0	3	3
	Tiffany	TIF	9	Subadult (4–5 yrs)			3	0	0	3	3
Alexander 97–98	Fanny (2)	FAN2	86	Old (wrinkles)	√	√	4	0	1	5	4
	Judy	JUD	86	Fully adult	√	√	4	0	1	5	4

(Continued)

39

Table 3–2 Continued

OMU—Name of Leader Male & Observation Season	Name of Female	Shortened Name (for subsequent tables)	Number of Scan Samples	Estimated Age	Had Infant during Study Period[1]	Cycling during Study Period[2]	Number of Females in OMU	Number of Follower Males Associated with OMU	Number of Juveniles Associated with OMU	Total Number of Potential Social Partners[3]	Potential Adult or Subadult Social Partners[4]
	Katy	KAY	86	Subadult (4–5 yrs)		✓	4	0	0	4	4
	Netty	NET	86	Young adult (5–6 yrs)		✓	4	0	0	4	4
Clive 96–97	Claire	CLA	54	Fully adult	✓		4	2	0	7	6
	Mirjam	MIR	54	Fully adult	✓		4	2	0	6	6
	Seline	SEL	56	Fully adult			4	2	0	6	6
	Tÿna	TYN	55	Young adult (5–6 yrs)			4	2	0	6	6
Felix 96–97 (1)	Ellie (1)	ELL	3	Fully adult			4	0	0	4	4
	Goldie (1)	GOL	3	Fully adult			4	0	0	4	4
	Josie (1)	JOS	3	Fully adult	✓		4	0	0	5	4
	Polly (1)	POL	3	Fully adult			4	0	1	5	4
Ike 97–98	Belinda	BEL	148	Fully adult		✓	4	0	0	4	4
	Patsy	PAT	144	Subadult (4–5 yrs)		✓	4	0	0	4	4
	Raquel	RAQ	152	Fully adult	✓		4	0	1	5	4
	Whoopie (3)	WHO3	162	Fully adult	✓	✓	4	0	1	5	4
Jack 97–98	Holly	HOL	6	Fully adult	✓		4	0	0	4	4
	Meryl	MER	3	Older adult			4	0	1	4	4
	Mira	MIA	1	Young adult (5–6 yrs)			4	0	0	4	4
	Talia (2)	TAL2	3	Fully adult	✓		4	0	0	4	4
Quincy 96–97	Iris	IRI	42	Fully adult	✓		4	0	0	4	4
	Rose	ROS	42	Fully adult	✓		4	0	0	4	4
	Violet	VIO	42	Fully adult			4	0	1	5	4
	Zennia	ZEN	42	Fully adult	✓		4	0	0	5	4

Group	Name	Code	No.	Age								
Leonardo 97–98	Anabella	ANA	83	Fully adult			√	5	0	0	5	5
	Chiara (2)	CHI2	83	Fully adult		√		5	0	1	6	5
	Gina	GIN	83	Older adult		√	√	5	0	0	5	5
	Isabella	ISA	83	Fully adult		√		5	0	0	5	5
	Roma (2)	ROM2	83	Fully adult		√		5	0	1	6	5
Max 97–98	Anja (2)	ANJ2	122	Older adult		√		5	0	0	5	5
	Elena	ELE	121	Older adult		√		5	0	0	5	5
	Kaja	KAJ	122	Subadult (4–5 yrs)			√	5	0	0	5	5
	Sylvia (2)	SYL2	122	Young adult (5–6 yrs)			√	5	0	0	5	5
	Tonja	TON	122	Juvenile (3–4 yrs)			√	5	0	0	5	5
Sylvester 96–97	Beatrice (1)	BEA	3	Fully adult	√			5	0	0	5	5
	Dorothy (1)	DOR	3	Old (wrinkles)				5	0	1	6	5
	Hazel (1)	HAZ	3	Fully adult				5	0	0	5	5
	Irma	IRM	3	Fully adult				5	0	0	5	5
	Whoopie (1)	WHO	3	Fully adult				5	0	1	6	5
Felix 96–97 (2)	Beatrice (2)	BEA2	28	Fully adult			√	6	0	0	6	6
	Ellie (2)	ELL2	28	Older adult		√		6	0	0	7	6
	Goldie (2)	GOL2	28	Fully adult				6	0	0	6	6
	Hazel (2)	HAZ2	28	Fully adult		√		6	0	0	6	6
	Josie (2)	JOS2	28	Fully adult		√		6	0	0	7	6
	Polly (2)	POL2	28	Fully adult		√		6	0	1	8	6
Max 96–97	Dorothy (2)	DOR2	3	Old (wrinkles)				7	1	1	9	8
	Bertie	BER	4	Very old				8	0	1	9	8
	Elsa	ELS	4	Older adult				8	0	1	9	8
	Gloria (1)	GLO	3	Old (wrinkles)		√		8	0	0	8	8

(Continued)

Table 3–2 Continued

OMU—Name of Leader Male & Observation Season	Name of Female	Shortened Name (for subsequent tables)	Number of Scan Samples	Estimated Age	Had Infant during Study Period[1]	Cycling during Study Period[2]	Number of Females in OMU	Number of Follower Males Associated with OMU	Number of Juveniles Associated with OMU	Total Number of Potential Social Partners[3]	Potential Adult or Subadult Social Partners[4]
	Loretta	LOT	0	Young adult (5–6 yrs)	√		8	0	0	9	8
	Natasha	NAS	3	Young adult (5–6 yrs)			8	0	0	8	8
	Sylvia (1)	SYL	3	Young adult (5–6 yrs)		√	8	0	0	8	8
	Victoria	VIC	0	Older adult	√		8	0	0	9	8
	Yesennia	YES	3	Older adult	√		8	0	1	9	8
Leonardo 96–97	Anja (1)	ANJ	27	Older adult			9	0	2	11	9
	Chiara (1)	CHI	25	Older adult	√		9	0	2	11	9
	Fiona	FIO	20	Fully adult		√	9	0	1	10	9
	Maria	MAI	22	Young adult (5–6 yrs)			9	0	0	9	9
	Pia	PIA	22	Young adult (5–6 yrs)	√		9	0	1	10	9
	Roma (1)	ROM	27	Fully adult			9	0	1	9	9
	Sophia	SOP	21	Fully adult		√	9	0	0	9	9
	Talia (1)	TAL	27	Fully adult	√		9	0	0	9	9
	Verena (1)	VER	22	Older adult	√		9	0	0	9	9

*More than one occurrence of the same name indicates different conditions for the same female (i.e., a different leader male or a different number of females in her OMU).

[1] Had a black infant at the beginning of the study period or gave birth to an infant during the study period.

[2] Underwent one or more estrus cycles during the study period.

[3] Leader male + other females in OMU + follower males + juveniles.

[4] Leader male + other females in OMU + follower males.

not marked or tagged in any way, so only 13 females could be identified with confidence from one season (November 1996–May 1997) to the next (December 1997–September 1998). Consequently, I collected data on 43 females during the first observation season, renamed most females at the beginning of the second season (in December 1997), and then collected data on 55 females during the second observation season, only 13 of which had the same name as during the first season. Some names in Table 3–2, therefore, most certainly represent the same female over two observation seasons, but are treated as different females for the purpose of these analyses because there is no way to know for certain which pairs are actually the same individual. It is important to note that, because of this problem, some females contribute two data points to all analyses reported in this book. Also, females that were in more than one type of OMU during the study period (e.g., in cases in which a leader male gained another female during another female's tenure) are listed multiple times, once for each type of OMU to which they belonged (e.g., there are three listings for Angie, two listings for Antonia, etc.).

COLLECTION OF REPRODUCTIVE DATA

Estrus

Many primate taxa, including baboons, show physiological signs of estrus (see Chapter 2 for a discussion of the estrus concept), such as sexual swellings and face color changes, that correspond with behavioral estrus (cf. Beach 1976; see Chapter 2). In baboons (*P. h. anubis* and *P. h. cynocephalus*), sexual swellings have been shown to correspond closely with levels of ovarian hormones and to occur during the period just before, during, and just after ovulation (Shaikh et al. 1982). Although my study did not involve the collection of samples for hormone analyses to confirm the hormonal basis of sexual swellings, I assumed that sexual swellings in this population were a sign of the periovulatory period.

I defined *sexually swollen* as that period of time during which a female's sexual skin (i.e., the area immediately surrounding her vulva, medial to her ischial callosities) was tumescent. As shorthand, I used the term *swollen* to mean sexually swollen or having a tumescent sexual skin, and the term *flat* to indicate a nonswollen state, or not having a tumescent sexual skin. I divided sexual swellings into the following stages: the "going up" phase—visibly swollen and increasing in size but not yet at its maximum size; the "fully swollen" phase—the point of maximal tumescence; and the "going down" phase—after detumescence, or deflation, of the swelling, while it is decreasing in size but not yet back to its nonswollen state. The going up and fully swollen phases were often determinable only in retrospect, as I often was not sure if a female was fully swollen until I had seen her up to the time of detumescence. Individual females varied in the size of their maximal swelling in that some females consistently had larger swellings than others, which was not related solely to female age but also varied among fully adult females. Consequently, there was no consistent size measure of maximal swelling without knowing that of each individual female.

I defined *estrus* as that period during which a female was both sexually swollen and displayed estrus behavior, i.e., behavior that facilitated or involved copulation, such as soliciting copulations (via sexual presentations) as well as being receptive to and engaging in multi-mount copulations (cf. Beach 1976). While a few copulations occurred when females were not sexually swollen, females never solicited copulations when they were not swollen, nor did any multiple-mount copulations, or copulations that included ejaculation, occur when females were not swollen (see Chapter 6 for further discussion of sexual behavior and estrus).

Calculation of Female Reproductive Parameters

Female reproductive cycles were inferred from observational data. Sexual swellings were the most obvious visual cue. Menstrual blood on the perineum was also observed on two occasions. Sexual cycle lengths were measured from the first day of maximal swelling to the day before the first day of maximal swelling in the following cycle. For cases in which a female was not under observation during the first part of this period, cycle length was measured from the last day of full swelling (i.e., just before detumescence) to the day before the last day of full swelling during the next cycle. Pregnancies were inferred from an apparent cessation in sexual cycles (i.e., no sexual swellings for a period of at least one and a half times that female's normal cycle length, based on previously observed cycles) accompanied by obvious weight gain and/or a reddening of the perineal area (shown by Altmann 1970 to indicate pregnancy in baboons).

The birth of an infant was assumed to have taken place from the observation of a black infant with a female that had been pregnant (based on the signs just noted) on the last day she was observed prior to the appearance of the infant. If I had not observed that female on the day prior to the appearance of the infant, I assumed the birth to have taken place midway between the last day on which I saw her pregnant and the day on which I observed her with the newborn infant. In a few cases, I adjusted this estimated birth date in one direction or the other based on how old the infant appeared to be compared to other infants of known age. Conception dates were estimated by counting 181 days back from the actual or inferred date of birth. A gestation length of 181 days has been reported for captive hamadryas baboons at the German Primate Center (mean 181.3 days, range 171–191 days, N=52; Kaumanns et al. 1989) and is similar to that reported for wild populations of other baboon subspecies (*P. h. anubis* at Gilgil, Kenya: mean 180.2 days, N=13; Smuts & Nicolson 1989; *P. h. cynocephalus* at Tana River, Kenya: mean 181.5 days, N=28; Bentley-Condit & Smith 1997).

COLLECTION OF BEHAVIORAL DATA

Before commencing behavioral data collection (while I was habituating the study animals and learning individual identities), I recorded the various elements of the behavioral repertoire exhibited by this population of baboons and compiled them into an ethogram for the purposes of reference during behavioral data collection. Appendix I lists only the behavioral elements shown by females and those shown by males in the context of interacting with females; behavioral elements that occurred exclusively in male-male, male-juvenile, or juvenile-juvenile interactions are not included, as I did not collect data on male or juvenile behavior. After one month of ad libitum observations on patterns of proximity and social interactions, I decided to use a distance of 1 meter to define an "approach" and a distance of 10 cm to define "sitting close" (see Appendix I). I chose a distance of 10 cm for "sitting close" because it appeared to most consistently reflect social engagement between two individuals, whereas greater distances (such as 1 meter) were common among individuals that were in the same OMU but rarely interacted socially. I considered sitting close to be a form of affiliative behavior because it was often interspersed with grooming bouts and appeared to mainly characterize dyads that showed other evidence of a close social relationship, such as frequent grooming and lip smacking. In other primate taxa, such close spatial proximity has been shown to be a valid measure of social relationships and also to function as reconciliatory behavior after a conflict (Cords 1993, 1997).

Behavioral observations were made every day that the study group had slept at the Filoha cliff the previous night. Before February 1997, I conducted behavioral observations only when the baboons were on or around the Filoha sleeping cliff and limited my data collection to those individuals whom I could identify with confidence by that time. By mid-February 1997, I had learned to distinguish (and was collecting data on) most females in the group and began to follow the baboons away from the sleeping cliff. During the second observation season, in addition to follows from the Filoha Cliff, I also followed the baboons on some days when they had slept at the Wasaro cliff the previous night. (I only discovered the Wasaro sleeping cliff in late May 1997, just before the end of the first observation season.) Observation days at Wasaro were only possible when I had access to a vehicle, that is, during parts of July, August, and September 1998. Follows began at dawn and lasted as long as possible each day, though the majority were cut short of a full day because (1) the group was traveling too fast to keep up with it, (2) the group traveled through an area of marshy swamp or hot springs that I could not cross, (3) my scout and I became completely separated and had to stop following the baboons in order to find one another, (4) continuous heavy rain made observation impossible, or (5) it became obvious that the baboons were traveling to another sleeping cliff than the one from which they had come that morning and I had to leave them by late afternoon in order to get back to Filoha (or the truck, if we were at Wasaro) before dark.

During follows, I recorded the general group activity (e.g., resting, foraging, traveling, drinking) or combination of activities (e.g., resting and foraging; traveling and foraging) every 10 minutes. When the group was traveling, I recorded the direction of travel and all changes in direction of travel as they occurred, using a compass. I also made ad libitum observations (Altmann 1974) on mating and agonistic behavior among adult individuals, recording who was involved in each copulation or fight, if known. Whenever a known one-male unit came into view, I immediately conducted a scan sample of that OMU, recording the activity of all of its members, each female's nearest adult or subadult neighbor, and each female's proximity to the leader male. I repeated these OMU scan samples at 10-minute intervals for as long as that unit was in view. When a known female was in view, I conducted a continuous focal animal sample on that female (Altmann 1974). If more than one known female was in view, I chose a focal female based on two criteria: reproductive condition and

The author observing baboons southeast of the Wasaro Cliff. *(Photo by Julian Saunders)*

time since the last sampling. The focal samples were intended to be 30 minutes long, and were always terminated after 30 minutes, but were often cut short when the focal female went out of view during the sample period; about 55% of focal samples were less than 30 minutes. I never conducted two samples in a row on the same female, but always waited 30 minutes before beginning a new sample on her (e.g., when only one female was visible for a period of an hour or two and another focal female could not be found). During the focal samples, all social interactions of the focal female with any other adult or subadult individual, excluding infants and juveniles, were recorded continuously. During all focal samples, I scanned the focal female's one-male unit, and the group as a whole, every 10 minutes and recorded the general group activity (rest, travel, forage, etc.), the activity of all other members of the focal female's OMU within view, the focal female's proximity to all adult or subadult males within 3 meters, and the focal female's nearest neighbor.

DATA ANALYSIS

Group Scan Samples and Ranging Data

To obtain an estimate of group activity patterns, I first divided group scan sample data into the seventy-two 10-minute time slots between 0600 and 1800. I then selected 10-minute group scan samples from the largest uninterrupted blocks of observation time, that is, full observation days and partial days that included the longest periods of continuous data collection. I selected samples so that the entire data set consisted of an equal number of samples for each 10-minute time slot during the day and was also representative of as many months of the year as possible. By these methods, the total number of group scan samples used for analysis was 1,239. These data were used to determine general activity budgets of this population of hamadryas baboons (as described in Chapter 4).

For analysis of ranging patterns, I constructed a map of the Filoha-Sabure area using topographic maps based on satellite images obtained from the Ethiopian Mapping Authority in Addis Ababa (see Figure 3–2). Landmark data were collected with a handheld Magellan 2000 GPS unit (with 100 meter error) and used to fit points on the map to known locations in the baboons' home range. Travel directions and durations recorded during daily follows were transcribed onto the map and path lengths were calculated using a known scale (see Chapter 4).

One-Male Unit Scan Samples

I divided one-male unit scan sample data according to female identity and the type of unit to which the female belonged at the time. For example, if a female was in two different units (i.e., had two different leader males) at different times during the study period, data from each time period were tabulated separately. Likewise, if, for example, a female was in a three-female unit for several months and then her leader male acquired a fourth female, the data from the time during which she was in a three-female unit were tabulated separately from the data from the time during which she was in a four-female unit. For analyses of overall patterns of female social activity and comparisons between females in different sized units, the data for each female in each condition were analyzed separately. For analyses that included comparisons between individual females, data from different conditions for each female were pooled and averaged into per-female counts.

During exploratory data analysis, I examined the data in several ways: (1) using all available scan sample data; (2) using only scan sample data from females for whom I had at least a specified number of scan samples (e.g., at least 20, at least 50, or at least 100); and (3) using only scan samples during which females did not have sexual swellings. Using these different criteria did not produce wide variation in the results. When results were compared between tabulations that included females for whom I had at least 20, at least 30, at least 50, and at least 100 scan samples, across-female averages for percentage of samples spent in each type of social activity never varied by more than 2.8 points. Correspondingly, across-female averages for percentage of samples spent with each type of individual as her nearest neighbor did not vary by more than 3.0 points when I compared totals for females for whom I had at least 20, at least 50, and at least 100 scan samples. In most cases, results using females for whom I had at least 20 scans differed from those for whom I had at least 30 scans to a greater extent than results from females for whom I had at least 30 scans did from those from whom I had at least 50 scans or at least 100 scans. It thus seemed that once a minimum of 30 scans was reached, general patterns of female social activity and proximity (as shown in scan data tabulations; see Table 5–5) changed only minimally as more data were added.

As an additional means of examining the data, I divided scan sample data sets for each female randomly into two halves and compared them to evaluate consistency in patterns of results for each female. Each random half of data sets that consisted of at least 30 scans did not differ from the other in its broad patterns. Data sets of fewer than 30 scans, on the other hand, could not consistently be divided randomly to produce qualitatively similar halves.

Based on the results of these two analyses, I set the per-female minimum at 30 scans. Table 3–3 lists the 45 females for whom I had more than 30 scans and who were therefore included in analyses of patterns of behavior reported in Chapters 5, 6, and 7. Of these 45 females, data from

12 were collected during the 1996–1997 observation season over a period of three months. Data from the remainder of the females were collected during the 1997–1998 observation season, each over a period of at least nine months. Data for three females—Fanny, Venus, and Serena—were subdivided due to changes in the size and composition of their OMUs. Data on Fanny (FAN) from the first season, when she was the only female in her OMU, were considered separately from data from the second season, when her OMU consisted of four females. Likewise, information on Serena and Venus was subdivided into data collected when they were the only two females in their unit (SER and VEN) and data collected when a third female, Luna, was temporarily a member of their unit (SER2 and VEN2). Consequently Fanny, Serena, and Venus each count as two females for the purposes of most of these analyses.

Patterns of Proximity within One-Male Units. To calculate patterns of proximity between females and their leader males, the distance of each female from her leader male was averaged across all scan samples obtained for that female. To obtain general patterns of proximity between females and other individuals in their units (i.e., not just their leader males), I tabulated nearest neighbor data from the scan samples. The number of scan samples during which each other individual was a female's nearest neighbor was divided by the total number of scan samples for that female, resulting in a per-female percentage of total scan samples in which each other individual was her nearest neighbor. Patterns of proximity, including females' distances to their leader males and females' nearest neighbors, are reported in Table 5–2 and discussed in Chapters 5, 6, and 7.

Female Activity Patterns. From the OMU scan sample data, I tabulated per female totals for each type of activity. I eliminated the behavioral categories walking, running, traveling, foraging, eating, and drinking from the analysis because the baboons were typically less visible when engaged in these activities and their relative frequency would therefore have been underestimated (for general group activity patterns, I used the group scan samples, discussed earlier). The elimination of these categories resulted in a new total for each female that represented the number of scan samples during which she was in view but not walking, running, traveling, foraging, eating, or drinking, that is, when she was essentially "free" and available for social activity. This method not only eliminated those scans in which the baboons were less visible, but also focused the analysis on those times when females were not engaged in subsistence activities and when their behavior would more likely be motivated by social rather than ecological factors. The number of scan samples spent resting or engaged in each type of social activity was divided by this new total, which resulted

Table 3–3 Females Used in Analyses of Patterns of Proximity and Social Interactions

OMU	Name of Female	Number of Scan Samples	Distribution of Samples over Observation Period	Estimated Age (yrs)	Had Infant during Study Period	Cycling during Study Period	Number of Females in OMU	Number of Follower Males in OMU	Number of Juveniles in OMU	Total Potential Social Partners	Potential Adult or Subadult Social Partners
Alexander 96–97	FAN	34	35% from Mar. 97; rest from Dec. 96, Jan. 97, Feb. 97, and early Apr. 97	Old (wrinkles)		√	1	0	1	3	1
Ximeno 97–98	JUA	31	55% from Mar. 98, 23% from Apr. 98; rest (totaling 22%) from Feb., May, June, and July 98 (none from Dec. 97, Jan. 98, Aug. 98, or Sep. 98)	Young adult (5–6)			1	0	0	1	1
Rudy 97–98	JUL	69	13% from Apr. 98, 16% from May 98, 20% from June 98, 12% from July 98, 19% from early Sep. 98; rest (totaling 20%) from Dec. 97, Feb. 98, Mar. 98, and Aug. 98 (none from Jan. 98)	Fully adult	√	√	1	0	1	4	1
Hank 97–98	URS2	83	11% from Feb. 98, 17% from Mar. 98, 17% from Apr. 98, 20% from May 98, 11% from June 98; rest (totaling 23%) from Dec. 97, Aug. 98, and early Sep. 98 (none from Jan. or Jul.)	Young adult (5–6)	√	√	1	0	0	1	1
Orion 97–98	VIR	81	17% from May 98, 17% from June 98, 19% from July 98, 22% from early Sep. 98; rest (totaling 25%) from Feb., Mar., Apr., and Aug. 98 (none from Dec. or Jan.)	Fully adult		√	1	0	1	2	1

Emilio 97-98	ANT	72	18% from Apr. 98, 29% from May 98, 15% from June 98, 18% from July 98, 13% from early Sep. 98; rest (totaling 7%) from Mar. & Aug. 98	Fully adult	√		2	0	1	4	2
	LIN	72	18% from Apr. 98, 29% from May 98, 15% from June 98, 18% from July 98, 13% from early Sep. 98; rest (totaling 7%) from Mar. & Aug. 98	Fully adult		√	2	0	1	3	2
Darth 97-98	AUD2	218	12% from Mar. 98, 26% from Apr. 98, 19% from May 98, 19% from June 98, 9% from July 98, 8% from early Sep. 98; rest (totaling 7%) from Dec. 97, Feb. 98, and Aug. 98 (none from Jan. 98)	Fully adult	√	√	2	0	1	4	2
	VER2	218	12% from Mar. 98, 26% from Apr. 98, 19% from May 98, 19% from June 98, 9% from July 98, 8% from early Sep. 98; rest (totaling 7%) from Dec. 97, Feb. 98, and Aug. 98 (none from Jan. 98)	Older adult		√	2	0	1	3	2

(Continued)

Table 3-3 Continued

OMU	Name of Female	Number of Scan Samples	Distribution of Samples over Observation Period	Estimated Age (yrs)	Had Infant during Study Period	Cycling during Study Period	Number of Females in OMU	Number of Follower Males in OMU	Number of Juveniles in OMU	Total Potential Social Partners	Potential Adult or Subadult Social Partners
Sebastian 97-98	MAR	123	34% from Apr. 98, 24% from May 98, 14% from July 98; rest (totaling 18%) from Feb., Mar., Jun., Aug., and Sep. 98 (none from Dec. 97 or Jan. 98)	Fully adult	√		2	0	0	3	2
Sebastian 97-98	CLE	123	34% from Apr. 98, 24% from May 98, 14% from July 98; rest (totaling 18%) from Feb., Mar., Jun., Aug., and Sep. 98 (none from Dec. 97 or Jan. 98)	Fully adult		√	2	0	1	3	2
Jupiter 97-98 (1)	VEN	118	6% from Feb. 98, 12% from Mar. 98, 16% from Apr. 98, 36% from May 98, 8% from June 98, 10% from July 98, 2% from Aug. 98, 11% from Sep. 98 (none from Dec. 97 or Jan. 98)	Fully adult	√		2	1	0	4	3
Jupiter 97-98 (1)	SER	108	9% from Mar. 98, 18% from Apr. 98, 39% from May 98, 8% from June 98, 11% from July 98, 2% from Aug. 98, 12% from Sep. 98 (none from Dec. 97, Jan. or Feb. 98)	Fully adult		√	2	1	0	3	3

Group	Name	No.	Origin of samples	Age							
Boris 96–97	KAT	50	20% from Dec. 96, 24% from Feb. 97, 44% from Jan., Feb., & Apr. 97	Fully adult	√		3	1	0	5	4
	NAT	50	20% from Dec. 96, 24% from Feb. 97, 44% from Jan., Feb., & Apr. 97	Older adult	√	√	3	1	0	5	4
	OPH	50	20% from Dec. 96, 24% from Feb. 97, 44% from Jan., Feb., & Apr. 97	Fully adult	√		3	1	0	5	4
Jupiter 97–98 (2)	LUN	39	69% from June 98, 31% from July 98	Fully adult			3	1	0	4	4
	SER2	39	69% from June 98, 31% from July 98	Fully adult		√	3	1	0	4	4
	VEN2	39	69% from June 98, 31% from July 98	Fully adult	√		3	1	0	5	4
Quincy 96–97	IRI	42	43% from Mar. 97, 29% from early Apr. 97; rest (totaling 18%) from Dec. 96, Jan. 97, and Feb. 97	Older adult	√		4	0	0	5	4
	ROS	42	43% from Mar. 97, 29% from early Apr. 97; rest (totaling 18%) from Dec. 96, Jan. 97, and Feb. 97	Fully adult	√		4	0	0	5	4
	VIO	42	43% from Mar. 97, 29% from early Apr. 97; rest (totaling 18%) from Dec. 96, Jan. 97, and Feb. 97	Fully adult		√	4	0	1	5	4
	ZEN	42	43% from Mar. 97, 29% from early Apr. 97; rest (totaling 18%) from Dec. 96, Jan. 97, and Feb. 97	Fully adult	√		4	0	0	5	4

(Continued)

Table 3-3 Continued

OMU	Name of Female	Number of Scan Samples	Distribution of Samples over Observation Period	Estimated Age (yrs)	Had Infant during Study Period	Cycling during Study Period	Number of Females in OMU	Number of Follower Males in OMU	Number of Juveniles in OMU	Total Potential Social Partners	Potential Adult or Subadult Social Partners
Clive 96–97	CLA	54	22% from Dec. 96, 5% from Jan. 97, 24% from Feb. 97, 18% from Mar. 97, 31% from early Apr. 97	Fully adult	√		4	2	1	7	6
	MIR	54	22% from Dec. 96, 5% from Jan. 97, 24% from Feb. 97, 18% from Mar. 97, 31% from early Apr. 97	Fully adult	√		4	2	0	7	6
	SEL	56	22% from Dec. 96, 5% from Jan. 97, 24% from Feb. 97, 18% from Mar. 97, 31% from early Apr. 97	Fully adult	√		4	2	0	6	6
	TYN	55	22% from Dec. 96, 5% from Jan. 97, 24% from Feb. 97, 18% from Mar. 97, 31% from early Apr. 97	Young adult (5–6)			4	2	0	6	6
Alexander 97–98	FAN2	86	24% from July 98, 27% from Sep. 98; rest from Mar., Apr., May, June, and Aug. 98 (none from Jan. or Feb.)	Old (wrinkles)		√	4	0	1	5	4
	JUD	86	24% from July 98, 27% from Sep. 98; rest from Mar., Apr., May, June, and Aug. 98 (none from Jan. or Feb.)	Fully adult	√	√	4	0	1	5	4
	KAY	86	24% from July 98, 27% from Sep. 98; rest from Mar., Apr., May, June, and Aug. 98 (none from Jan. or Feb.)	Subadult (4–5)		√	4	0	0	4	4

	N	Timing	Age class							
Ike 97–98										
NET	86	24% from July 98, 27% from Sep. 98; rest from Mar., Apr., May, June, and Aug. 98 (none from Jan. or Feb.)	Young adult (5–6)	√		4	0	0	4	4
BEL	148	31% from May 98, 21% from June 98, 19% from July 98, 18% from early Sep. 98; rest (totaling 11%) from Mar., Apr. and Aug. 98 (none from Dec. 97, Jan. or Feb. 98)	Fully adult	√		4	0	0	4	4
PAT	144	31% from May 98, 21% from June 98, 19% from July 98, 18% from early Sep. 98; rest (totaling 11%) from Mar., Apr., and Aug. 98 (none from Dec., Jan. or Feb.)	Subadult (4–5 yrs)	√		4	0	0	4	4
RAQ	152	31% from May 98, 21% from June 98, 19% from July 98, 18% from early Sep. 98; rest (totaling 11%) from Mar., Apr., and Aug. 98 (none from Dec., Jan. or Feb.)	Fully adult		√	4	0	1	5	4
WHO3	162	28% from May 98, 19% from June 98, 17% from July 98, 16% from early Sep. 98; rest (totaling 20%) from Dec. 97, Feb., Mar., Apr., and Aug. 98 (none from Jan.)	Fully adult	√	√	4	0	1	5	4

(Continued)

Table 3-3 (Continued)

OMU	Name of Female	Number of Scan Samples	Distribution of Samples over Observation Period	Estimated Age (yrs)	Had Infant during Study Period	Cycling during Study Period	Number of Females in OMU	Number of Follower Males in OMU	Number of Juveniles in OMU	Total Potential Social Partners	Potential Adult or Subadult Social Partners
Leonardo 97–98	ANA	83	22% from Apr. 98, 39% from May 98, 27% from June 98; rest (totaling 12%) from Mar., July, Aug., and Sep. 98 (none from Dec. 97, Jan. or Feb. 98)	Fully adult		√	5	0	0	5	5
	CHI2	83	22% from Apr. 98, 39% from May 98, 27% from June 98; rest (totaling 12%) from Mar., July, Aug., and Sep. 98 (none from Dec. 97, Jan. or Feb. 98)	Fully adult	√		5	0	1	7	5
	GIN	83	22% from Apr. 98, 39% from May 98, 27% from June 98; rest (totaling 12%) from Mar., July, Aug., and Sep. 98 (none from Dec. 97, Jan. or Feb. 98)	Older adult	√	√	5	0	0	6	5
	ISA	83	22% from Apr. 98, 39% from May 98, 27% from June 98; rest (totaling 12%) from Mar., July, Aug., and Sep. 98 (none from Dec. 97, Jan. or Feb. 98)	Older adult	√		5	0	0	6	5
	ROM2	83	22% from Apr. 98, 39% from May 98, 27% from June 98; rest (totaling 12%) from Mar., July, Aug., and Sep. 98 (none from Dec. 97, Jan. or Feb. 98)	Fully adult	√		5	0	1	6	5

ANJ2	122	11% from Mar. 98, 25% from Apr. 98, 23% from May 98, 10% from June 98, 18% from July 98; rest (totaling 13%) from Aug. and Sep. 98 (none from Dec. 97, Jan. or Feb. 98)	Older adult	√		5	0	0	6	5
ELE	121	11% from Mar. 98, 25% from Apr. 98, 23% from May 98, 10% from June 98, 18% from July 98; rest (totaling 13%) from Aug. and Sep. 98 (none from Dec. 97, Jan. or Feb. 98)	Older adult	√		5	0	0	6	5
KAJ	122	11% from Mar. 98, 25% from Apr. 98, 23% from May 98, 10% from June 98, 18% from July 98; rest (totaling 13%) from Aug. and Sep. 98 (none from Dec. 97, Jan. or Feb. 98)	Subadult (4–5 yrs)		√	5	0	0	5	5
SYL2	122	11% from Mar. 98, 25% from Apr. 98, 23% from May 98, 10% from June 98, 18% from July 98; rest (totaling 13%) from Aug. and Sep. 98 (none from Dec. 97, Jan. or Feb. 98)	Young adult (5–6 years)		√	5	0	0	5	5
TON	122	11% from Mar. 98, 25% from Apr. 98, 23% from May 98, 10% from June 98, 18% from July 98; rest (totaling 13%) from Aug. and Sep. 98 (none from Dec. 97, Jan. or Feb. 98)	Juvenile (3–4 yrs)		√	5	0	0	5	5

Max 97–98

in a per-female percentage of "available social time" (calculated as a percentage of scan samples) spent in each type of social activity. The following activities were compared: sitting alone, sitting close to another individual, grooming another individual, and being groomed by another individual. "Sitting alone" was defined as sitting at least 10 cm from any other individual and not interacting socially. "Sitting close to" another individual was defined as sitting so that one's torso, arm, leg, or head (i.e., any body part except the tail) was within 10 cm of another adult or subadult individual (see also Appendix I). While the 10 cm distinction between "sitting alone" and "sitting close" was somewhat arbitrary, preliminary observations suggested that this distance reflected the presence or absence of social engagement among individuals (see page 45). Results of analyses of female activity patterns are reported in Table 5–5 and discussed in Chapters 5, 6, and 7.

Analysis Based on Reproductive State.   To compare female activity patterns across reproductive states, I divided per-female totals from scan sample tabulations into categories based on whether the female was swollen, was cycling but not currently swollen (flat), was pregnant (inferred as described earlier), or had an infant and was presumably lactating. Samples from a female's swollen phase were then again divided into categories based on whether the female's swelling was going up or whether the female was fully swollen. Preliminary analysis of female behavior during each phase showed no significant differences in patterns of behavior across all females for whom I had scan samples from each of these two conditions. I therefore collapsed scan data into a single swollen category that included going up and fully swollen, and compared swollen to flat in my analyses of the effects of sexual swellings on female behavior. Because it was unclear whether females in the going down phase of their cycle were in behavioral estrus, and because I had so few such samples for their inclusion or exclusion to make a difference in patterns observed, I excluded going down samples from comparisons of female behavior between reproductive states.

Continuous Focal Samples

The females for whom I have continuous focal samples are listed in Table 3–4. Due to problems of visibility and habituation, the amount of focal data obtained were limited and varied widely among females. Therefore, I used focal data for two main purposes: (1) to provide qualitative data to add to interpretations of female activity patterns in Chapters 5, 6, and 7; and (2) to provide behavioral sequence data related to mating behavior, reported in Chapter 6.

Table 3-4 Continuous Focal Sample Data

Name of Female[1]	Minutes of Focal Data	Minutes of Focal Data When Swollen	Minutes of Focal Data When Not Swollen
ANA	237.0	225	12.0
AUD	102.0	0	102.0
AUD2	20.0	0	20.0
BEL	541.0	99	442.0
CLE	453.0	323	130.0
FAN	49.0	0	49.0
HAR	63.0	48	15.0
JUD	30.0	30	0.0
JUL	18.5	0	18.5
KAJ	187.0	187	0.0
KAY	89.0	89	0.0
LIN	101.0	0	101.0
LUN	30.0	0	30.0
NAT	122.0	122	0.0
PAT	65.0	65	0.0
SEL	120.0	0	120.0
SER	337.0	268	69.0
SOP	43.0	43	0.0
SYL2	97.0	47	50.0
TAL	28.0	0	28.0
URS	58.0	0	58.0
URS2	33.5	0	33.5
UTE	44.0	30	14.0
VER2	589.0	276	313.0
VIO	46.0	0	46.0
VIR	175.0	115	60.0
WHO2	73.0	73	0.0
WHO3	26.0	0	26.0

[1]See Table 3–2 for details on individual females.

Statistical Analyses

Because the variables measured did not meet the assumptions required for parametric statistics, nonparametric statistical tests were used for all analyses (Siegel & Castellan 1988). The SAS Statview statistical software package was used to generate results. Unless otherwise indicated, all tests were two-tailed and the level of significance was set at alpha <0.05.

4

Hamadryas Behavioral Ecology: Negotiating a Hostile Land[1]

GEOGRAPHY, DISTRIBUTION, AND GROUP SIZES

The topography of the northern part of Awash National Park reflects the history of the dormant volcano Mt. Fantalle, consisting largely of volcanic rocky outcrops, rolling hills, and several kilometer-long cliffs. The Filoha outpost lies about 20 km north of Mt. Fantalle, in the far north of the park, and the area immediately surrounding the outpost is dominated by hot springs, doum palm trees (*Hyphaene thebaica*), palm scrub, and tall marsh grasses (Figure 3–2). The surrounding region resembles typical hamadryas habitat (Kummer 1968a) in that it is a semiarid thornscrub dominated by several species of shrubby *Acacia*. The mean annual rainfall at the park headquarters, 45 km south of Filoha, is 500–600 mm (most of which falls between June and September), and the mean afternoon shade temperature at Filoha is 34°C (93°F). The drier months (October through June) are generally about two degrees warmer (mean afternoon shade temperature 34.4°C) than the rainy months (32.7°C), with a peak of aridity and temperature (averaging 36°C) in May and June, just before the beginning of the wet season (July through mid-September).

At least five groups, or "bands" (Kummer 1968a), range throughout the Filoha-Sabure area (see Figure 3–2). As noted in Chapter 3, my main study

---

[1]A portion of the text of this chapter, as well as Table 4–1, was previously published in "Ranging Behavior, Group Size and Behavioral Flexibility in Ethiopian Hamadryas Baboons *(Papio hamadryas hamadryas)*," *Folia Primatologica 73* (2002): 95–103, and is reprinted with permission from Karger AG Publishers.

Much of the area around the Filoha hot springs is dominated by volcanic rock and an open thornscrub consisting of various *Acacia* species. *(Photo by the author)*

group, Group 1, consisted of about 150 individuals in November 1996 and about 170 in September 1998 (and numbers over 200 as of the writing of this book). Group 2 and Group 3 consisted of about 200 and 220 individuals, respectively, in 1998, but Group 3 has since become much larger, now comprising over 300 individuals (see Chapter 5). I have also seen in this area a group of about 100 individuals, a group of about 50 individuals, and small groups of fewer than 30 individuals. Unfortunately, I was never able to determine whether these small groups were stable bands or just temporary subgroups ("clans," perhaps, in Kummer and Abegglen's terms) of a larger band.

The group sizes in the Filoha area are, on average, substantially larger than those reported for most other hamadryas populations (see Table 4–1). In the Erer Gota area, about 180 km to the northeast of Filoha, Kummer (1968a) observed bands of 30 to 90 individuals; Sigg and Stolba (1981) observed bands of 62 to 95 individuals; and Abegglen (1984) observed bands of 52 to 90 individuals. In Awash Canyon near Awash Station, Nagel's (1973) two hamadryas study groups consisted of 51 and 57 individuals. In surveys of hamadryas baboons in southwestern Saudi Arabia, Kummer et al. (1981) found groups of 13 to 70 individuals and Biquand et al. (1992b) found groups of 9 to 102 individuals. In a survey in Yemen, Al-Safadi (1994) found groups of 22 to 89 individuals. A. Mori (pers. comm.), on the other hand, found larger groups of 120 to 190 individuals on cliffs along the Wabi-Shebeli River, south of Awash, which are similar

Table 4–1 Group Size, Home Range Size, and Daily Path Length of Filoha Hamadryas Compared to Other Populations[1]

	Filoha (this study)	Erer Gota (Kummer 1968a)	Erer Gota (Sigg & Stolba 1981)	Erer Gota (Abegglen 1984)	Awash Station (Nagel 1973)	Saudi Arabia (Kummer et al., 1981)	Saudi Arabia (Biquand et al., 1992 & Boug et al., 1994)	Yemen (Al-Safadi 1994)
Group (band) Sizes Observed	50–220	30–90	62–95	52–90	51–57	13–70	9–102	22–89
Estimated Home Range Size	30 km²	N/R[a]	28 km²	N/R[a]	N/R[a]	N/R[a]	9.31 km²	N/R[a]
Daily Path Lengths	3.2–11.2 km mean 7.5 km (N=27)	4.1–19.2 km mean 13.2 km (N=9)	mean 8.6 km (Band I; N=57) & 10.4 km (Band II; N=13)	N/R[a]	mean 6.5 km (N=7)	N/R[a]	1.04–14.03 km (mean N/R[a])	N/R[a]

[a]N/R = not reported.

[1]From "Ranging Behavior, Group Size and Behavioral Flexibility in Ethiopian Hamadryas Baboons (*Papio hamadryas hamadryas*)," *Folia Primatologica* 73 (2002): 95–103; used with permission from Karger AG Publishers.

to the group sizes observed in the Filoha-Sabure area. Further evidence of large group sizes comes from the work of Zinner and colleagues in Eritrea, where bands of 25 to 327 individuals, averaging 139, have been observed (Zinner et al. 2001b; Zinner, pers. comm.).

RANGING PATTERNS

Home Range Size

The shaded area in Figure 4–1 shows the minimum home range of Group 1, based on the areas through which they traveled while I was following them in 1996, 1997, and 1998. I previously estimated this area to be about 30 square kilometers (Swedell 2002b). I suspect that Group 1's home range is actually much larger than this, however, because I often lost or left the group as they were traveling away from these areas. There were also several periods, including 25 days during the 1998 wet season (see p. 32), when Group 1 could not be found at any of their known sleeping sites and I suspected that they were ranging southwest of Wasaro, closer to Mt. Fantalle and outside of my estimated home range area.

Estimated home range sizes for other hamadryas populations are 28 km^2 at Erer Gota (Sigg & Stolba 1981) and 9.3 km^2 in the Alhada Mountains of Saudi Arabia (Boug et al. 1994a). These are the only figures I have found so far, though, as Kummer (1968a) and Nagel (1973) did not report home range sizes; Abegglen (1984) did not follow his study group away from the sleeping sites; and neither Kummer et al. (1981), Biquand et al. (1992a,b), Al-Safadi (1994), nor Zinner et al. (2001a,b) reported ranging data (Table 4–1).

Daily Path Length

On 30 days I was able to map a complete daily route for Group 1, that is, I knew for certain where they both started and ended the day and was able to follow them for most or all of their route. On these days, path lengths varied from 3.2 km to 11.2 km, with an average of 7.5 km. Some daily path lengths are minimum figures because there were days on which I was unable to follow the group all the way to their sleeping site (because dusk was approaching) but was able to confirm their final destination by driving there the next morning; that is, I assumed that the baboons followed the shortest path from where I left them to their sleeping site, but they may not have. Therefore, a mean daily path length of 7.5 km is probably a slight underestimate.

On average, the Filoha path lengths are shorter than those reported by Kummer (1968a) for the White Rock troop near Erer Gota, who ranged from 4.1 to 19.2 km a day, averaging 13.2 km for the nine daily routes that Kummer and Kurt were able to map (Kummer 1968a). Filoha path lengths are comparable, however, to those of Nagel's hamadryas study group

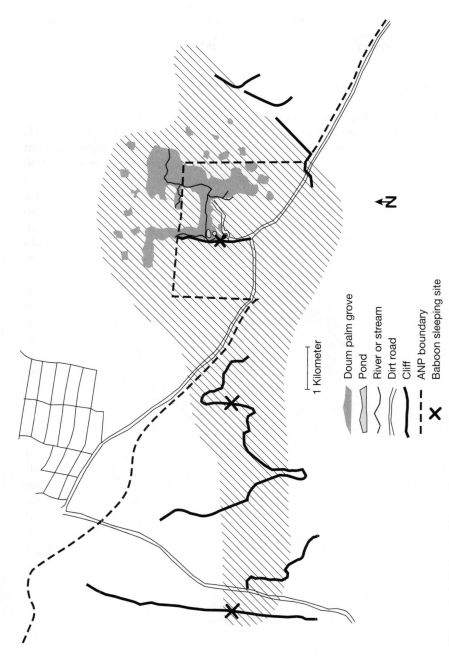

Figure 4–1 Estimated Home Range of Group 1

Legend:
- Doum palm grove
- Pond
- River or stream
- Dirt road
- Cliff
- ANP boundary
- **X** Baboon sleeping site

1 Kilometer

N

near Awash Station, which averaged 6.5 km over 7 routes; Sigg and Stolba's study groups at Erer Gota, which averaged 8.6 km over 57 routes for Band I and 10.4 km over 13 routes for Band II; and Boug's population in the Alhada Mountains of Saudi Arabia, which ranged from 1.04 km to 14.03 km (Table 4–1).

Travel Route Patterns

Figures 4–2, 4–3, and 4–4 show the complete daily path lengths that I was able to map. Figure 4–2 shows the 13 daily travel routes of Group 1 that started and ended at Filoha, Figure 4–3 shows the 15 daily travel routes of Group 1 that started at Filoha and ended at Wasaro, and Figure 4–4 shows

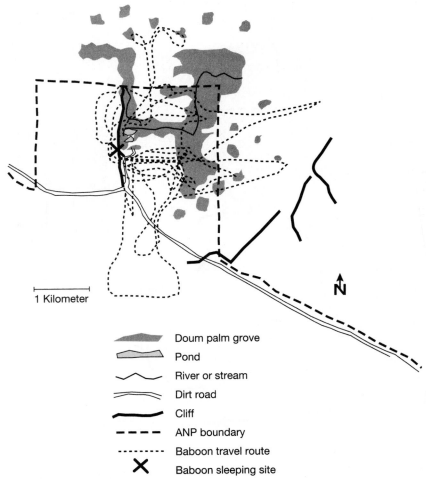

1 Kilometer

Doum palm grove
Pond
River or stream
Dirt road
Cliff
ANP boundary
Baboon travel route
Baboon sleeping site

Figure 4–2 Travel Routes from the Filoha Cliff

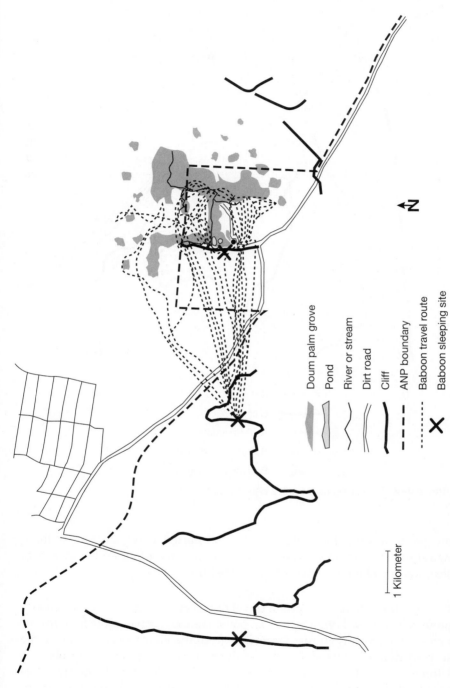

Figure 4–3 Travel Routes between Filoha and Wasaro

Doum palm grove
Pond
River or stream
Dirt road
Cliff
ANP boundary
Baboon travel route
Baboon sleeping site

N

1 Kilometer

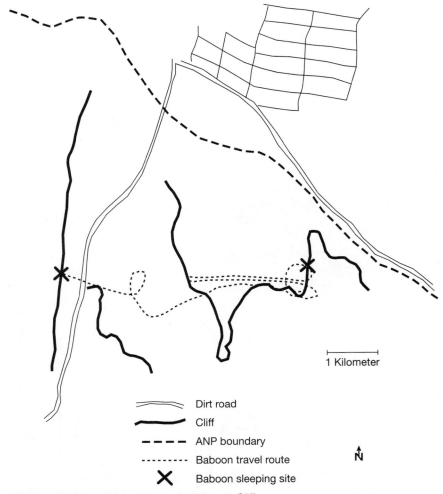

Dirt road
Cliff
ANP boundary
Baboon travel route
Baboon sleeping site

1 Kilometer

N

Figure 4–4 Travel Routes from the Wasaro Cliff

the two routes that I was able to map that started at Wasaro. One of these two routes also ended at the Wasaro cliff, and the other ended at a third sleeping site along a cliff southwest of Sabure.

Preferred Travel Routes. Certain travel routes and foraging areas are clearly preferred and used often by the baboons. The main travel route for Group 1 in the Filoha area is an east-west route from the Filoha sleeping cliff to the strip of doum palms along the north-south running hot spring about a kilometer east of camp (see Figures 3–2 and 4–2). Most of the group's preferred foraging and resting spots in the Filoha area, where they have spent at least an hour at a time on more than one occasion, are about a kilometer east of camp, in the eastern north-south palm strip.

On leaving their sleeping site each morning, the baboons tend to travel along cliffs for longer parts of their route than might be expected based on their final destination. After having slept at the Filoha cliff, the baboons always leave the sleeping site by first traveling either north or south along the cliff, and then, once at least 500 meters north or south of the sleeping site, turning away from the cliff and heading east or west (usually east when traveling from Filoha and west when traveling from Wasaro). At Filoha, this attraction to cliffs appears to be at least partially related to the fact that there are hot springs and palm trees in front of most of the length of the 2 km-long cliff that includes the Filoha sleeping site (see Figure 3–2). The baboons spend a significant amount of time foraging on palm fruit, and part of the group would usually forage in the palms as they traveled along the cliff. At Wasaro, however, there are no palm trees along the cliff and yet the group often still follows the cliff for several hundred meters before turning away from it. My sample size for the Wasaro sleeping site is still very small, however, and is probably not indicative of habitual ranging patterns in that area.

Despite the fact that Group 1 often crosses or travels along the route of hot spring streams and rivers in the Filoha area (Figure 3–2), the baboons nevertheless actively avoid the water itself. When their route requires that they cross a waterway, they usually travel along it until they find a spot where it is narrow enough to jump across. This is done even if the waterway is a shallow stream that can easily be waded across without swimming. When the waterway is too wide to jump over, they often climb one of the palm trees that line the waterway and jump across to a tree on the other side. Only when the baboons travel across extensive areas of tall marsh grass in water do they travel through the water itself, and in those cases they jump quickly from grass clump to grass clump so as to avoid contact with the water as much as possible. The baboons' active avoidance of water may be related to potential sources of danger in the water, such as crocodiles or water snakes (see p. 78).

Coordination of Travel among Bands. Both Kummer (1968a) and Abegglen (1984) reported that hamadryas bands, having shared a sleeping cliff the night before, would often depart from the cliff at the same time and travel away from it in the same direction for the first part of their foraging route. After traveling a short distance together, the baboons would then split along band lines and travel in different directions for the remainder of their daily foraging route (Kummer 1968a; Abegglen 1984). This pattern also characterizes the hamadryas at Filoha. Although I have not yet collected any systematic data on ranging patterns of other bands, I have noticed that when Group 1 shares the Filoha sleeping cliff with Group 3, the two bands almost invariably leave the sleeping cliff at about the same time and travel in the same direction, one band in front of the other, for at least 500 meters, often a kilometer or more, before one band either turns in a different direction or pauses while the other band moves ahead. This initial coordination in movement between two bands is probably the result of social facilitation.

Group Spread.   When resting, the individuals of Group 1 are typically all within an area of less than 100 meters in diameter. While traveling, they typically spread out over 50–100 meters in both directions. While foraging, however, they usually spread out over 100, often over 200, meters. This is consistent with previous reports that hamadryas baboons spread out and split up into smaller parties, along one-male unit lines, while foraging (Kummer 1968a; Kummer et al. 1981; Biquand et al. 1992b). Kummer and Kurt, in fact, reported that, during their daily foraging routes, groups often spread out over an area of almost 1 square kilometer (Kummer 1968a). That the splitting of groups into foraging parties is related to an avoidance of food competition is supported by the fact that, in Saudi Arabia, wild hamadryas split into significantly smaller foraging parties than do commensal hamadryas (i.e., those living and foraging near human developments, where garbage dumps provide an abundant food resource), and that wild hamadryas groups have fewer females per OMU than do commensal groups (Biquand et al. 1992b).

Group 1 traveling and foraging southeast of the Wasaro sleeping cliff. *(Photo by the author)*

Seasonality

The 7 wet season routes that I was able to map in 1998 averaged 8.1 km and ranged from 5.0 to 10.0 km. The 23 dry season routes that I was able to map averaged 7.3 km and ranged from 3.0 to 11.2 km. On average, the dry season routes were slightly, though not statistically significantly, shorter than the wet season routes. There was a greater range for the dry season routes (8.2 km) than for the wet season routes (5.0), however. The only routes that were longer than 10 km (N=3) occurred during the dry season, and the only routes that were less than 5 km (N=4) also occurred during the dry season. A greater range for wet season routes (similar to that for dry season routes) would most likely result from a larger sample size, as it is unlikely that my sample of 7 wet season routes is representative for this population of hamadryas.

Boug et al. (1994b) found a similar relationship between seasonality and daily path length for the hamadryas in Alhada Mountain of Saudi Arabia. There, the baboons had the smallest home range and shortest daily path length in August, the driest month, and the longest daily path lengths in April, when vegetation was more abundant.

During the 1998 wet season, Group 1 spent more time away from Filoha than during the dry season. For a period of 25 days from August 4 to August 28, 1998, Group 1 did not sleep at the Filoha cliff at all; on the days that I was able to drive or walk to the Wasaro cliff, I did not find them there either. It is during this time that I suspected they were using a fourth sleeping site somewhere to the southwest of Wasaro (see p. 73).

The Filoha hot springs are a reliable year-round source of water for baboons. During the dry season, the baboons may need to come to Filoha if only to obtain drinking water. During the wet season, however, there is standing water available elsewhere. Although the baboons clearly use other resources in the Filoha area besides the water (e.g., doum palm fruits), they are not as dependent on Filoha as a water source during the wet season and may be more flexible in their ranging behavior during that time than in the drier months.

SLEEPING CLIFF USE

Throughout their geographic range, hamadryas baboons sleep on cliffs (Kummer 1968a; Nagel 1973; Kummer et al. 1981; Biquand et al. 1992a; Zinner et al. 2001a). There are few trees in hamadryas habitat that would be suitable for sleeping, and it is presumably as a result of this need to guard against predation that they sleep on cliffs instead. A relationship between sleeping on cliffs and predation risk is suggested by the observation that in some parts of Saudi Arabia, where natural predators of baboons are

The Filoha sleeping cliff is about 20 meters high and is lined with palm trees and Acacia thornscrub. At the bottom of the portion of the cliff shown here lies one of the sources of the Filoha hot springs and a bathing pool commonly used by the local Afar. *(Photo by the author)*

The Wasaro sleeping cliff is over 80 meters high and the only large mammals found regularly on the cliff itself are baboons and rock hyraxes. The area along the bottom of the cliff, however, is occasionally frequented by spotted hyenas and lions. *(Photo by the author)*

extremely rare or completely absent, hamadryas were observed to sleep on shallow hills and slopes rather than on vertical or near-vertical cliff faces (Kummer et al. 1981, Kummer et al. 1985).

On the many several-kilometer-long cliff faces in the Filoha-Sabure area, only certain areas are habitual sleeping sites for baboons. There appears to be nothing distinguishing these particular areas from other parts of the cliffs other than brownish stains, presumably from years of baboon urine and feces dropping along it. These stains, as well as the regularity in sleeping site choice by every group that I observed, suggest that hamadryas baboon sleeping sites remain highly consistent over time.

Each of the hamadryas groups that ranges throughout the Filoha-Sabure area uses more than one sleeping site. The two main sleeping cliffs of Group 1 are the cliff at Filoha and the cliff near the village of Wasaro, a little over 4 km away from Filoha. These two cliffs differ from one another in potentially important ways: the Filoha cliff, while only about 20 meters high, is located next to a permanent water source and an abundance of doum palm trees, whereas the Wasaro cliff is close to 100 meters high—and thus offers greater protection—but is much farther from a permanent source of water. It is thus no surprise that the Wasaro cliff is used by Group 1 and other bands more often during the rainy season whereas the Filoha cliff is used more often during the dry season.

A third sleeping cliff is located southwest of the town of Sabure, about 10 km from Filoha and almost 6 km due west of the Wasaro cliff (see Figures 3–2 and 4–1). A fourth sleeping site is located somewhere to the southwest of the Wasaro and Sabure cliffs and was used primarily during the peak of the long rains in August. A possible fifth sleeping site is located along the cliff to the east of Filoha, and a sixth site—used by Group 3 and possibly Group 1 as well—consists of tall trees instead of a cliff and has been reported by the local Afar but not yet seen by any of the researchers at Filoha.

Group 1 often alternates between the Filoha and Wasaro sleeping cliffs on a daily basis; equally often, the group sleeps on either the Filoha or the Wasaro cliff for several days at a time. Of the 394 nights I was at Filoha between 1996 and 1998, at least one group of baboons slept at the Filoha sleeping cliff on 261 nights. On 220 nights, there was a single group (band) of baboons at Filoha. Group 1 slept there on at least 146 nights, Group 3 slept there on at least 36 nights, Group 2 slept there on at least 15 nights, and another group (Group 4, Group 5, or an unknown group) slept there on at least 13 nights. On 10 nights in October 1996, before I had learned to distinguish the groups, an unidentified group slept at the Filoha sleeping site.

Sometimes two or more groups share the Filoha cliff. Group 1 shared the Filoha cliff with Group 3 on 26 of the nights they were at Filoha and with Group 2 on 10 of the nights they were at Filoha between 1996 and 1998. On 5 nights, two groups other than Group 1 slept at the Filoha cliff together. There appears to be variation in relationships among groups. Some pairs of groups (e.g., Group 1 and Group 3) share the same sleeping site relatively often (and often travel near one another as well) and do so relatively peaceably, whereas other pairs of groups, on both arriving at the same sleeping cliff, engage in aggressive intergroup encounters. Following the encounter, one or both groups leaves the site and travels to another sleeping cliff for the night. This pattern of inter-group relationships, varying from antagonism to tolerance at sleeping sites, was also observed by Kummer (1968a) and Abegglen (1984).

When both Group 1 and Group 3 share the Filoha or Wasaro cliffs, they are spatially separated into two distinct groups. When they share the Filoha cliff, Group 1 consistently sleeps on the right side of a regularly used Afar trail that goes up the cliff, and Group 3 sleeps on the left side of the trail. Likewise, when Group 1 shares the Filoha cliff with any other group, it always sleeps on the right side of the trail and the other group always sleeps on the left side. When Group 1 sleeps alone at the Filoha cliff, however, it uses both the right and left sides of the cliff.

ACTIVITY PATTERNS

Categorization of group activity is not straightforward because group members are usually not all engaged in the same activity at the same time. The two most common combinations are *travel-forage* and *rest-groom-forage*. Travel-foraging consists of the group gradually but consistently moving in a particular direction while individual one-male units pause to forage for periods of up to several minutes. During travel-foraging, there are no times when the entire group is either exclusively traveling or exclusively forag-ing. Likewise, rest-groom-foraging consists of some group members rest-ing and/or grooming and others foraging. Less common combinations of activities are *rest-groom-travel*, when part of the group is resting and/or grooming and part of the group is traveling, and *rest-groom-travel-forage*, when part of the group is resting and/or grooming, part of the group is traveling, and yet another part of the group is foraging.

In 1996, 1997, and 1998, between the hours of 6:00 A.M. and 6:00 P.M., Group 1 spent 29% of its time exclusively resting and grooming, 19% of its time exclusively traveling, 19% of its time rest-groom-foraging, and 16% of its time travel-foraging. Only 6% of the group's time was spent exclusively foraging, 5% of its time was spent rest-groom-travel-foraging, and 4% of its time was spent rest-groom-traveling. A remaining 2% of the group's time was spent in a combination of one or more of the above activities and drinking, the most common combination being rest-groom-drinking.

DIET

Although I did not collect systematic data on feeding behavior during the 1996–1998 study period, I did record the identity (if known) of all food items that I observed baboons eating during focal samples (see Table 4–2). The main food items eaten year-round are the outer layer of the fruits of doum palm trees (*Hyphaene thebaica*) and the leaves, flowers, pods, and seeds of *Acacia senegal* and *A. mellifera*. Other common food items are grass seeds, blades, and flowers; *A. nubica* leaves and seeds; and *Grewia* berries. I have also occasionally seen the baboons eating grass corms and roots, *A. tortilis* seeds and flowers, and sap from *A. senegal*. Both the doum palms and most *Acacia* species appear to be variable enough in their reproductive cycles so that there are ripe palm fruits as well as young leaves and flowers of *Acacia* species available year-round. As of the writing of this book, CUNY graduate students Getenet Hailemeskel and Amy Schreier have begun studies of the feeding ecology and ranging behavior, respectively, of Group 3 at Filoha, and their dissertation research promises to offer more details on the feeding behavior and dietary composition of hamadryas in this area.

On three occasions, I observed two adult male and one adult female baboons eating Abyssinian hares (*Lepus capensis habessinicus*). On one of these occasions, I witnessed the predation event. An adult male chased the hare down, captured it, held it to his chest briefly, and then started tearing meat from the hare's thigh while it was still alive. After consuming most

The fruits of doum palm trees *(Hyphaene thebaica)* are a favorite food source for hamadryas baboons. *(Photo by the author)*

Table 4–2 Food Types Observed Being Eaten by Filoha Hamadryas*

Name	Plant Part	How Often Observed
Hyphaene thebaica	Outer layer of fruit	Frequent
Acacia mellifera	Leaves, pods, seeds, flowers	Frequent
Acacia nubica	Leaves, seeds	Occasional
Acacia senegal	Leaves, pods, seeds, flowers	Frequent
Acacia tortilis	Seeds, flowers	Occasional
Grewia spp.	Fruit	Frequent
Dobera glabra	Fruit	Rare
Grasses	Blades, seeds, roots, flowers	Frequent
Acacia senegal	Sap	Rare
Insects		Occasional
Small mammals (e.g., Lepus capensis habessinicus)		Rare

*Based on ad libitum observations of feeding behavior.

of the hare himself, he left parts of it scattered around, which were then investigated and eaten by other individuals who had watched the predation event.

Kummer (1968a) reported a possible predation event by hamadryas on a dik-dik (*Rhynchotragus kirki*), and many other baboons have been reported to hunt and eat meat as well (Rowell 1966; Harding 1975; Peters & Mech 1975; Strum 1981; Strum & Mitchell 1987; Hill 1999). The most common prey items for baboons appear to be small mammals such as dik-diks and hares as well as the infants of larger ungulates such as gazelles. Although the Filoha baboons try to catch hares whenever they see them, some small mammals are, for whatever reason, not considered food sources by the baboons. Rock hyraxes (*Procavia habessinica*), for example, live on both the Filoha and the Wasaro sleeping cliffs and are frequently in view within 1–2 meters of baboons, but I have never observed a baboon attempting to catch or eat a hyrax.

FEEDING COMPETITION

Direct competition over food is rare in this population. Usually an entire one-male unit feeds at the same time, and food sources (and the members of the OMU) are sufficiently dispersed so that all members of the unit simultaneously have access to food. In contrast to the pattern found in other baboons, I have never observed competition over food among hamadryas females. When food competition does occur, it typically consists of a leader male displacing one of his females at a food source or a female displacing a juvenile at a food source. That leader males exploit their dominance over females to obtain food resources has also been observed by Sigg (1980) in wild hamadryas and Gore (1993) in captive hamadryas. In an experimental study of foraging competition in captive hamadryas baboons and rhesus macaques, Gore found that when food was clumped, hamadryas males would often monitor female group members and displace them if the females found a clump of food. Gore also found that, on a few occasions, while a female was sorting the contents of her cheek pouches on the ground in front of her, her leader male would displace her and eat the food himself.

Food competition and differential access to food resources among hamadryas females has been observed to varying degrees in captivity (Sigg 1980; Kaumanns et al. 1987; Gore 1991) but rarely in the wild (Kummer 1968a; Sigg 1980). Sigg (1980) reported that, in two-female units, one female takes advantage of the leader male's access to food resources and stays near him to exploit those resources, whereas the other female remains more peripheral to the unit and exploits resources that are farther away from the leader male. Sigg suggests that the peripheral female may not gain access to as much food as the central female, but that the peripheral female may compensate for this by being more experienced at finding food (due to always being in the peripheral role), more efficient in feeding, and better able than the central female to monopolize food for herself without the leader male detecting her and displacing her at the food source. Females in two-female units may therefore avoid food competition by assuming different spatial and foraging roles within the OMU (Sigg 1980).

In the Filoha population, I have never observed one female displace another female at a food resource or fight in the context of feeding. Although I did not collect systematic data on feeding behavior, it also did not appear that females differed in the rate at which they were able to obtain food. The only exception to this occurred when a female was sexually swollen. A swollen female was more closely guarded by her leader male than other females in the unit and was therefore probably forced to limit her food options to those resources within a smaller radius of the leader male, whereas the other females in the unit had a wider radius around the leader male within which to forage. (I discuss the effect of sexual swellings on female behavior in more detail in Chapter 6.)

One way to infer feeding competition is through the existence of dominance hierarchies, commonly thought to be a means to mediate competitive relationships. Although hamadryas females do show dominance relationships in captivity, especially in the absence of males (Stammbach 1978; Sigg 1980; Stammbach & Kummer 1982; Coelho et al. 1983; Chalyan et al. 1991; Vervaecke et al. 1992; Gore 1994; Leinfelder et al. 2001), wild hamadryas females rarely show such relationships (Kummer 1968a; Sigg 1980). Even in captivity, dominance rank among hamadryas females is not usually determined based on approach-retreat or agonistic interactions but on a difference in each female's relationship with her leader male—a different, and somewhat problematic, operational definition of dominance than that used for females of other baboon subspecies (Kaumanns et al. 1987; Gore 1993).

At Filoha, I also have not observed any consistently unidirectional interactions among females that would be indicative of dominance relationships. Females at Filoha do occasionally fight, but these fights appear to be almost exclusively over grooming access to the leader male rather than over food. Fights do not typically result in the withdrawal or submission of one female, but instead usually draw both females closer to the leader male, after which the agonism eventually subsides. An absence of direct competition over food combined with a lack of dominance relationships suggests that females in the Filoha population, and possibly other populations of wild hamadryas as well, do not experience feeding competition with one another.

PREDATION

Potential predators of hamadryas baboons in the Filoha-Sabure area and elsewhere include lions (*Panthera leo*), leopards (*Panthera pardus*), spotted hyenas (*Crocuta crocuta*), jackals (*Canis* spp.), crocodiles (*Crocodylus niloticus*), and birds of prey (e.g., Verreaux's eagles, Zinner & Peláez 1999). Snakes—such as puff adders and cobras—also inhabit the region, and snake bites were a suspected cause of at least one observed death (see Chapter 5). All of these predators, though no actual predation attempts, have been observed within the home range of Group 1. It is likely that predator pressure on this population has decreased in recent years, as the abundance of large carnivores within the park (and presumably in the surrounding areas as well) has decreased substantially in the past four decades (Kummer, pers. comm.; Hailemeskel, pers. comm.).

Visual detection of predators appears to be perceived by the baboons as a greater indication of predation risk than auditory detection alone, as lion and hyena calls are often heard close to the baboon sleeping cliff but the baboons only give alarm calls when a lion or hyena is actually in view of the cliff. When snakes or crocodiles are nearby, the baboons watch them continuously but do not run away. When a single hyena is nearby and the baboons are not safely on a cliff, they stay at least 50 meters away from the hyena but do not run away. On encountering three hyenas at the sleeping cliff, which I observed only once, the baboons ran from the sleeping site and did not stop until they were over a kilometer away.

Although no predation events on this population have been observed, it is likely that predation has been an important selective factor in the evolution of hamadryas behavior. Not only is the multilevel social structure of hamadryas suggestive of a flexibility in grouping patterns that has evolved in response to varying levels of feeding competition and predator pressure, but the baboons do seem to split up and then coalesce into larger and smaller social units in response to these very factors. When foraging on widely dispersed resources, as noted earlier, the baboons are less cohesive and the group spread is much larger. When a potential source of danger (such as an Afar nomad) is perceived and alarm call is given, however, the group immediately coalesces and the group spread becomes much smaller as the group moves away from the potential predator.

EFFECT OF HUMANS ON BABOON RANGING PATTERNS

Awash National Park, especially the region north of the Addis-Harar highway (see Figures 1–1 and 3–1), is heavily used by nomadic Afar, Itu, and Kereyu pastoralists. The Filoha-Sabure region in particular is frequented by Afar nomads, who bathe and water their livestock at the Filoha hot springs. The Afar and their herds of cattle, camel, goats, and sheep, as well as their donkeys and dogs, are thus a common sight in the area and often come into contact with the baboons. The baboons cross paths with Afar nomads and/or their livestock at least once, and usually several times, each day. When this occurs, the baboons usually change their direction of travel, at least temporarily (e.g., when approaching Afar and/or their livestock or when Afar are blocking their path), or move to another area (when Afar are passing through an area where the baboons are foraging or resting). As the

The baboons often cross paths with Afar nomads, such as these women and their camels. *(Photo by the author)*

Afar nomads barely tolerate the baboons and generally regard them as competitors for the grazing land used by their livestock, they often react to the baboons' presence by shouting and/or throwing rocks at them. When this happens, the baboons run quickly away from the area of the encounter and usually do not return to the area that day.

While herds of camels, cattle, goats, or sheep are almost always an indicator that the Afar are nearby, it is the Afar people themselves who elicit a response from the baboons. If I, and presumably the baboons as well, can hear or see a herd of livestock but cannot see or hear any Afar people, the baboons do usually avoid the livestock more than they would wild animals. Nevertheless, they do not run away until the Afar themselves are visible or audible.

Although the Afar often have a pronounced immediate effect on the baboons' direction and/or speed of travel when their paths cross, the baboons still return to the same areas on subsequent days. Often they only travel about 100 meters away and then return to the same area after the Afar have left, but only if their arrival was not accompanied by any aggressive acts toward the baboons. In general, I doubt that the baboons' overall ranging patterns or their choice of sleeping cliff at the end of each day are strongly affected by the Afar.

OVERALL PATTERNS AND INTERPRETATIONS

The main ecological difference between Filoha hamadryas and other hamadryas populations appears to be the frequency with which baboons at Filoha eat doum palm fruits. Palm fruits are presumably high in fat and probably satisfy a large portion of a baboon's daily caloric requirements. The high abundance of palm fruits in the Filoha area and the baboons' dependence on them as a food resource may be factors that allow the large group sizes observed in this area compared to other areas where hamadryas have been studied.

Although palm fruits appear to be a key resource for these baboons and are available within a short distance of one of their primary sleeping cliffs, the baboons still travel up to 11 km or more each day. Thus, there may be some critical nutrient, not available in palm fruits, that the baboons are seeking in these other areas. Although I have not observed the baboons eating anything in these other areas that is obviously unavailable at Filoha, I have not collected systematic data on feeding behavior and so could easily have overlooked some component of their diet that they obtained from these other areas. Results from Getenet Hailemeskel's and Amy Schreier's studies of hamadryas feeding ecology and ranging patterns promise to elucidate this issue.

An alternate explanation for the long travel routes of the Filoha baboons may be that they are simply constrained by their phylogenetic history.

Due to their presumable evolution in a semiarid environment where food resources are scarce (Kummer 1971), hamadryas baboons may be genetically predisposed to travel a certain minimum distance per day, or at least a minimum distance over a several day period, even if food resources are readily available. Many aspects of hamadryas behavior, such as male herding and "notifying" behavior, appear to be invariable under a wide array of environmental conditions (Kummer & Kurt 1965; Colmenares 1990), and hamadryas ranging behavior may be no exception to this pattern. Lackman-Ancrenaz (1994) found that a group of hamadryas baboons in Taif, Saudi Arabia, still traveled long distances each day and exhibited a fission-fusion system typical of wild hamadryas even though they could probably meet all of their food requirements by feeding at the city garbage dump. This observation suggests that the hamadryas multilevel social system, although it may be ecologically based, does not readily revert back to a social system with more cohesive groups and shorter travel lengths even when ecological conditions are favorable.

On the other hand, Nagel (1973) found that his hamadryas study group near Awash Station had a significantly shorter mean daily path length than the hamadryas near Erer Gota. Compared to Erer Gota, a semiarid area more characteristic of typical hamadryas habitat, Nagel's hamadryas group inhabited an area of gallery forest along the Awash River, and its home range probably also included the Awash Station garbage dump, a site at which baboons have often been observed foraging (Jolly and Phillips-Conroy, pers. comm.). Because the habitat near Awash Station appears to be richer in resources than that around Erer Gota, Nagel's results suggest that there may in fact be a relationship between local environmental conditions and hamadryas ranging patterns. The mean daily path length of Filoha hamadryas (7.5 km) is intermediate between that shown by the Awash Station hamadryas (6.5 km) and the Erer Gota hamadryas (8.6 km, 10.4 km, & 13.2 km; see Table 4–1). If Filoha is also intermediate in habitat quality between Awash Station and Erer Gota (which is likely, as the area around Filoha is largely a semidesert thornscrub much like typical hamadryas habitat with the addition of doum palms as an additional food resource), then the relationship between habitat quality and daily path length between these three sites suggests that hamadryas baboons may indeed be at least somewhat flexible in their ability to adjust their ranging patterns to resource availability.

CHAPTER

5

Hamadryas Social Organization: The Haves and the Have-Nots

In this chapter, I will describe and discuss the social structure and social organization of Group 1 at Filoha. I define *social structure* as the size and composition of a social group, which, for these purposes, will include the size and composition of Group 1 and the one-male units therein. I define *social organization* as the patterns of association and interaction among the members of a social group, which will be described both at the level of the band and the level of the OMU. In the first half of the chapter, I will describe the social structure and social organization of Group 1 at Filoha. In the second half of the chapter, I will discuss takeovers of OMUs that occurred during the study period and patterns of social relationships between females and males. Sexual behavior between females and males and the effects of sexual swellings and parturition on female behavior will be discussed in Chapter 6, and social relationships among females will be discussed in Chapter 7.

METHODS SPECIFIC TO THIS CHAPTER

Both one-male unit scan sample data and *ad libitum* observations (described in Chapter 3) were used to generate the results reported in this chapter. Unless otherwise noted, average values of activity and proximity patterns represent swollen and nonswollen females combined and adult and sub-adult females combined. As described in Chapter 3, patterns of activity and proximity (including nearest neighbors) were calculated as a percentage of those scan samples that represented "available social time," and were then compared among females. Counts of age-sex classes of individuals were obtained as the group was leaving the sleeping cliff, at the beginning of their daily travel route, on those occasions when they all departed relatively slowly but at the same time and in the same direction. Age estimates were based on those of Sigg et al. (1982), the only published report of multiple years of data from wild hamadryas baboons (Table 5–1).

Table 5–1 Age Classes Used in This Study*

Age Class	Estimated Age Range (years)	Description	Corresponding Age Class of Sigg et al. (1982)
Black infant	0–1	Hair completely or partially black; face and perineal region pink	Infant N
Small juvenile	1–2	Hair brown; longer snout; sitting height 25–30 cm; no differences between sexes	Juvenile 1
Medium juvenile male	2–5	Sitting height 30–45 cm; smaller than an adult female; no testicular bulges	Juvenile 2 male
Medium–large juvenile female	2–4	Sitting height 30–45 cm; very first sexual swellings	Juvenile 2 female
Large juvenile male or "young male"	5–6	Sitting height 45–55 cm; around same size as an adult female; canine fossae evident; testes descending	Juvenile 3 male
Subadult or adolescent female (sometimes called large juvenile female when not cycling)	4–5.5	Sitting height 45–50 cm; reproductively cycling	Juvenile 3 female
Subadult male	6–10	Sitting height 55–60 cm; partial growth of mantle; pendulant scrotum but no clear separation of testes	Subadult male
Young adult female	5.5–7	Sitting height 50–55 cm; cycling regularly; muzzle shorter than adult females	Adult female
Adult male	10+	Sitting height 65 cm; mantle fully developed; testes clearly separated	Adult male
Fully adult female	7+	Sitting height 50–55 cm; cycling regularly	Adult female

* Based on Sigg et al., 1982.

SOCIAL STRUCTURE OF GROUP 1

Demography

Group 1 at Filoha (as well as Groups 2 and 3) was, by Kummer's (1968a) definition, a *band*. In April 1997, by which point an accurate estimate of its size could be obtained, Group 1 consisted of about 155 individuals: approximately 45 adult and subadult females; approximately 35 adult and subadult males, about 16 of whom were leader males; and about 75 young males, juveniles, and infants. One year later, in April 1998, Group 1 consisted of about 175 individuals: 46 adult females; 10 subadult females; about 30 adult males, 24 of whom were leader males; about 10 subadult males; and at least 80 young males, juveniles, and infants (see Table 5–1 for age classes). The ratio of adult females to adult males ranged from 1.3 to 1.8 over the course of the study period.

Because females mature more quickly than males, males have longer periods of growth and development and are therefore not considered subadult until at least the age of 6 years or adult until the age of 10 years. Females, on the other hand, are reproductively cycling and therefore subadult (or "adolescent") at about the age of 4 years and then reach adult body size at 5 or 6 years. There were thus many more juvenile males than females, as well as more adult females than adult males, over both observation seasons. Given the differences in maturation rates and the high female-to-male sex ratio in most baboon populations (1.36 to 1.42 near Erer Gota, 2.07 to 2.87 in Eritrea, and 1.4 to 4.0 in *P. h. anubis*, *P. h. cynocephalus*, and *P. h. ursinus* populations; Kummer et al. 1985; Zinner et al. 2001b; Melnick & Pearl 1987), the sex ratio of the Filoha population was not atypical.

The size of Group 1 increased by about 20 individuals over the one-year period between April 1997 and April 1998, and increased by another 25 individuals over the subsequent three years. This 12% increase over one year represents a higher population growth rate than the 12% increase over 5.5 years reported for the only other hamadryas population that has been observed for a period of a year or more (Sigg et al. 1982). Some of the increase in group size at Filoha appears to have resulted from a high birth rate coupled with an apparently high infant survival rate. Between December 1996 and April 1997, at least 10 infants were born to females in Group 1; between December 1997 and September 1998, 19 infants were born to females in Group 1. Of the infants in Group 1, only two are known to have died, one from each season. In addition, two medium juveniles are known or presumed to have died as well: one from an injury, which I assumed died after I observed it unable to move due to a serious wound, and one, which I observed dead, from an unknown cause. It is not known how many other juveniles died during the study period, though, as they were not individually identified and it was very difficult to get accurate counts of juveniles due to visibility problems and the large group size. One very old female from the first season was no longer present in the group at the beginning of the second season, and another very old female disappeared during the second season. Due to their old age, it is presumed that they both died rather than transferred to other groups.

Immigration of both males and females into the group during this time may also have contributed to the increase in group size (see Chapter 8). I did not see Group 1 for a period of seven months (late May to early December 1997) between the two observation seasons, and both Group 1 and Group 3, as well as at least one other group, were trapped by the Awash National Park Baboon Research Project in July 1997, during which time I could not be there to identify the trapped individuals. It is unlikely that trapping provided opportunities for transfer between groups that would not have existed otherwise, as Groups 1 and 3 often sleep on the same cliff and travel together in the mornings (see Chapter 4). Nevertheless, trapping may have affected the social structure of Group 1 by providing opportunities for the takeover of females between groups when those females' leader males were trapped.

Sub-Band Social Structure

Within hamadryas bands, the two subgroupings that have been observed are *one-male units* and *clans*. In Ethiopian populations, membership in one-male units, clans, and bands is consistent over time, and social units are both spatially and socially distinct from one another at each level of social structure. In Saudi Arabian populations, however, bands, clans, and one-male units are neither as cohesive in space nor as consistent over time as they are in Ethiopian populations (Kummer et al. 1981, 1985; Biquand et al. 1992b). Some of this flexibility in Arabian populations may be due to commensalism, and some (in noncommensal Arabian populations) may be due to a higher ratio of females to males, which Biquand et al. (1992b) have suggested to be the result of commensalism. In Saudi Arabia, adult sex ratios range from 2.06 to 3.00 females per male, whereas in Ethiopia they range from 1.36 at Dire Dawa to 1.42 at Erer Gota (Kummer et al. 1985) and, as noted above, were about 1.5 at Filoha in 1998. A lower percentage of adult males in Arabian hamadryas populations may lead to their subgroupings being looser and less structured because hamadryas social structure is maintained largely by the behavior of males. It is unlikely that the female-biased sex ratio is the only factor contributing to the greater flexibility in Arabian populations, however, as Zinner et al. (2001) observed distinct and cohesive OMUs in Eritrea and the sex ratio there was as female-biased as the Arabian populations (2.07 to 2.87 females per male). Zinner et al. (2001) suggest that the strongly female-biased sex ratio in Eritrea may be the result of climatic fluctuations (and, in particular, a drought several years prior to their demographic sampling) or of antipredator behavior of males leading to higher mortality among males than among females.

One-Male Units.   Consistent with previous observations of wild hamadryas, Group 1 was subdivided into one-male units that were constant over time in both their size and composition. Each unit consisted of one leader male, one to nine adult and/or subadult females, and up to five juveniles and infants. Every adult or subadult female was a member of an OMU, whereas only about 60% of the adult or subadult males were leader males of OMUs. The remaining adult and subadult males in the group were either "solitary" males, i.e., not affiliated with any OMU in particular but interacting with other males and juveniles in the band, or "follower" males of one particular OMU. About 30% of OMUs had follower males. Infants and juveniles were associated with their natal unit until they were 2–3 years of age (based on age estimates of Sigg et al. 1982), at which point juvenile males associated mainly with solitary subadult and adult males and juvenile females had been incorporated into another OMU (often an "initial unit"— consisting of a subadult male and a juvenile female—as described by Kummer 1968; Sigg et al. 1982; and Abegglen 1984).

During the 1996–1997 observation season, there were at least 16 OMUs in Group 1; the average number of females per unit was 2.8, and the range was 1 to 9 females per unit. During the 1997–1998 season, there were 24 one-male units; the average number of females per unit was 2.3, and units ranged from 1 to 5 females. The average over both observation seasons was 2.5 females per unit. Figure 5–1 shows a frequency distribution of the number of females per OMU over both observation seasons.

The maximum number of females per unit was no higher at Filoha than elsewhere, as Sigg et al. (1982) also found maximum unit sizes of 9 females and Kummer (1968a) found one unit with 10 females in his broad sample. The average number of 2.5 females per unit in Group 1 is slightly higher than that found for previously studied groups of wild hamadryas baboons in Ethiopia. In his study group near Erer Gota, Kummer (1968a) found an average of 2.3 females per OMU, and an even lower average, 1.9, when juvenile females were excluded from the tallies. Nagel (1973) found averages of 2.29 and 2.13 females per OMU in his two study groups near Awash Station, Ethiopia. In Saudi Arabia, Biquand et al. (1992b) found average OMU sizes to be even larger than those at Filoha: 2.62 females per OMU for 32 wild groups of hamadryas and 3.31 females per OMU for 16 commensal groups. As discussed earlier, however, the female-to-male ratio in Saudi Arabian populations is higher than in Ethiopian populations, which would usually result in a greater number of females per OMU.

Units with two adult leader males and multiple females have been observed in hamadryas populations in Saudi Arabia (Biquand et al. 1992b)

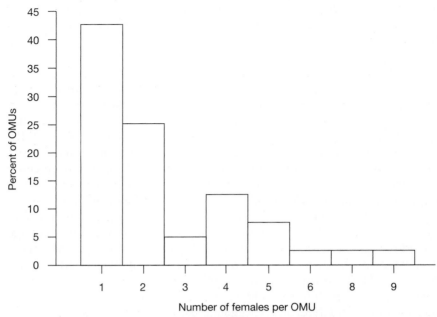

Figure 5–1 Frequency Distribution of Percentage of OMUs Containing Various Numbers of Females over Both Observation Seasons

and Eritrea (Zinner et al. 2001b). At Filoha, however, I never observed more than one adult male consistently associated with and copulating with a group of females.

Clans. As described in Chapter 1, Abegglen (1984) and Stolba (1979) observed another level of social structure in hamadryas society—the *clan*— consisting of two or more OMUs whose members tended to be spatially and socially distinct from other clans and whose leader males were presumably closely related. Although I did not collect systematic data on proximity between OMUs, I have noticed in Group 1 at Filoha a facial resemblance among three leader males in particular (Boris, Alex, and Sting) and I often observed their OMUs near one another, both during daily travel and on the sleeping cliff at night. Also, Group 1 typically splits into smaller groupings, each consisting of several OMUs, while foraging, and these smaller groupings may be clans. Whether these smaller groupings consist of the same sets of OMUs each day, however, is not yet known.

All-Male Groups. Although I never observed all-male groups except as temporary grooming associations within bands, Lackman-Ancrenaz (1994) found all-male groups of hamadryas baboons at a garbage dump in Saudi

Arabia. These groups were apparently stable and were independent from other heterosexual groups. Based on my own observations as well as previous reports of Ethiopian hamadryas (e.g., Kummer 1968a; Abegglen 1984), all-male aggregations are unusual for hamadryas baboons and may, in the above case, be related to commensalism (Lackman-Ancrenaz 1994). That commensalism may lead to abnormal social structure in hamadryas is supported by the fact that Lackman-Ancrenaz (1994) also observed a troop of 1,500 baboons, by far the largest aggregation of hamadryas ever seen, at a Saudi Arabian garbage dump.

SOCIAL ORGANIZATION OF GROUP 1

Overall, hamadryas social organization appears to be based on two types of social bonds: (1) those between leader males and their females and (2) those among adult males of the same band or clan. The structure of hamadryas society as a whole, in fact, appears to be primarily a result of the behavior of males. Not only is the cohesiveness of individual one-male units maintained by male herding behavior, but the OMU social structure itself appears to be largely the result of social relationships and negotiations among adult males. Relationships among males, both among leader males and between leader males and their followers, appear to form the basis for hamadryas social organization in that males both compete and cooperate with one another over access to and control of females (Kummer 1968a; Abegglen 1984).

Social Interactions among Males and between One-Male Units

The vast majority of social interactions in a hamadryas group occur within one-male units and among solitary or follower males, but not between OMUs. The social separation of OMUs appears to be largely enforced by leader males, and even leader males limit their social interactions mainly to individuals within their units. Although I did not collect systematic data on male behavior, my qualitative observations agree with those of Kummer (1968a) in suggesting that adult and subadult males associate with and groom one another frequently when they are solitary but usually cease all grooming interactions with one another once they acquire females (Kummer 1968a; Abegglen 1984). Interactions between leader males of OMUs thus consist mainly of facial gestures, occasional fights, and formalized "notifying" behavior. Kummer (1968a) attributes the almost complete lack of interaction among leader males, compared to the frequent interaction among solitary males, to the "leaders' strong tendency to keep their units from intermingling" (p. 47). That is, it is probably more important for a leader male to keep his females nearby, so as to maintain exclusive reproductive access to them, than to sustain his grooming relationships with other males, to whom he is probably closely related (Kummer 1968; Abegglen 1984).

Females of separate OMUs also rarely interact, either affiliatively or agonistically. I rarely observed agonism between females of different units. When agonism occurred, it usually consisted of a few stare threats and sometimes screams. On the one occasion in which I witnessed the cause of the conflict, it appeared to be over space on a sleeping ledge. In such situations, one or both leader males may also become involved. Twice I observed conflicts between several members of one OMU and a juvenile, and on one of these occasions the juvenile solicited aid from the leader male of another unit (who was probably his father, based on the juvenile's frequent association with one of the females in that unit). On several occasions I observed females from different OMUs engaging in affiliative interactions. These interactions are described more fully and discussed in Chapter 7.

Patterns of Spacing and Proximity within One-Male Units

My qualitative observations suggested that individuals were generally more spread out when traveling and foraging than when resting, both within one-male units and between them. I do not, however, have enough quantitative proximity data from times when the group was traveling and foraging to compare these conditions statistically. Results from Amy Schreier's dissertation research (beginning in February 2005) will provide quantitative data to address group cohesion while traveling and foraging and should thus elucidate this issue.

Females' Nearest Neighbors.　Table 5–2 shows proximity and nearest neighbor data for the 45 females used in this analysis (see Chapter 3 for methodological details). On average, a female's nearest neighbor was her leader male 37% of the time. A female's nearest neighbor was another female an average of 45% of the time, a follower or solitary male 8% of the time, and a member of another OMU 0.6% of the time. Both a female's leader male and either another female or a follower/solitary male were equidistant from her 9% of the time, and both another female and a follower/solitary male were equidistant from her 0.5% of the time.

Proximity to the Leader Male.　The average distance between a female and her leader male was 2.2 meters. As shown in Table 5–2 and Table 5–3, however, this distance varied greatly among females. Some of this variation appeared to be related to unit size, as a female's average distance to her leader male was weakly but statistically significantly correlated with the number of females in her unit (r_s=.365, p=.015, N=45). Correspondingly, the likelihood of a female's nearest neighbor being her leader male was

Table 5–2 Mean Distance to Leader Male and Frequency That Each Other Individual Was a Female's Nearest Neighbor (NN)*

Size of OMU	Name of Female[1]	N	Mean Distance to Leader in Meters (st. dev.)	NN Leader Male	NN Female	NN Non-leader Male	NN Member of Another OMU	NN Non-leader Male + Female(s) (equidistant)	NN Leader + Other (equidistant)
1 female	FAN	34	0.6 (0.9)	79	12	0	3	0	6
	JUA	31	1.8 (5.7)	97	0	0	3	0	0
	JUL	69	1.6 (2.7)	80	2	14	0	0	5
	URS2	83	1.4 (2.4)	94	1	0	2	0	2
	VIR	81	1.6 (2.9)	94	1	4	1	0	1
2 females	ANT	72	2.4 (4.3)	37	38	6	0	0	20
	LIN	72	2.6 (4.3)	38	38	7	0	0	18
	AUD2	218	2.8 (3.4)	29	16	11	3	1	43
	VER2	218	1.0 (1.7)	76	12	2	1	0	9
	MAR	123	2.3 (3.4)	41	28	6	0	0	25
	CLE	123	1.3 (1.5)	64	20	0	4	1	16
	VEN	118	2.5 (2.5)	31	27	24	1	0	17
	SER	108	2.2 (2.9)	51	31	8	0	0	10
3 females	KAT	50	1.9 (2.5)	19	19	54	0	0	8
	NAT	50	2.0 (4.1)	58	26	14	0	0	2
	OPH	50	1.4 (2.0)	40	18	20	0	0	23
	LUN	39	1.3 (1.9)	68	14	0	0	0	18
	SER2	39	2.0 (3.3)	30	55	9	3	0	6
	VEN2	39	2.6 (2.2)	3	37	54	0	3	3
4 females	IRI	42	1.2 (1.7)	15	64	0	3	0	18
	ROS	42	1.1 (1.2)	40	47	0	0	0	13
	VIO	42	1.7 (3.5)	38	44	3	0	0	15

(Continued)

Table 5-2 Continued

Size of OMU	Name of Female[1]	N	Mean Distance to Leader in Meters (st. dev.)	NN Leader Male	NN Female	NN Non-leader Male	NN Member of Another OMU	NN Non-leader Male + Female(s) (equidistant)	NN Leader + Other (equidistant)
	ZEN	42	1.0 (1.3)	37	51	0	0	0	11
4 females	CLA	54	2.2 (3.3)	30	51	8	0	11	0
	MIR	54	1.6 (1.5)	19	60	19	0	2	0
	SEL	56	1.4 (1.3)	35	33	28	0	0	4
	TYN	55	1.7 (1.4)	2	64	31	0	2	2
	FAN2	86	3.9 (6.0)	30	58	0	0	0	12
	JUD	86	4.5 (7.1)	25	71	0	0	0	3
	KAY	86	4.1 (5.4)	27	67	4	1	1	1
	NET	86	4.2 (5.2)	11	79	5	0	0	5
	BEL	148	1.7 (2.8)	47	46	1	2	1	6
	PAT	144	2.7 (3.0)	17	73	3	0	1	5
	RAQ	152	4.2 (6.2)	11	81	2	0	0	5
	WHO3	162	2.5 (3.2)	29	59	1	0	0	11
5 females	ANA	83	3.0 (4.4)	31	66	2	0	0	2
	CHI2	83	2.4 (4.2)	43	46	0	2	0	9
	GIN	83	2.9 (3.7)	16	73	0	0	0	12
	ISA	83	4.0 (5.2)	9	85	2	0	0	5
	ROM2	83	2.6 (3.4)	31	54	0	0	0	16
	ANJ2	122	2.4 (3.7)	17	70	0	0	0	13
	ELE	121	2.1 (3.1)	20	74	0	0	0	6
	KAJ	122	1.4 (1.8)	40	53	1	0	0	7
	SYL2	122	2.1 (3.4)	23	68	0	0	0	8
	TON	122	3.1 (2.6)	1	94	5	0	0	0
Mean Values:			2.2	23.1	68.3	1.0	0.2	0.0	7.8

* Calculated as a percentage of scan samples.
[1] See Table 2–2 for details on individual females.

negatively correlated with the number of females in her unit ($r_s = -.553$, p<.001, N=45). Females in larger units thus appear to stay farther away from their leader males, on average, than females in smaller units. Much of this pattern, however, can be accounted for by the fact that females in one-female units were consistently closer to their leader male (mean 1.42 meters, N=5) than females in multiple-female units (mean 2.32 meters, N=40). When females in one-female units are excluded from the analysis, there is no longer a significant correlation between the number of females in a unit and the average distance between a female and her leader male ($r_s = .265$, p=.098, N=40).

Despite the general correlation between unit size and proximity to the leader male, females varied greatly within unit size categories. Table 5–3 shows this variation, much of which appeared to be the result of individual variation among females. For example, within Ike's unit, three females were, on average, 2.7 meters or less from Ike, whereas one female (RAQ) was, on average, 4.16 meters from Ike. Likewise, four of the five females in Leonardo's unit typically stayed within 3 meters of Leonardo, but one female (ISA) averaged almost 4 meters from Leonardo, a full meter more than the other females in her unit.

Variation *between* OMUs of the same size also appeared to account for much of the variation observed. Both the four 4-female units and the two 5-female units showed wide variation in this respect. Of Quincy's, Clive's, and Alexander's units, all consisting of four females, the mean distances between females and their leader males differed so greatly that the ranges of the three units do not even overlap (Quincy's females: .69 to 1.23 meters; Clive's females: 1.38 to 2.18 meters; Alexander's females: 3.89 to 4.45 meters). As shown in Table 5–3, there was no apparent relationship between these differences in female proximity patterns and the age or reproductive status of the females in each of these three units.

Alexander's unit in particular was characterized by the greatest distances between females and their leader male. On one occasion, I observed one of Alexander's females (JUD) more than 100 meters from him, a distance over twice as great as I observed for any other female during the study period. This observation and the above proximity data suggest that some characteristic of Alexander himself, such as less frequent herding and/or a more tolerant personality, may have contributed to the proximity patterns observed for his unit. Although I did not observe fewer neck-bites by Alexander than by other males in Group 1, he may well have had a history of herding his females less often than other males.

Of the four 2-female OMUs, two showed a similar pattern to that described by Sigg (1980) for two-female OMUs near Erer Gota (see Chapter 4). In Sigg's model, one female in the unit, the "central" female, is consistently closer to the leader male, and the other "peripheral" female is consistently farther away from him. Both my qualitative observations and

Table 5–3 Mean Distance between Females and their Leader Males, Broken Down by One-Male Units, with Potential Correlating Factors

Name of Leader Male of OMU	Name of Female[1]	N	Age	Number of Follower Males in OMU	Number of Juveniles in OMU	Pregnant or Lactating during Study Period	Cycling during Study Period	Mean Distance to Leader Male (meters)[2]
Units with one Female:								
Alexander*	FAN	34	Old (wrinkles)	0	1		√	0.6
Ximeno	JUA	31	Young adult (5–6 yrs)	0	0		√	1.8
Julie	JUL	69	Fully adult	1	1	√	√	1.7
Hank	URS2	83	Young adult (5–6 yrs)	0	0	√	√	1.4
Orion	VIR	81	Fully adult	0	1		√	1.6
						AVERAGE FOR ONE-FEMALE UNITS:		1.4
Units with Two Females:								
Emilio	ANT	72	Fully adult	0	1			2.4
	LIN	72	Fully adult	0	1	√	√	2.6
Darth	AUD2	218	Fully adult	0	1	√		2.8
	VER2	218	Fully adult	0	1		√	1.0
Sebastian	CLE	123	Fully adult	0	1		√	1.3
	MAR	123	Fully adult	0	0	√		2.3
Jupiter	SER	108	Fully adult	1	0		√	2.2
	VEN	118	Fully adult	1	0	√		2.5
						AVERAGE FOR TWO-FEMALE UNITS:		2.1

Units with Three Females:

Unit	ID	Age		Size				Mean
Boris*	KAT	Fully adult	1	50			0	1.9
	NAT	Older adult	1	50	√		0	2.0
	OPH	Fully adult	1	50	√	√	0	1.4
Jupiter	LUN	Fully adult	1	39			0	1.3
	SER2	Fully adult	1	39			0	2.0
	VEN2	Fully adult	1	39	√	√	0	2.6
		AVERAGE FOR THREE-FEMALE UNITS:						1.9

Units with Four Females:

Unit	ID	Age		Size				Mean
Quincy*	IRI	Fully adult	0	42	√		0	1.2
	ROS	Fully adult	0	42	√		0	0.9
	VIO	Fully adult	0	42		√	1	1.6
	ZEN	Fully adult	0	42	√		0	0.7
Clive*	CLA	Fully adult	2	54	√		0	2.2
	MIR	Fully adult	2	54	√		0	1.6
	SEL	Fully adult	2	56	√		0	1.4
	TYN	Young adult (5–6 yrs)	2	55	√		0	1.7
Alexander	FAN2	Old (wrinkles)	0	86		√	1	3.9
	JUD	Fully adult	0	86		√	0	4.5
	KAY	Subadult (4–5 yrs)	0	86		√	0	4.1
	NET	Young adult (5–6 yrs)	0	86		√	0	4.2
Ike	BEL	Fully adult	0	148		√	0	1.7
	PAT	Subadult (4–5 yrs)	0	144		√	0	2.7
	RAQ	Fully adult	0	152		√	0	4.2
	WHO3	Fully adult	0	162		√	1	2.5
		AVERAGE FOR FOUR-FEMALE UNITS:						2.4

(Continued)

Table 5-3 Continued

Name of Leader Male of OMU	Name of Female[1]	N	Age	Number of Follower Males in OMU	Number of Juveniles in OMU	Pregnant or Lactating during Study Period	Cycling during Study Period	Mean Distance to Leader Male (meters)[2]
Units with Five Females:								
Leonardo	ANA	83	Fully adult	0	0		√	3.0
	CHI2	83	Fully adult	0	1	√		2.4
	GIN	83	Older adult	0	0	√	√	2.9
	ISA	83	Fully adult	0	0	√		4.0
	ROM2	83	Fully adult	0	1	√		2.6
Max	ANJ2	122	Older adult	0	0	√		2.4
	ELE	121	Older adult	0	0	√		2.1
	KAJ	122	Subadult (4–5 yrs)	0	0		√	1.4
	SYL2	122	Young adult (5–6 yrs)	0	0		√	2.1
	TON	122	Juvenile (3–4 yrs)	0	0		√	3.1
						AVERAGE FOR FIVE-FEMALE UNITS:		2.6

* One-male units from the first observation season (November 1996–May 1997).

[1] See Table 3–2 for full names and other details of females.

[2] See Table 5–2 for standard deviations.

their quantitative difference in average distance to the leader male suggest that both Darth's females (AUD2 and VER2) and Sebastian's females (MAR and CLE) showed such a pattern of spatial differentiation (see Table 5–3). Both of the females who had shorter average distances to their leader male (VER2 and CLE), however, were sexually swollen for a larger proportion of the study period than the other females, and swollen females usually stay closer to their leader males than do nonswollen females (discussed later and in Chapter 6). The differences in proximity to the leader male in these two OMUs may therefore be related to the reproductive condition of each female and may thus be temporary. These two OMUs are discussed in more detail with regard to the patterns of interaction shown by each of their females, both with their leader male and also with non-leader males, in Chapter 6.

Other factors besides unit size and individual differences affected the average distance of a female to her leader male. First, as mentioned earlier, swollen females were consistently closer to their leader male—and more closely guarded by their leader male—than were nonswollen females. Second, females with newborn infants tended to stay closer to their leader males than they did when they did not have newborn infants or when their infants were older (see Chapter 6). Third, females that had been more recently incorporated into a unit usually stayed closer to the leader male than females who had been in that unit for longer periods, undoubtedly as a result of increased herding by the leader male during this time (see Chapter 6). Neither a female's age nor the number of follower males associated with her unit, however, appeared to be related to the average distance between that female and her leader male.

The average distance between a female and her leader male at Filoha is considerably greater than that reported by Kummer and Kurt (1963) for the hamadryas near Erer Gota. There, the average distance between a female and her leader male was 0.7 meters, and no female was ever observed farther than 3.2 meters from her leader male in the sample reported by Kummer and Kurt (1963). At Filoha, on the other hand, six females had an average proximity to their leader male of greater than 3.2 meters, and I occasionally observed female–leader male distances of 20 meters or more. Although these differences in proximity patterns between the females of Filoha and Erer Gota suggest differences between the two sites in spatial cohesion of one-male units, I have no evidence to suggest that OMUs at Filoha are any less *socially* cohesive than those at Erer Gota, as interactions between OMUs were equally rare at Filoha as they were at Erer Gota.

Differences observed in patterns of proximity between females and their leader males at Filoha compared to Kummer and Kurt's sample at Erer Gota are probably due to the fact that most of Kummer and Kurt's observations were made at the sleeping cliffs, where individuals are typically in closer proximity to one another than they are during the day. Sigg (1980), who calculated distances between females and leader males during the daily travel route, found that central females were, on average, 8.3 meters from their leader male and peripheral females were, on average, 13.6 meters from their leader male. These distances, although they are only from two-female units, are considerably greater than the mean distances at Filoha (see Table 5–3), which included both the daily travel route and time spent at the sleeping cliff.

Patterns of Social Interaction within One-Male Units

Kummer (1968a) describes social activity within one-male units as occurring along two main avenues: (1) between the leader male and each of his females and (2) between females and their offspring. In contrast to Kummer's observations, however, only about half of the females in Group 1 (23 out of 45; see Table 5–5) engaged in grooming interactions with their leader male more often than they did with other females, and only 10 engaged in more grooming interactions with their offspring than they did with other non-leader unit members (e.g., other females or follower males). Grooming interactions among females at Filoha occurred, on average, about as often as those between leader males and females and more often than those between females and their offspring.

The two sociograms in Figure 5–2 show the distribution of grooming activity among the members of two OMUs in Group 1, Leonardo's unit with

A one-male unit on the edge of the Filoha cliff. Two females are grooming on the left and the third female, accompanied by her young infant, is grooming the leader male on the right. *(Photo by the author)*

five females and Alexander's unit with four females, both of which remained stable in membership for the entire length of the second observation season. Patterns of social interaction in these two OMUs (along with the data presented in Table 5–5) show that social activity within the OMUs at

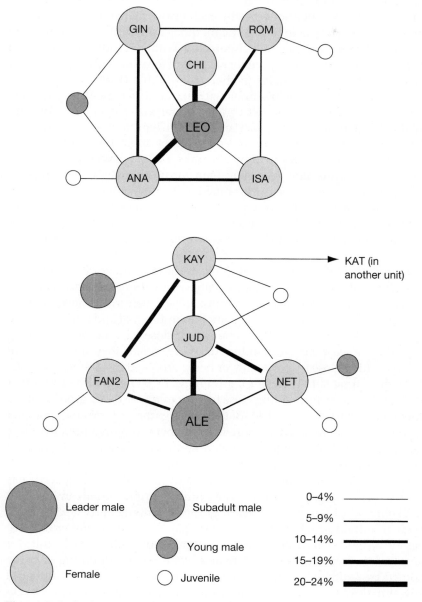

Figure 5–2 Sociograms of Leonardo's and Alexander's Units

Filoha was more evenly distributed across all members of an OMU than it was at Erer Gota. Analyses of social interactions among females, as well as comparisons to interactions with leader males and a further examination of the star-shaped sociogram, are presented and discussed in Chapter 7.

Social Interactions of Leader Males.   Table 5–4 lists the percentage of scan samples spent in various activities by each leader male for whom I had at least 30 scan samples, using the same methods as described for females in Chapter 3. Leader males rarely interacted with individuals other than females (i.e., other males or juveniles), and all females with whom leader males interacted were females in their own OMU. (I did not include a column in Table 5–4 for interactions with extraunit females because there were no such interactions.) On average, leader males spent 40% of their available social time sitting alone (i.e., at least 10 cm from another individual and not interacting socially) and 59% of their time sitting close to, grooming, or being groomed by a female. With the exception of Darth, who spent far more time grooming than most other males, and Jupiter, who spent far *less* time being groomed than most other males, leader males did not vary widely in their frequencies of interaction. Leader males with more females tended to receive more grooming than leader males with fewer females, but this difference was not statistically significant.

Social Interactions of Females.   Table 5–5 lists the percentage of scan samples that each female spent interacting socially with various categories of individuals. On average, females spent about 38% of their available social time sitting alone (i.e., at least 10 cm from another individual and not interacting socially) and about 63% of their time sitting close to, grooming, or being groomed by at least one other individual. On average, they spent 24.5% of their time sitting close to, grooming, or being groomed by their leader male; 25% of their time sitting close to, grooming, or being groomed by other females; 6% of their time sitting close to, grooming, or being groomed by a follower or solitary male; and 4% of their time grooming or being groomed by a juvenile or an infant. The more females there were in a unit, the more likely it was that females in that unit were sitting close to another individual rather than sitting alone (r_s=.491, p=.001, N=45).

A female's likelihood of being involved in grooming interactions was not affected by her age, parity, or the number of individuals in her unit. Her likelihood of being involved in grooming interactions with specific classes of individuals, however, was correlated with the number of those types of individuals in her unit. The number of females in a unit, for example, was correlated with a female's likelihood of grooming or being groomed by another female (r_s=.608, p=.0001, N=45), and the number of follower males associated with a unit was correlated with a female's likelihood of grooming or being groomed by a non-leader (follower or solitary) male (r_s=.690, p=.0001, N=45).

Table 5-4 Percentage of Scan Samples Spent by Leader Males in Various Social Activities

Name	N	Number of Females in OMU	Sitting Alone	Sitting Alone, Self-Grooming	Sitting Alone, Sleeping	Sitting Alone TOTAL	Sitting Close to At Least One Female	Grooming a Female[1]	Being Groomed by At Least One Female[1]	Sitting Close to, Grooming, or Being Groomed by At Least One Female[1]	Sitting Close to Another Male	Grooming Another Male	Being Groomed by Another Male	Grooming or Being Groomed by a Juvenile
Alexander*	32	1	34	3	0	38	31	6	25	63	0	0	0	0
Hank	68	1	41	2	3	46	19	10	24	53	0	0	0	2
Orion	70	1	43	1	4	49	19	13	20	52	0	0	0	0
Rudy	56	1	30	0	9	39	16	16	20	52	0	2	2	5
Ximeno	29	1	28	0	4	31	28	14	28	69	0	0	0	0
Darth	180	2	26	2	4	32	18	27	22	67	1	0	0	0
Emilio	60	2	45	0	7	52	20	5	22	47	0	2	0	0
Sebastian	102	2	30	0	11	41	20	13	26	58	0	0	1	0
Jupiter	133	2.5[2]	44	0	1	45	31	6	14	51	2	2	1	0
Boris*	48	3	35	0	0	35	19	4	42	65	0	0	0	0
Alexander	70	4	41	0	7	49	13	11	24	49	0	1	1	0
Clive*	57	4	44	2	2	48	16	12	25	53	0	0	0	0
Ike	133	4	37	0	9	46	31	4	20	54	0	0	0	0
Quincy*	41	4	22	0	0	22	32	10	37	78	0	0	0	0
Leonardo	70	5	34	0	0	34	17	13	36	66	0	0	0	0
Max	99	5	27	1	1	29	19	9	42	71	0	0	0	0
Mean values:			35.2	0.7	3.8	39.7	21.7	10.8	26.5	59.1	0.1	0.4	0.3	0.4

* One-male units from the first observation season (1996–1997).

[1] May also be sitting close to another individual at the same time.

[2] Jupiter had two females for part of the study period and three females for part of the study period.

Table 5-5 Percentage of Available Social Time Spent by Females Sitting Close to, Grooming, or Being Groomed by Each Type of Other Individual

Size of OMU	Name of Female	N	Sit Alone	Sitting Close to (SC) At Least One Other Individual:						
				SC Leader	SC Female	SC Non-leader Male	SC Juv	SC Non-leader Male + Female (on either side)	SC Leader + Other (on either side)	SC TOTAL
1 female	FAN	34	21	27	0	0	0	0	6	33
	JUA	31	23	27	0	0	0	0	0	27
	JUL	69	28	15	0	2	0	0	2	19
	URS2	83	53	14	0	0	0	0	1	15
	VIR	81	38	20	0	0	2	0	0	22
2 females	ANT	72	51	11	9	4	0	0	5	29
	LIN	72	39	8	8	5	0	0	5	26
	AUD2	218	58	9	1	2	0	0	1	13
	VER2	218	31	19	0	0	0	0	4	23
	MAR	123	48	14	8	0	4	0	2	28
	CLE	123	50	9	9	0	0	0	2	20
	VEN	118	48	15	3	19	0	0	5	42
	SER	108	55	13	5	2	0	0	3	23
3 females	KAT	50	49	5	0	23	0	2	2	32
	NAT	50	28	7	2	2	0	0	2	13
	OPH	50	54	13	4	4	0	0	0	21
	LUN	39	56	17	3	0	0	0	9	29
	SER2	39	44	15	9	0	0	3	3	30
	VEN2	39	20	6	6	31	0	3	3	49

4 females	IRI	42	33	0	25	0	0	0	8	33
	ROS	42	38	8	10	3	0	0	8	29
	VIO	42	44	15	15	0	3	0	3	36
	ZEN	42	40	15	18	0	0	0	3	36
	CLA	54	46	9	15	4	0	0	0	28
	MIR	54	21	6	17	4	0	0	0	27
	SEL	56	43	6	0	4	0	0	4	14
	TYN	55	37	0	19	7	0	0	2	28
	FAN2	86	34	5	12	0	0	0	8	25
	JUD	86	20	2	24	0	0	2	0	28
	KAY	86	36	5	17	2	0	0	0	22
	NET	86	43	2	21	0	0	0	0	25
	BEL	148	45	10	14	0	1	1	8	34
	PAT	144	41	6	19	2	0	2	7	36
	RAQ	152	45	4	25	0	1	1	6	37
	WHO3	162	41	5	17	1	0	0	5	28
5 females	ANA	83	18	2	30	2	0	0	6	40
	CHI2	83	32	11	33	0	0	0	0	44
	GIN	83	38	3	31	0	0	0	2	36
	ISA	83	33	3	32	2	2	0	2	41
	ROM2	83	38	5	27	0	0	0	2	34
	ANJ2	122	29	2	34	0	0	0	11	47
	ELE	121	26	8	33	0	0	0	5	46
	KAJ	122	34	6	13	0	0	0	8	27
	SYL2	122	31	4	27	0	0	0	7	38
	TON	122	45	1	17	0	0	0	1	19
Mean values:			32.4	4.5	27.7	0.4	0.2	0.0	4.4	37.2

(Continued)

103

Table 5-5 Continued

Size of OMU	Name of Female	N	Grooming (GM)						Being Groomed by (GM by):				
			Self GM	GM Leader	GM Female	GM Non-Leader Male	GM Juv or Infant	GM TOTAL	GM by Leader	GM by Female	GM by Non-Leader Male	GM by Juv or Infant	GM by TOTAL
1 female	FAN	34	0	21	6	3	3	33	6	6	0	0	12
	JUA	31	0	27	0	0	10	37	13	0	0	0	13
	JUL	69	0	21	0	2	11	34	17	0	0	4	21
	URS2	83	5	22	0	0	0	22	10	0	0	0	10
	VIR	81	5	19	0	0	8	27	14	0	0	0	14
2 females	ANT	72	0	7	2	0	6	15	0	4	2	0	6
	LIN	72	5	17	2	0	10	29	5	2	0	0	7
	AUD2	218	1	5	0	8	13	26	2	0	6	1	9
	VER2	218	2	20	0	0	3	23	26	0	0	0	26
	MAR	123	1	12	2	2	1	17	4	0	4	0	8
	CLE	123	4	15	0	0	7	22	9	2	0	2	13
	VEN	118	0	3	1	0	0	4	1	3	1	0	5
	SER	108	0	15	3	0	0	18	6	1	0	0	7
3 females	KAT	50	0	5	0	9	0	14	0	5	2	0	7
	NAT	50	7	35	5	5	2	47	7	0	2	0	9
	OPH	50	0	10	0	6	4	20	0	0	4	0	4
	LUN	39	6	6	0	0	0	6	6	0	0	0	6
	SER2	39	0	3	15	0	0	18	0	9	0	0	9
	VEN2	39	0	0	9	11	0	20	0	14	3	0	17

	Code	N											
			1.0	10.4	8.9	0.4	1.6	21.3	2.4	7.6	0.0	0.4	10.4
4 females	IRI	42	0	15	3	0	8	26	0	8	0	5	13
	ROS	42	5	18	0	0	8	26	3	0	0	0	3
	VIO	42	0	10	3	0	8	21	0	0	0	5	5
	ZEN	42	3	3	8	0	3	14	8	3	0	0	11
	CLA	54	0	13	4	0	4	21	2	4	2	0	8
	MIR	54	0	8	6	6	0	20	4	21	10	0	35
	SEL	56	7	9	6	9	0	24	7	6	10	0	23
	TYN	55	0	0	19	10	2	31	0	4	2	0	6
	FAN2	86	0	8	11	0	3	22	6	14	0	0	20
	JUD	86	0	19	15	0	2	36	7	15	0	2	24
	KAY	86	2	0	17	2	3	22	0	14	0	0	14
	NET	86	2	5	13	2	2	22	0	13	0	2	15
	BEL	148	2	14	6	0	0	20	2	3	0	0	5
	PAT	144	2	5	7	0	1	13	0	3	0	1	4
	RAQ	152	0	3	2	0	3	8	0	12	0	2	14
	WHO3	162	2	8	7	0	14	29	2	4	0	0	6
5 females	ANA	83	5	18	15	2	2	37	3	10	0	0	13
	CHI2	83	0	14	0	0	0	14	10	0	0	0	10
	GIN	83	0	5	10	2	0	17	0	10	0	0	10
	ISA	83	0	3	8	0	9	20	0	11	0	0	11
	ROM2	83	0	12	13	0	0	25	2	2	0	2	6
	ANJ2	122	0	12	4	0	2	18	0	10	0	0	10
	ELE	121	0	13	9	0	1	23	0	9	0	0	9
	KAJ	122	2	15	7	0	1	23	7	7	0	1	15
	SYL2	122	2	12	11	0	0	23	2	9	0	1	12
	TON	122	1	0	12	0	1	13	0	8	0	0	8
Mean values:			1.0	10.4	8.9	0.4	1.6	21.3	2.4	7.6	0.0	0.4	10.4

(Continued)

105

Table 5-5 Continued

Size of OMU	Name of Female	N	Grooming (GM) or Being Groomed by (GM by):				
			GM or GM by Leader	GM or GM by Female	GM or GM by Non-Leader	GM or GM by Juv or Infant	Grooming or Being Groomed by
1 female	FAN	34	27	12	3	3	45
	JUA	31	40	0	0	10	50
	JUL	69	38	0	2	15	55
	URS2	83	32	0	0	0	32
	VIR	81	33	0	0	8	41
2 females	ANT	72	7	6	2	6	21
	LIN	72	22	4	0	10	36
	AUD2	218	7	0	14	14	35
	VER2	218	46	0	0	3	49
	MAR	123	16	2	6	1	25
	CLE	123	24	2	0	9	35
	VEN	118	4	4	1	0	9
	SER	108	21	4	0	0	25
3 females	KAT	50	5	5	11	0	21
	NAT	50	42	5	7	2	56
	OPH	50	10	0	10	4	24
	LUN	39	12	0	0	0	12
	SER2	39	3	24	0	0	27
	VEN2	39	0	23	14	0	37

	IRI	42	15	11	0	13	39
	ROS	42	21	0	0	8	29
	VIO	42	10	3	0	13	26
	ZEN	42	11	11	0	3	25
	CLA	54	15	8	2	4	29
	MIR	54	12	27	16	0	55
4 females	SEL	56	16	12	19	0	47
	TYN	55	0	23	12	2	37
	FAN2	86	14	25	0	3	42
	JUD	86	26	30	0	4	60
	KAY	86	0	31	2	3	36
	NET	86	5	26	2	4	37
	BEL	148	16	9	0	0	25
	PAT	144	5	10	0	2	17
	RAQ	152	3	14	0	5	22
	WHO3	162	10	11	0	14	35
	ANA	83	21	25	2	2	50
	CHI2	83	24	0	0	0	24
	GIN	83	5	20	2	0	27
	ISA	83	3	19	0	9	31
5 females	ROM2	83	14	15	0	2	31
	ANJ2	122	12	14	0	2	28
	ELE	121	13	18	0	1	32
	KAJ	122	22	14	0	2	38
	SYL2	122	14	20	0	1	35
	TON	122	0	20	0	1	21
Mean values:			12.8	16.5	0.4	2.0	31.7

(Continued)

Table 5-5 Continued

Size of OMU	Name of Female	N	SC/GM/ GM by Leader	SC/GM/ GM by Female	SC/GM/GM by Non-Leader Male	Sitting Close Grooming or Being Groomed
1 female	FAN	34	54	12	3	78
	JUA	31	67	0	0	77
	JUL	69	53	0	4	74
	URS2	83	46	0	0	47
	VIR	81	53	0	0	63
2 females	ANT	72	18	15	6	50
	LIN	72	30	12	5	62
	AUD2	218	16	1	16	48
	VER2	218	65	0	0	72
	MAR	123	30	10	6	53
	CLE	123	33	11	0	55
	VEN	118	19	7	20	51
	SER	108	34	9	2	48
3 females	KAT	50	10	5	34	53
	NAT	50	49	7	9	69
	OPH	50	23	4	14	45
	LUN	39	29	3	0	41
	SER2	39	18	33	0	57
	VEN2	39	6	29	45	86

Sitting Close to, Grooming, or Being Groomed by:

4 females					
IRI	42	15	36	0	72
ROS	42	29	10	3	58
VIO	42	25	18	0	62
ZEN	42	26	29	0	61
CLA	54	24	23	6	57
MIR	54	18	44	20	82
SEL	56	22	12	23	61
TYN	55	0	42	19	65
FAN2	86	19	37	0	67
JUD	86	28	54	0	88
KAY	86	5	48	2	58
NET	86	7	47	4	62
BEL	148	26	23	0	59
PAT	144	11	29	2	53
RAQ	152	7	39	0	59
WHO3	162	15	28	1	63
5 females					
ANA	83	23	55	4	90
CHI2	83	35	33	0	68
GIN	83	8	51	2	63
ISA	83	6	51	2	72
ROM2	83	19	42	0	65
ANJ2	122	14	48	0	75
ELE	121	21	51	0	78
KAJ	122	28	27	0	65
SYL2	122	18	47	0	73
TON	122	1	37	0	40
Mean values:		17.3	44.2	0.8	68.9

Patterns of social interaction between females and leader males, as well as those between females and non-leader males, are discussed in more detail in Chapter 6. Social interactions among females are compared to those between females and leader males and discussed further in Chapter 7.

UNIT TAKEOVERS

The cohesion of one-male units is broken only when females transfer into a new unit. Transfer between units occurs mainly through unit takeovers, instigated and carried out by males, rather than through voluntary dispersal by females. A minimum of 10 takeovers occurred in Group 1 between November 1996 and September 1998, at least 6 of which took place between May 1997 and December 1997, when Group 1 was not under observation. During this seven-month lapse in observation, the composition of the OMUs in Group 1 changed more than it did between December 1996 and April 1997 (5 months) and between December 1997 and September 1998 (10 months) combined. These changes may be related to the trapping season that took place in July 1997, as trapping provides an opportunity for takeovers to occur if leader males are trapped without their females or if

A leader male looks up the cliff at his females, waiting for them to follow him. After takeovers, females are herded more frequently than at other times and are thus quickly conditioned to follow their new leader male.

females are trapped without their leader males. The two most notable changes that occurred between May and December 1997 were a reduction in size of the two largest OMUs from eight and nine, respectively, to five females each. Several other rearrangements of females among OMUs also occurred during this time.

The majority of takeovers in Group 1 occurred when that OMU, or the group as a whole, was not under observation. Two takeovers were witnessed, however: one in December 1996, at the very beginning of the study period, and another in September 1998, on the last day of observation on Group 1 until July 2000 (Swedell 2000). Several more takeovers have been witnessed by either me or my field assistant, Teklu Tesfaye, since July 2000, two of which are reported in Swedell and Tesfaye (2003). In the following section, I describe four observed takeovers in detail.

Takeover #1: December 1996

Because this takeover occurred before all-day follows and systematic data collection had begun, I observed the events surrounding it only during the mornings and evenings, when the group was in the vicinity of the sleeping cliff. The takeover consisted of the loss of all five of a leader male's females to three other males. Three of these females were taken over by another leader male, one was taken over by a solitary male, and one was taken over by an unknown male. One of the three females taken over by the other leader male subsequently returned to the deposed leader male within two weeks of the takeover.

Before the takeover, Sylvester was the leader male of five females: Dorothy, Beatrice, Hazel, Whoopie, and Irma. At the time of the takeover, Beatrice had a black infant and Dorothy was pregnant. On the evening of December 7, 1996, Sylvester was spending much of his time lying down, unusual postural behavior for a leader male, and had what appeared to be dried blood on his torso and legs, indicating a possible injury. At 5:45 P.M. that evening, Ike, a solitary male, and Sylvester were threatening one another with yawns, stare threats, and eyebrow-raises after Ike somehow provoked one of Sylvester's females to scream (I did not see what Ike did to provoke this). Subsequent to the agonism between Sylvester and Ike, the latter then did something to provoke a scream by a female of Quincy, another leader male. This was followed by a fight between Ike and Quincy, after which Ike sat down two meters from Sylvester's unit and stayed there until dark.

On the evening of December 8, Dorothy was sitting spatially within another OMU, which consisted of Felix and four females. She was not, however, interacting with any of these individuals. All four of Sylvester's other females were sitting with him, and Sylvester was again lying down on a cliff ledge. At 5:40 that evening, Beatrice saw Ike coming toward the sleeping cliff and quickly moved from her position in front of Sylvester and his other females to a position behind Sylvester. When Ike arrived, he got into a fight with Quincy, and then sat down several meters away. Sylvester then stood up and watched Ike, as if to be ready to defend his females should the need arise, but no further fighting took place before dark and Sylvester eventually lay down again.

On the morning of December 9, Dorothy was again sitting among the members of Felix's unit rather than with Sylvester's unit. Sylvester's other four females, however, were still with him and followed him as they departed from the sleeping cliff. At 5:00 P.M. on the evening of December 9, Sylvester had arrived back at the sleeping cliff and was lying face down, alone, on a cliff ledge. Felix then arrived at the sleeping cliff with his own four females as well as Dorothy, Beatrice and Hazel, who were now members of his unit. Felix and his females sat about one meter away from Sylvester, who remained lying down. Of Felix's seven females, the three whom he had taken over from Sylvester followed Felix more closely and sat closer to him than Felix's other females. Felix also exhibited possessive behavior, including possession grips and genital inspection (see Appendix I), with these females but not with his other females. Felix displayed the most possessive behavior with Beatrice, whom he frequently held close to him and genitally inspected.

Of Sylvester's remaining two females, Whoopie had been taken over by Ike and Irma had been taken over by an unknown male (unknown because this takeover occurred so early in the study period). Whoopie, however, did not follow Ike as closely as Beatrice followed Felix: she often only followed him to about 3 meters and then sat down, whereas Beatrice followed Felix at a distance of 1 meter or less. Probably as a result of Whoopie's failure to follow Ike closely enough, he threatened and neckbit her repeatedly, sometimes pulling her up by her head hair to do so. At about 5:30 P.M. that evening, Ike threatened Felix several times, who threatened back. After that Sylvester got up from his prone position, walked to the top of the cliff, and gazed at Felix's unit for about five minutes before returning to his previous spot and lying down again.

Later, on December 20 (after an eight-day gap in observation), Beatrice had a sexual swelling and Hazel was starting to develop one, and Beatrice's infant had disappeared. At the sleeping cliff on the evening of December 20, Sylvester was sitting alone, still had dried blood on his torso, and looked older and thinner than he had before the takeover. The closest member of Felix's unit to Sylvester, Hazel, was only one meter away from him. Dorothy, Beatrice, and Hazel were all still in Felix's unit.

On December 25, Beatrice and Hazel were both fully swollen and were copulating with Felix. Whoopie was also fully swollen and was copulating with Ike. Dorothy, however, was sitting with Sylvester, the deposed leader male, rather than with Felix, and after this date was never observed to interact with Felix again. Beatrice's black infant was still missing and presumed dead.

On January 3, I observed Dorothy copulating with Sylvester. She was not swollen and was in fact pregnant at the time (see below). Beatrice and Hazel were both still swollen, and Beatrice had fresh wounds on her left cheek. On January 6, Dorothy had developed a small swelling and was again observed copulating with Sylvester. Beatrice was no longer swollen, and Hazel's swelling was going down. On February 27, Dorothy gave birth to an infant. This infant must have been conceived more than three months prior to the takeover and Sylvester was thus the likely sire.

Dorothy stayed with Sylvester for at least five months after the takeover. Beatrice and Hazel stayed with Felix for at least five months after the takeover. Whoopie stayed with Ike for at least 21 months after the takeover, and it is not known how long Irma stayed with her new leader male. For about a month after the takeover, Sylvester's and Felix's units associated closely with one another: although Felix's females never interacted with Sylvester and Dorothy never interacted with Felix, the two units were nevertheless often almost spatially indistinguishable. After that time, the two units continued to coordinate their movements more closely than with any other unit and were usually closer to one another than either was to any other unit. Also, despite the fact that Dorothy and Hazel were now in different units, they often sat close to one another when both of their leader males were at least a meter away and/or when Felix in particular was out of their line of sight.

The takeover of Sylvester's females appeared to have been instigated by one or more solitary males, including Ike, before or after Sylvester's injury. Sylvester had probably sustained a wound to his torso during the day on December 7, either in a fight with Ike or another solitary male or from an accident. This injury probably weakened him enough so that Ike began to challenge him for possession of his females. That Sylvester was weak and may not have been physically capable of fighting is suggested by several factors: (1) the fact that Quincy fought with the solitary challenger, Ike, whereas Sylvester did not; (2) that Sylvester's main interactions with Ike on December 7 and 8 were to threaten him and watch him rather than to chase him or fight with him (as Quincy did and as leader males typically do); (3) that Sylvester was observed lying down on his stomach several days in a row, which is an unusual posture for hamadryas, especially for leader males; and (4) that Sylvester eventually lost all five of his females on December 9.

The fact that three of five females in this takeover went to another leader male rather than to solitary or follower males (cf. Kummer 1968; Sigg et al. 1982; Abegglen 1984) may be related to Sylvester's apparent injury. The usual inhibition of leader males from taking over the females of other leader males (as suggested by Kummer et al. 1974) may be released when a leader male becomes injured and is suddenly unable to defend his females. In this case, the male who took over the majority of Sylvester's females, Felix, was not observed to fight or interact agonistically with Sylvester either before or after the takeover. Rather, the takeover appeared to be initiated by one or more solitary males, but somehow Felix, rather than a solitary male, ended up with three of Sylvester's females. Felix may simply have outfought Ike for the females once Sylvester had already lost them. Ike was not yet fully adult, and Felix was probably capable of defeating him. Ike's threats to Felix on the evening of the takeover suggest that Ike had been fighting with Felix for control of Sylvester's females, but that he was only capable of obtaining one of them (Whoopie) for himself. As demonstrated by both Whoopie's failure to follow Ike closely and Ike's relentless neckbiting, it was probably difficult for Ike to take over and control more than one female at once, especially when they were relatively uncooperative like Whoopie.

Alternatively, it may have been easier for Felix than for other males to gain access to Sylvester's females because the two males—and/or the females in their units—may have had a close social and/or kin relationship. This possibility is suggested by the close association between the two units both before and after the takeover. Such an association may have allowed Felix to take over Sylvester's females easily and without much opposition from the females themselves. Sylvester's females were probably already familiar with Felix and his females and may have been more willing to be subsumed into his unit than to be taken over by an unfamiliar solitary male.

Takeover #2: September 1998

Prior to takeover #2, Bruce was the leader male of five females: Carolyn, Linda, Ralaine, Gloria, and Janice. At the time of the takeover, Ralaine had a six-week old female infant.

On the morning of September 15, 1998, Bruce suffered an injury that impaired his ability to move around. The lack of blood or wounds and Bruce's apparent young age and good health suggested that he was probably bitten by a snake. This injury resulted in Bruce's apparent inability to defend his females and the subsequent loss of all five females to other males. By 7:00 A.M., when I first observed them that day, Carolyn, Linda, and Ralaine had been taken over by three different leader males in the group: Darth, Emilio, and Jupiter, respectively. Each of these males already had two females of his own prior to the takeover. Gloria had been taken over by a solitary male, Pluto, and Janice had been taken over by an unknown solitary male. Because this was the last day of observation on Group 1, I do not know which solitary male took over Janice nor how long any of Bruce's females stayed with their new leader males.

At 8:00 A.M. that morning, at least an hour after the takeover, Ralaine's infant was taken from her by a solitary subadult male, who played with the infant for at least an hour and a half without returning it to her. Ralaine's new leader male, Jupiter, neither defended the infant nor tried to retrieve it, as leader males typically do, and the infant probably died from dehydration shortly thereafter.

At 9:00 A.M., Group 1 left the vicinity of the sleeping cliff. Bruce traveled with the group about one kilometer, at which point he fell behind the group and died at 1:30 P.M. that day. Prior to his death, Bruce lay nearly motionless on the ground for at least two hours, suggesting that he may have been incapacitated by snake venom. After his death, no blood or visible wounds were found on his body.

As with takeover #1, takeover #2 was also preceded by an injury to the leader male, in this case most likely a snake bite. Also similar to takeover #1, in takeover #2 three females were taken over by other leaders and two females were taken over by solitary or unknown males. As noted earlier, this pattern contrasts with previous reports of hamadryas takeovers suggesting that most females are taken over by solitary or follower males (Kummer 1968a; Sigg et al. 1982; Abegglen 1984). In Bruce's case, because each of his females was taken over by a different male, the recipients of his females were probably determined by two factors: (1) chance, that is, who happened to be nearby when Bruce was injured and suddenly incapable of defending his females; and (2) fighting ability, that is, which of those males that were nearby could outcompete the others for access to Bruce's females. Because I could not locate Group 1 between this day and my last day at Filoha on October 2, observations on Group 1 after this takeover could not be made and further consequences of the takeover beyond the day on which it occurred are not known.

Takeover #3: August 2002

Prior to this takeover, Natalie had been one of 2 or 3 of Boris's females since at least October 1996. At the time of the takeover, Boris had two females, Natalie and Katrina, and Natalie had a black infant. On August 1, Boris was seen with fresh wounds on his face. On August 2, Natalie was aggressively taken from Boris by Kim. Kim herded and neckbit Natalie repeatedly and held her in a possession grip, almost completely hiding her from view, sometimes walking with her underneath him. (It is not known who took over Katrina, as Boris was seen alone after the takeover and Katrina was not seen again.)

On August 4, Natalie was seen with her infant on her belly, sitting about one meter from Kim. I next observed her on August 13, at which time she no longer had an infant with her. She also had many new scars all over the back of her head, undoubtedly from the repeated neckbites she had received from Kim since the takeover. Natalie's infant was still missing on August 16, the last day of observation of that field season, and so was presumed dead.

Takeover #4: September 2002

This takeover was witnessed by my field assistant, Teklu Tesfaye. Prior to the takeover, Marigold was one of four females of the leader male Herb. She gave birth to an infant male on August 22, 2002, and was observed with Herb's unit through September 12. When observations commenced on the morning of September 13, Marigold had been taken over by Park, a leader male with one other female. Park's face was bloody, and Herb had a new wound on his ear. Marigold had some hair missing on the back of her head (presumably from receiving frequent neckbites), and Marigold's infant had blood on its head and fresh wounds on its face. Marigold was apparently attempting to stay near Herb's unit, but Park kept herding her away and would neckbite and mount her each time she moved more than a meter away from him. He also held her in a possession grip while she crouched and screamed. At least five times, Park grabbed Marigold's infant and bit its head and ears while the infant screamed. This same pattern of behavior was observed on September 14 as well.

On September 17, Marigold was observed following Park, carrying her dead infant. She was next seen on September 27, without her infant. At that time, she had a medium-sized swelling, which was sufficiently large enough that it must have started inflating a few days earlier.

Effects of the Takeovers on Female Reproduction

Of the four infants of females involved in these takeovers, all were either known or likely to have died shortly after the takeover. Beatrice's and Natalie's infants both disappeared within 11 days of the takeover, Marigold's infant appears to have been killed by her new leader male within 4 days of the takeover, and Ralaine's infant was kidnapped for a prolonged period of time and likely died as well. A fifth takeover of a known female (Catherine) that occurred in October 2003, though the takeover itself was not actually witnessed, also involved the disappearance (and presumed death) of Catherine's six-month-old infant within a week of the takeover.

In addition to infant mortality, several females came into estrus (i.e., developed a swelling and began copulating) within two weeks of their takeover. Of the four females in the first event that were observed on days subsequent to their takeover, three—Beatrice, Hazel, and Whoopie—came into estrus within two weeks of the takeover. The fourth female, Dorothy, came into estrus two weeks after she returned to Sylvester, despite the fact that she was pregnant at the time. In addition, Marigold developed a sexual swelling within two weeks of takeover #4. Unfortunately, I could not identify the cycle stage of these females at the time of the takeover and therefore do not know whether they came into estrus sooner than they would have had they *not* been taken over, nor do I know the age of Beatrice's infant so as to ascertain whether she began cycling sooner than she would have had her infant survived. Marigold developed a sexual swelling 36 days after her infant's birth (and 10 days after its death), however, which is far shorter than the 9–16 month lactational amenorrhea reported for wild hamadryas baboons (Sigg et al. 1982; Chapter 6). It is thus likely that Marigold's interbirth interval was shortened by at least nine months as a result of her infant's death. In addition, of possible importance is the fact that the two shortest ovarian cycles observed among Filoha females were those of Hazel and Whoopie immediately after their takeover by Felix and Ike, respectively (see Chapter 6 for details). The effects of takeovers #2 and #3 on female reproduction are not known because they each occurred so close to the end of their respective observation seasons.

Similar changes in reproductive condition following takeovers have been reported for other wild populations as well as for captive groups of hamadryas baboons. At Erer Gota, three infants died while their mothers were still in lactational amenorrhea (one of these was stillborn), and in all three cases the females came into estrus less than one month later (Sigg et al. 1982). Also at Erer Gota, a female who was transferred to another band *with* her infant (who survived) resumed estrus cycling within only six months, which is four months fewer than the minimum amenorrhea observed for other females in that population following the birth of a surviving infant (range 10–16 months, mean 14 months, N=13; Sigg et al. 1982).

Zinner (1997, 1998) reported that captive hamadryas females showed a significantly reduced postpartum amenorrhea after being taken over by a new leader male compared to periods of stable group membership. Similarly, Colmenares and Gomendio (1988) reported that takeovers of females in their colony of hamadryas and hybrid baboons in Madrid caused lactating females to resume estrus cycles within two weeks and pregnant females to either abort or give birth prematurely.

RELATIONSHIPS BETWEEN FEMALES AND LEADER MALES

The relationship between a female and her leader male defines the one-male unit and is the most obvious relationship in hamadryas society. Given that the most common type of OMU is that consisting of one male and one female (see Figure 5–1), many hamadryas females have no social relationships with adults other than their leader male. Females in one-female units spent an average of 36% of their available social time in grooming interactions with their leader male (range 27%–40%; N=5), whereas females in multi-female units spent, on average, only 13% of their time in grooming interactions with their leader male (range 0%–26%; N=40).

Duration of Bonds

Sigg estimates that 70% of the bonds between females and their leader males last a minimum of three years, and that females change OMUs two to three times during their lifetimes (Sigg 1980; Sigg et al. 1982). Because of the changes in the composition of Group 1 between May and December 1997, I could not confidently identify most of the females from one observation season to the next and therefore cannot reliably estimate how long each female was with her leader male over the course of the entire study period. I do know that at least 36 females (64% of females in Group 1 during 1997–1998) were with the same leader male for a minimum of 9 months (December 8, 1997, through September 15, 1998), and at least 6 females (about 11% of Group 1 females)—Audrey, Chiara, Fanny, Roma, Sylvia, and Whoopie—were with the same leader male for a minimum of 21 months (i.e., the entire study period). Since September 2002, when Teklu Tesfaye began observing Group 1 full-time during my absence, we have been able to record unit membership over time once again, and these more recent observations have shown that at least 27 out of the 55 known adult females in Group 1 have remained with the same leader male for at least 18 months and at least 5 females have remained with the same leader male for four years or more.

Herding Behavior

Bonds between leader males and their females are established and maintained by the male's herding behavior, in that females are essentially conditioned by their leader male's threats and neckbites to stay closer to him than to any other adult or subadult individual, particularly those outside the unit and sometimes even those within the unit. Kummer (1968a) reported that a leader male responds aggressively when his female (1) becomes separated from him physically; (2) becomes separated from him socially, that is, when she allows another individual to come between her and her leader male; or (3) engages in social interactions with an outside individual (Kummer 1968a). Even in captivity, "hamadryas females are actively discouraged from interactions not directed towards the adult male or their own young offspring" (Gore 1994 p. 391). As a consequence of male herding, the vast majority of the aggression that a hamadryas female receives is from her leader male. Gore (1994) compared hamadryas and rhesus macaque (*Macaca mulatta*) females in captivity and found that rhesus females received only 8% of their dyadic aggression from subadult or adult males, whereas hamadryas females received 32% of their dyadic aggression from their leader male alone. In the wild, these differences appear to be much greater.

The females at Filoha showed signs of male-inflicted aggression in the form of scars on the napes of their necks, the back of their heads, and their faces. Ad libitum observations of neck bites suggested that head and face wounds received by females were primarily, if not exclusively, from attempted neck bites by leader males. As if anticipating his aggression, females appeared to be constantly aware of the location of their leader male and their own proximity to him, and would typically look back at their leader male periodically as they moved farther away from him, for example, while foraging or approaching another individual. Also, when a female had been farther away from her leader male than normal for a short period, she usually ran toward him afterwards, kecking, and he would often respond by chasing and neckbiting her. My subjective impression overall was that females were often not self-motivated to maintain proximity to their leader male and only did so because of the threat of physical aggression from him (or from another individual). As will be discussed in Chapter 7, females often chose to interact with other females in their unit over their leader male and apparently did not necessarily prefer him as a social partner.

Grooming Interactions

Table 5–6 shows the percentage of scan samples that each female spent sitting close to or in grooming interactions with her leader male, as well as each female's average proximity to her leader male. Females ranged from 0% to 46% in their amount of available social time spent grooming or being groomed by their leader male. On average, females spent 15% of their available social time in grooming interactions with their leader male.

Grooming Reciprocity. Both Kummer (1968a) and Sigg (1980) reported that female hamadryas more often take the active than the passive role in grooming relationships with their leader male. Females in the Filoha population also spent more time grooming their leader (79%, on average) than being groomed by him (21%). With only 3 exceptions of 41 females, each individual female also spent more time grooming her leader than being groomed by him. Scan sample data for leader males (see Table 5–4) also

Table 5–6 Percentage of Available Social Time Spent by Females in Social Interactions* with Males, Broken Down by One-Male Units, with Potential Correlating Factors

Name of Leader Male	Name of Female[1]	N	Age	Number of Follower Males in OMU	Pregnant or Lactating during Study Period	Cycling during Study Period	SC/GM/GB Leader Male:					SC/GM/GB Non-Leader Male:			
							SC Leader	GM/GB Leader	SC/GM/GB Leader	NN Leader	MEAN DISTANCE TO LEADER MALE[2]	SC Non-leader	GM/GB Non-leader	SC/GM/GB Non-leader	NN Non-leader
Alexander	FAN	34	Old (wrinkles)	0		√	27	27	54	79	0.6	0	3	3	0
Ximeno	JUA	31	Young adult (5–6 yrs)	0			27	40	67	97	1.8	0	0	0	0
Rudy	JUL	69	Fully adult	0	√	√	15	38	53	80	1.7	2	2	4	14
Hank	URS2	83	Young adult (5–6 yrs)	0	√	√	14	32	46	94	1.4	0	0	0	0
Orion	VIR	81	Fully adult	0		√	20	33	53	94	1.6	0	0	0	4
Emilio	ANT	72	Fully adult	0	√		11	7	18	37	2.4	4	2	6	6
	LIN	72	Fully adult	0		√	8	22	30	38	2.6	5	0	5	7
Darth	AUD2	218	Fully adult	0		√	9	7	16	29	2.8	2	14	16	11
	VER2	218	Fully adult	0	√		19	46	65	76	1.0	0	0	0	2
Sebastian	MAR	123	Fully adult	0	√		14	16	30	41	2.3	0	6	6	6
	CLE	123	Fully adult	0		√	9	24	33	64	1.3	0	0	0	0
Jupiter	VEN	118	Fully adult	1	√		15	4	19	31	2.5	19	1	20	24
	SER	108	Fully adult	1		√	13	21	34	51	2.2	2	0	2	8
Boris**	KAT	50	Fully adult	1	√		5	5	10	19	1.9	23	11	34	54
	NAT	50	Older adult	1	√		7	42	49	58	2.0	2	7	9	14
	OPH	50	Fully adult	1	√		13	10	23	40	1.4	4	10	14	20

Jupiter	LUN	39	Fully adult	1			17	12	29	68	1.3	0	0	0	0
	SER2	39	Fully adult	1		√	15	3	18	30	2.0	0	0	0	9
	VEN2	39	Fully adult	1	√		6	0	6	3	2.6	31	14	45	54
Quincy**	IRI	42	Fully adult	0	√		0	15	15	15	1.2	0	0	0	0
	ROS	42	Fully adult	0	√		8	21	29	40	0.9	3	0	3	0
	VIO	42	Fully adult	0		√	15	10	25	38	1.6	0	0	0	3
	ZEN	42	Fully adult	0	√		15	11	26	37	0.7	0	0	0	0
Clive**	CLA	54	Fully adult	2	√		9	15	24	30	2.2	4	2	6	8
	MIR	54	Fully adult	2	√		6	12	18	19	1.6	4	16	20	19
	SEL	56	Fully adult	2	√		6	16	22	35	1.4	4	19	23	28
	TYN	55	Young adult (5–6 yrs)	2			0	0	0	2	1.7	7	12	19	31
Alexander	FAN2	86	Old (wrinkles)	0	√		5	14	19	30	3.9	0	0	0	0
	JUD	86	Fully adult	0		√	2	26	28	25	4.5	0	0	0	0
	KAY	86	Subadult (4–5 yrs)	0	√		5	0	5	27	4.1	0	2	2	4
	NET	86	Young adult (5–6 yrs)	0	√		2	5	7	11	4.2	2	2	4	5
Ike	BEL	148	Fully adult	0	√		10	16	26	47	1.7	0	0	0	1
	PAT	144	Subadult (4–5 yrs)	0	√		6	5	11	17	2.7	2	0	2	3
	RAQ	152	Fully adult	0		√	4	3	7	11	4.2	0	0	0	2
	WHO3	162	Fully adult	0	√		5	10	15	29	2.5	1	0	1	1
Leonardo	ANA	83	Fully adult	0	√		2	21	23	31	3.0	2	2	4	2
	CHI2	83	Fully adult	0		√	11	24	35	43	2.4	0	0	0	0
	GIN	83	Older adult	0		√	3	5	8	16	2.9	0	2	2	0
	ISA	83	Fully adult	0	√		3	3	6	9	4.0	2	0	2	2
	ROM2	83	Fully adult	0	√		5	14	19	31	2.6	0	0	0	0

(Continued)

Table 5–6 Continued

Name of Leader Male	Name of Female[1]	N	Age	Number of Follower Males in OMU[1]	Pregnant or Lactating during Study Period	Cycling during Study Period	SC/GM/GB Leader Male:					SC/GM/GB Non-Leader Male:			
							SC Leader	GM/GB Leader	SC/GM/GB Leader	NN Leader	MEAN DISTANCE TO LEADER MALE[2]	SC Non-leader	GM/GB Non-leader	SC/GM/GB Non-leader	NN Non-leader
Max	ANJ2	122	Older adult	0	√		2	12	14	17	2.4	0	0	0	0
	ELE	121	Older adult	0	√		8	13	21	20	2.1	0	0	0	0
	KAJ	122	Subadult (4–5 yrs)	0		√	6	22	28	40	1.4	0	0	0	1
	SYL2	122	Young adult (5–6 yrs)	0		√	4	14	18	23	2.1	0	0	0	0
	TON	122	Juvenile (3–4 yrs)	0		√	1	0	1	1	3.1	0	0	0	5

* SC = Sitting close to

GM = grooming

GB = being groomed by

NN = nearest neighbor

** One-male units from the first observation season (1996–1997).

[1] See Table 3–2 for full names and other details on individual females.

[2] See Table 5–2 for standard deviations.

While most hamadryas females typically spend more time grooming their leader males than receiving grooming from them, this is not always the case. Leonardo and Chiara, shown here, had a particularly close relationship that involved a substantial amount of bi-directional grooming. *(Photo by the author)*

show that they received more grooming than they gave. With only three exceptions, each individual male was groomed by females at least twice as much as he groomed females. Both my qualitative observations and behavioral sequences from continuous focal data suggested that the two main social situations that prompted a female to groom her leader male were (1) conflict situations or times of uncertainty and (2) copulation. With the exception of estrus (see next section), though, no such specific social situations appeared to elicit grooming of females by leader males.

Grooming as Reassurance.   Despite the fact that a female's leader male is her main aggressor, he is also her main protector and provider of reassurance in times of conflict or uncertainty (Kummer 1968a; Sigg 1980). At Filoha, if there was a fight nearby, a female would immediately move closer to her leader male. On the rare occasions when a female was involved in a fight with another individual, typically another female or a juvenile, she would run to her leader male, groom him intently, and look over her shoulder at that individual periodically while grooming her leader male. This was similar to the "protected threat" triadic interaction described by Kummer (1968a) for captive hamadryas. Sigg (1980) found that, upon receiving electric shocks from a dog-training collar, a female would run to her leader male and groom him "frenetically." At Filoha, even after being neckbitten by the leader male himself, a female would usually run to him and groom him intently afterwards. Overall, grooming their leader male for a short period after a conflict appeared to function as a tension-reduction mechanism for females. Conflict likely increases levels of stress hormones, and grooming probably lowers those levels after a conflict (Terry 1970; Schino et al. 1988). That females run to their leader male for reassurance after being bitten by him illustrates not only the important role the leader male plays in reducing a female's stress after a conflict but also the powerful role neck bites play in conditioning females to stay near their leader male.

Variation among Females in Interactions with the Leader Male

As shown in Table 5–6, females varied widely in the amount of time they spent with their leader male. Neither her age nor the presence of a follower male in a female's unit was related to this variation among females. Rather, the main factor that appeared to affect a female's tendency to spend social time with her leader male was the number of other females in her unit. Females in larger units spent less time in grooming interactions with their leader male than females in smaller units, and the size of a one-male unit was negatively correlated with the amount of time females in that unit spent sitting close to, grooming, or being groomed by their leader male (Spearman Correlation $r_s = -.473$, p=.002, N=45). As with average proximity to the leader male (reported in Chapter 5), most of this correlation can be accounted for by the fact that females in one-female units spent consistently more social time with their leader males (mean 55%, N=5) than did females in multi-female units (mean 21%, N=40). When one-female units were excluded from the analysis, the correlation between the above two factors became weaker and was no longer statistically significant ($r_s = -.260$, p=.105, N=40).

Within unit size categories, there was also marked variation among females in how much social time they spent with their leader male. Females in two-female units varied from 16% to 65%, females in three-female units varied from 6% to 49%, females in four-female units varied from 0% to 29%, and females in five-female units varied from 1% to 35% (or from 6% to 35% if juvenile females are excluded) in the amount of time they spent sitting close to, grooming, or being groomed by their leader male. The least amount of variation can be seen in females in one-female units, who varied only from 46% to 67% in the amount of time they spent with their leader male.

Kummer (1968a) suggested that which females groom the leader male the most is determined by competition among females and preferences of the leader male. While females at Filoha did occasionally compete for grooming access to the leader male (see Chapter 9), this typically occurred during times of stress, when more than one female sought reassurance from the leader male simultaneously due to a conflict situation, and rarely resulted in one female losing grooming access to the leader male (i.e., both females would usually continue to groom the leader male afterward). Leader male preferences for one female over another may be a factor in determining which females spend more time in grooming interactions with him, but I could not test this for the Filoha population because I did not collect systematic data on male behavior. Sigg (1980), however, found that, although one female spent more time in grooming interactions with the leader male than the other female, leader males showed no consistent grooming preferences for either of their females.

In the Filoha population, it appeared that another factor played a large role in determining patterns of social interaction between females and their leader male: the stage of the female's reproductive cycle during the study period. This pattern is illustrated most clearly by the 4 two-female OMUs that were examined.

Table 5–6 shows all 4 two-female units and the comparative percentages of time that each female spent sitting close to, grooming, and being groomed by their leader male and by non-leader males. In all four units, one female spent more time grooming or being groomed by the leader male than did the other female, and the other female spent more time grooming with non-leader males than did the first female. In three of these units, the female that spent more time in grooming interactions with the leader male also spent more time closer to him and was more likely than the other female to have him as her nearest neighbor. By contrast, the female that spent *less* time in grooming interactions with the leader male was more likely than the other female to have a non-leader male, rather than the leader male, as her nearest neighbor.

As mentioned in Chapter 4, a similar pattern of differentiation in social behavior among the two females of an OMU was found by Sigg (1980). Sigg, who focused exclusively on two-female OMUs (three free-ranging at the sleeping cliff and three in enclosures), found that one "central female" was consistently closer to the center of a triangle formed by the two females and the leader male, whereas the other "peripheral female" was consistently farther away from the center of this triangle. In 5 of the 6 two-female OMUs on which Sigg focused his observations, the central female spent more time grooming the leader male than did the peripheral female in the unit; in 2 of the free-ranging OMUs, all 3 of which showed this pattern, the central female spent over four times as much time in grooming interactions with the leader male as did the peripheral female.

In each of the two-female units at Filoha, however, all four females who spent less time interacting with the leader male were pregnant and then gave birth at some point during the study period, whereas all four females who spent more time interacting with the leader male did not have infants and each underwent at least two estrus cycles during the study period. As will be discussed in Chapter 6, females with sexual swellings interact with their leader male more often than do nonswollen females. The higher frequency of interaction with the leader male shown by the above four cycling females, therefore, may be a result of a high percentage of scan samples during times when those females were swollen and therefore interacting more often than usual with their leader male. To test whether sexual swellings were the sole cause of the above differences, I excluded samples during which females were swollen and then again compared each pair of females with regard to their frequency of grooming interactions with their leader male; Table 5–7 shows these data. Among three pairs of females, a similar relationship still held. It thus appears that a female who is undergoing estrus cycles, regardless of whether she is actually swollen at the time, spends more time grooming with her leader male than a female who is pregnant or lactating. The differences observed among the above females in two-female units, therefore, are most likely a reflection of their differing stages of reproduction. While Sigg (1980) does not report reproductive states of the females in his study, his results may also have been affected by such factors.

Interestingly, these patterns do not hold when only "sitting close" is used as the behavior of comparison. Of the above pairs of females, two of the females who spent *less* time in grooming interactions with the leader male (ANT and MAR) actually spent *more* time sitting close to him than did the female who spent more time in grooming interactions with him.

Table 5–7 Percentage of Available Social Time Spent by Anestrous Females in Two-Female Units Sitting Close to or in Grooming Interactions with their Leader Male and with the Leader Male as their Nearest Neighbor

Name of Leader Male	Name of Female	N	Number of Follower Males in OMU	Pregnant or Lactating during Study Period	Cycling during Study Period	SC Leader	GM / GB by Leader	SC / GM / GB by Leader	NN Leader
Emilio	ANT	72	0	√		11	7	18	38
	LIN	72	0		√	8	22	30	40
Darth	AUD2	218	0	√		9	7	16	29
	VER2	124	0		√	16	40	56	70
			0						
Sebastian	MAR	123	0	√		14	16	30	43
	CLE	46	0		√	3	16	19	49
Jupiter	VEN	118	1	√		15	4	19	32
	SER	78	1		√	17	24	41	51

Females who are pregnant or have infants may not engage in grooming interactions with their leader male as much as females who are undergoing estrus cycles, but they do still sit close to their leader male as much, if not more, than cycling females. As will be discussed in Chapter 6, though they do not spend more time in grooming interactions with their leader male, females with newborn infants nevertheless appear to stay closer to their leader male than females without newborn infants, probably to ensure protection of their infants by their leader male.

The Effect of Female Tenure in a One-Male Unit

One factor that appeared to have at least a temporary effect on patterns of proximity and social interaction between a female and her leader male was the length of time she had been in his unit. As reported by Kummer (1968a), females at Filoha that had been recently acquired by their leader males were usually herded more frequently and guarded more closely than were females that had been with their leader males for longer periods of time.

Two examples in particular suggest that females that have recently been incorporated into an OMU stay much closer to (or are kept closer by) their leader male than females who have been in that unit for longer periods of time. One example, discussed earlier in this chapter, is that of Beatrice (BEA) and Hazel (HAZ), who were taken over from Sylvester by Felix in December 1996. As I do not have a minimum of 30 scan samples for the females in Felix's unit, they are not included in Table 5–6; an analysis using the samples I do have, however, shows that for about one month after the takeover, Beatrice and Hazel were consistently closer to Felix (BEA averaged .87 meters and HAZ averaged 1.4 meters) than were three of his other females (averaging 2.5 m, 3.9 m, and 4.6 m; the fourth female averaged 1.3 m; N=7). Scan samples over a four-month period after the takeover (N=28) show that both Beatrice and Hazel were, on average, closer to Felix than all four of his other females (BEA: 0.9 m; HAZ: 1.2 m; ELL: 1.3 m; POL: 1.8 m; GOL: 1.9 m; JOS: 2.5 m). During this period, Felix spent 7% of his time being groomed by Hazel, 29% of his time grooming or being groomed by Beatrice, and 29% of his time grooming or being groomed by his four other females combined.

A second example is that of Luna (LUN), who was a member of Jupiter's unit for about three weeks from late June through mid-July 1998. During Luna's short tenure, she was consistently closer to Jupiter than were Jupiter's other two females, Serena (SER) and Venus (VEN). Luna's mean proximity to Jupiter was 1.3 meters, whereas Serena's average proximity to Jupiter during Luna's tenure was 2.0 meters (2.2 meters overall, including the time before and after Luna's presence) and Venus' average proximity to Jupiter during Luna's tenure was 2.6 meters (2.5 meters overall). During Luna's tenure, Jupiter spent 10% of his time grooming or being groomed by Luna, whereas he spent only 2.5% of his time being groomed by Serena and none of his time grooming Serena or Venus or being groomed by Venus.

Kummer (1968a) suggests that more grooming occurs in situations in which social bonds are weaker or less certain. After a leader male acquires a new female, the bond between them is probably not yet cemented and requires a certain period of time to strengthen and develop, during which time the new female stays closer to her new leader male and grooms him (and is groomed *by* him) more frequently than females who have been with him for longer periods of time.

FEMALES AND NON-LEADER MALES

The vast majority of females in the Filoha population rarely interact with males other than their leader. Some females, however, often sit close to or engage in grooming interactions with non-leader males. These non-leader males are either follower males, defined as males that are consistently associated with a particular OMU, or solitary males, males that associate loosely with several OMUs and interact frequently with other solitary males and juveniles.

Types of Social Interaction between Females and Non-Leader Males

Table 5–6 lists the percentage of scan samples that each female spent sitting close to or in grooming interactions with non-leader males. Relationships between females and non-leader males were characterized mainly by time spent sitting close (mean 2.8%, N=45) and time spent in grooming interactions (mean 2.8%, N=45). Some relationships between females and non-leader males appeared to be motivated by an interest on the part of the non-leader male in the female's infant. Non-leader males, especially follower males, often attempted to take infants away from their mothers and sometimes succeeded in these attempts. Sexual behavior with non-leader males was infrequent (see Chapter 6). The implications of social and sexual interactions with non-leader males for hamadryas female reproductive strategies will be discussed further in Chapter 9.

Variation among Females in Interactions with Non-Leader Males

Females varied widely in the amount of social time they spent with non-leader males (see Table 5–6). Most females spent less than 5% of their available social time with these males. A few females, however, spent over 10%, even up to 45%, of their social time with non-leaders. The frequency with which females associated with non-leader males was strongly, but not completely, associated with the presence of a follower male in their one-male unit (Spearman Correlation r_s=.682, p<.0001, N=45). As shown in Table 5–6, some females who did have follower males in their unit rarely associated with those males (e.g., SER, SER2, LUN, CLA), and some females who did not have follower males in their unit nevertheless associated occasionally with non-leader males (e.g., AUD2, MAR, ANT). With only one exception (AUD2), however, all females who spent more than 6% of their available social time sitting close to, grooming, or being groomed by non-leader males (N=8) did so with the follower male associated with their unit.

As discussed earlier, in all four of the two-female units that were examined, one female in the unit spent more time than the other female in grooming interactions with the leader male and the other female spent more time in grooming interactions with non-leader males than the first female. Of the females who spent more time grooming with non-leader males, two of these females also spent more time than the other female in their unit sitting close to non-leader males (the other two spent equal amounts of time sitting close to non-leader males), and three of these females were also more likely than the other female in their unit to have a non-leader male as their nearest neighbor. All four of the females who spent more time grooming with non-leader males were pregnant and then gave birth during the study period.

Factors Affecting the Presence of Follower Males

In Group 1 at Filoha in April 1998 (see Table 3–1), 30% of one-male units had follower males. Across both observation seasons, 28% of units had follower males. Kummer (1968a) reported that 36% of OMUs at Erer Gota that contained adult females also had follower males; this figure for Group 1 at Filoha is 32%. Table 5–8 shows all OMUs, across both observation seasons, with the number of follower males associated with each unit and various aspects of reproduction of the females in each unit that might affect the presence of a follower male in that unit. The number of follower males in an OMU was relatively weakly correlated with the number of females in that unit (r_s=.390, p=.015, N=40). A female's age was significantly correlated with the number of follower males in her unit (r_s=.376, p<.001, N=96), although this can be at least partially accounted for by the fact that "initial units," consisting solely of juvenile females, never had follower males, either at Filoha or at Erer Gota (Kummer 1968a).

Although follower males rarely copulate with adult females in their units (see Chapter 6), they may nevertheless tend to associate with units that contain cycling females so as to maximize their potential reproductive opportunities. This notion is supported by a relatively weak but significant positive correlation between the number of follower males in an OMU and

Table 5–8 The Distribution of Follower Males across All One-Male Units over Both Observation Seasons, with Possible Correlative Factors to the Presence of a Follower Male in Each Unit

Name of Leader Male	Adult Females	Subadult / Adolescent Females	Total Females	Cycling Females	Pregnant Females	Male Infants	Female Infants	Total Infants	Male Juveniles	Female Juveniles	Total Juveniles	FOLLOWER MALES
Alexander 96–97*	1	0	1	1	0	0	0	0	1	0	1	0
Alexander 97–98	3	1	4	2	0	1	0	1	2	0	2	0
Boris 96–97*	3	0	3	1	1	0	2	2	0	0	0	2
Boris 97–98	2	0	2–3	0	0	1	0	0–1		1	2	1
Bruce	5	0	5	2	0–1		1	1–2	1		2	?
Casper	1	0	1	0	0–1	1	0	0–1	0	0	0	?
Clive*	3	1	4	1	1–2	1	0	1–2	0	0	0	2
Darth 96–97*	1	1	2	1	0	0	0	0	1	0	1	1
Darth 97–98	2	0	2	2	0–1	0	0–1	0–1	2	0	2	0–1[1]
Eddie*	1	0	1	1	0	0	0	0	0	0	0	0
Emilio	2	0	2	0	0		1	0–2	1		2	0
Felix*	6	0	6	0	0	1		1–3	1		3	0
Fred	1	0	1	0	1	0	0	0	1	0	1	1
George*	0	1	1	0	0	0	0	0	0	0	0	0
Gus	1	0	1	1	0	0	0	0	0	0	0	1
Hank	1	0	1	1	0	0	0	0–1	0	0	0	0
Hans*	1	0	1	0	0	0	0	0	1	0	1	0
Ike 96–97*	1	0	1	1	0	0	0	0	1	0	0	0
Ike 97–98	3	1	4	2	0	1	0	0–1	1	0	1	0
Jack	3	1	4	1	0	0	0	2	0	0	1	0
Jerry	1	1	2	1	0	0	0	0	0	0	0	0
Jupiter	2–3	0	2–3	1	0	0	1	0–1	0	0	0	1

Ken	2	0	2	2	1	0	0	0	0	0	0	1
Leonardo 96–97*	7	2	9	2	0	0	1	4		1	4	0
Leonardo 97–98	5	0	5	1–2	1	2	2	1–3	1	1	2	0
Max 96–97*	6	2	8	2	0	1	0	3		1	6	2
Max 97–98	3	2	5	2	0	2	0	0–2	0	0	0	0
Nick	1	0	1	0	0	0	1	0–1	0	0	0	0
Orion	1	0	1	1	0	0	0	0	1	1	1	0
Ozzie*	0	1	1	0	0	0	0	0	0	0	0	0
Pete	0	1–3	1–3	1	0	0	0	0	0	0	0	0
Quincy*	4	0	4	1	0	0	0	1–3			4	0
Ralph*	0	1	1	1	0	0	0	0	0	0	0	0
Roberto*	1	0	1	0	0	0	0	0	0	0	0	0
Rudy	1	0	1	1	0–1	1	0	0–1	1	1	1	0
Sebastian	2	0	2	1	0–1			0–1	1	1	1	0
Sting	1	2	3	2	1			1–2	0	0	0	1
Sylvester*	1	0	1	1	0			0–1	1	1	1	0
Ximeno	1	0	1	0	0	0	0	0	0	0	0	0
Zeus	2	0	2	2	0–1	0	1	0–1	0	0	1	1

* OMUs from the 1996–1997 observation season; all others from 1997–1998.

†Darth's unit had a follower male for part of the study period.

the number of females in that unit who were consistently undergoing estrus cycles during the study period (r_s=.343, p=.035, N=40). There was a much stronger positive correlation, however, between the number of follower males in an OMU and the number of *pregnant* females in that unit during the study period (r_s=.647, p<.0001, N=40).

An additional factor affecting the presence of a follower male in an OMU was the presence of a female infant or juvenile in that unit. The number of follower males associated with an OMU was positively correlated with the number of female infants (r_s=.542, p=.003, N=40) as well as with the number of female juveniles (r_s=.597, p=.0007, N=40). There was also a weaker but significant correlation between the number of follower males in an OMU and the number of infants in that unit (r_s=.346, p=.031, N=40). The number of follower males was not, however, correlated with the number of male infants in a unit, the number of male juveniles in a unit, or the total number of infants or juveniles in a unit.

To further examine this relationship between the number of follower males in an OMU and reproductive aspects of the females in that unit, I scored the presence or absence of a follower male in a unit and tested the association between the presence of a follower male and these factors using a Mann-Whitney U test. This analysis revealed a significant relationship between the presence of a follower male and the number of pregnant females in a unit (U=68.5, p=.018, N=40). There were no significant relationships, however, between the presence of a follower male and the number of females in a unit, the number of cycling females in a unit, the number of infants in a unit, the number of juveniles in a unit, the number of male infants or juveniles in a unit, or the number of female infants or juveniles in a unit.

Together, these correlations suggest, first, that follower males associate with OMUs that contain pregnant or cycling females, as opposed to units in which females are either too young to undergo estrus cycles or are not obviously reproducing and might be infertile. Secondly, these results suggest that follower males preferentially associate with OMUs that contain female infants and/or juveniles *or* pregnant females, but not units that contain solely male infants or juveniles. A follower male may be particularly interested in associating with an OMU with a female infant or juvenile (or a pregnant female who might soon give birth to a female) in order to establish a social relationship with the young female as well as with her mother. The development of both types of relationships would presumably give the follower male a greater chance of eventually acquiring the young female as the first female of his own "initial unit."

Both Kummer (1968a) and Abegglen (1984) emphasized relationships among males as a determining factor in the presence or absence, as well as the identity of, follower males in OMUs. Abegglen's results in particular suggest that follower males possess a social relationship, and possibly a kinship relationship as well, with the leader male of the unit with which they are associated, and that it is this relationship that determines which OMUs have follower males and which do not. As I did not focus my observations on males, I cannot examine relationships between leader males and their followers as possible determinants of follower male unit membership at Filoha. The results presented here, however, suggest that the reproductive condition of the females in OMUs, specifically whether females are pregnant or have recently given birth to *female* offspring, plays a role in patterns of membership in OMUs by follower males.

Kummer attributed the lack of follower males in initial units, that is, units consisting of subadult leader males and juvenile females, as a particular intolerance of these young leader males toward followers. Whether Kummer meant that such intolerance should be due to the fact that these are new, inexperienced leader males or that they are more motivated to keep their females than are other leader males is not clear. I suggest, however, that this pattern is due to the preferences of the follower males themselves rather than to the tolerance of leaders. Follower males probably prefer to associate with units that contain adult females over units consisting solely of juvenile females. If a follower male associates with an OMU to obtain surreptitious copulations and possibly inseminate a female, then OMUs without adult females would not provide him that opportunity because juvenile females cannot yet conceive. If, on the other hand, follower males associate with OMUs in order to eventually acquire their female offspring (as suggested earlier), then units without adult females would also be a poor choice, for the same reason: a follower male would have to wait much longer to obtain an infant from a unit consisting exclusively of juvenile females than he would from a unit containing adult females.

Van Schaik and Paul (1996) note that among gelada baboons, it is the follower male rather than the leader male who interacts frequently with infants (Mori 1979; Dunbar 1984a, 1984b), suggesting that follower males use affiliative interactions with infants to establish sexual relationships with their mothers. In hamadryas baboons, however, it appears more likely that follower males are trying to establish future sexual relationships with the infants themselves.

CHAPTER SUMMARY AND CONCLUSIONS

In summary, the social structure of Group 1 at Filoha is qualitatively very similar to that of other populations of wild hamadryas baboons (e.g., Kummer 1968a; Abegglen 1984; Biquand et al. 1992b; Zinner et al. 2001b). Two differences in particular—the larger band sizes and higher population growth rate at Filoha compared to other sites—may be due to the higher abundance of perennially-available food resources and presumable low predation rate (see Chapter 4) at Filoha, both of which would contribute to a high birth rate and high infant survival rate. The social organization of Group 1 also does not differ in its broad patterns from that of previously-studied wild hamadryas, with the important exception of the greater role of social interactions among females (discussed further in Chapter 7).

Four takeovers were observed in Group 1 during the study period. In contrast to the pattern described by Kummer (1968a) in which females are usually taken over by solitary or follower males, seven of the thirteen females involved in these four events were taken over by other leader males. In addition, all infants involved in the takeovers are known or suspected to have died shortly thereafter, and one appears to have been deliberately killed by its mother's new leader male. Moreover, five of the six females who were observed on days subsequent to the takeovers came into estrus within two weeks afterwards (or, in Dorothy's case, two weeks after she returned to Sylvester, her previous leader male).

Finally, the broad patterns of social interaction between females and males at Filoha are, overall, similar to those reported for other populations of wild hamadryas. An analysis of potential factors affecting the presence of follower males in OMUs suggests that it is the presence of a female infant or juvenile in an OMU—or a pregnant adult female that could potentially give birth to a female—that draws follower males to particular one-male units. This can be explained by the interest of follower males in establishing their own OMUs and the prospects that female infants or juveniles offer them in this regard. While Kummer (1968a) and Abegglen (1984) emphasized relationships between leader males and their followers as the primary determinant of the association of follower males with particular one-male units, results from Filoha suggest that females—and their infants—may play an equal or larger role.

6

Reproduction and Sexual Behavior

In this chapter, I will discuss female reproductive parameters, sexual behavior, and the effects of reproduction on female behavior. Definitions of terms and methods used to calculate reproductive parameters are outlined in Chapter 3. I will discuss hamadryas female reproductive strategies in more general terms in Chapter 9.

REPRODUCTION AND REPRODUCTIVE PARAMETERS

Menarche

It appears that wild hamadryas females undergo their first estrus (Beach 1976) at a slightly earlier age than do wild anubis (*P. h. anubis*) and yellow (*P. h. cynocephalus*) baboon females. As I did not know the ages of the females at Filoha, I do not have data on exact age at first estrus for my study population, but I estimate, using the age classes of Sigg et al. (1982), that all cycling females at Filoha were at least three and a half or four years old (Table 6–1; see Table 5–1 for age classes). The only longitudinal study of wild hamadryas, at Erer Gota, indicated that hamadryas females develop their first sexual swellings at four to five years of age (mean 4.3, N=13; Sigg et al. 1982), compared to four and a half to five years of age for Amboseli yellow baboons (mean 4.8, range 4–5.75, N=10; Altmann et al. 1977), five years for Awash hybrid baboons (mean 5.0, range 4.5–5.5, N=10; Beehner 2003), four and a half to five and a half years for Gombe anubis baboons (median

Table 6–1 Estimated Ages of First Reproductive Events for Subadult Females

Name	Age Class	Started Cycling[1]	Number of Estrus Periods During Study Period	Apparent Conception during Study Period	Gave Birth during Study Period	Surviving Offspring at End of Study Period
LIZ	Juvenile (3–4 yrs)	Not yet	0			
OLL	Juvenile (3–4 yrs)	During study period	2			
TON	Juvenile (3–4 yrs)	During study period	1			
JEW	Subadult (4–5 yrs)	Before study period	?		√	
KAJ	Subadult (4–5 yrs)	Before study period	7			
KAY	Subadult (4–5 yrs)	During study period	6			
PAT	Subadult (4–5 yrs)	During study period	5			
TIF	Subadult (4–5 yrs)	During study period	1	√		
ANG	Subadult (4–5 yrs)	During study period	1			
CAS	Young adult (5–6 yrs)	Before study period	0		√	√
JUA	Young adult (5–6 yrs)	Before study period	2	√		
NET	Young adult (5–6 yrs)	Before study period	>1	√		
SAM	Young adult (5–6 yrs)	Before study period	>2	√		
SYL	Young adult (5–6 yrs)	Before study period	6	√		
URS	Young adult (5–6 yrs)	Before study period	3	√	√	√

[1]For subadult females, estrus cycling was presumed to have started *before* the study period if the female had an estrus period within 40 days of the beginning of the study period (based on a 40-day average cycle length for subadult females); cycling was presumed to have started *during* the study period if the females had no estrus periods until at least two months into the study period (all subadult females fell into one of those two categories).

136

59.5 months, range 54–67 months; Packer 1979), and six years for Tana River yellow baboons (mean 6.0, range 4.4–7.5, N=6; Bentley-Condit & Smith 1997). In captivity, however, baboon females begin cycling at an earlier age than in the wild (Altmann et al. 1981), and hamadryas are no exception to this pattern. At the Gumista Primate Reserve in (former Soviet) Georgia, hamadryas females show their first swelling at three and a half years (Caljan et al. 1987), and at the German Primate Center (Deutsches Primatenzentrum) they show their first swellings at about three years of age (N=4; Kaumanns et al. 1989). Early sexual maturation and accelerated rates of reproduction (due to shorter interbirth intervals) are undoubtedly a result of the unlimited food supply in captivity and the consequent greater body weights of captive animals (Asanov & Mirvis 1972; Bercovitch 1987; Kaumanns et al. 1989).

First Conception and First Birth

Most adolescent females at Filoha who were undergoing estrus cycles had five or more cycles but were still not pregnant by the end of the study period. This is consistent with other observations that wild female baboons typically undergo sexual cycles for about a year before they first conceive (e.g., Altmann et al. 1981; Smuts & Nicolson 1989). At Filoha, I estimate that all females who conceived during the study period were at least four years old, and that all females who gave birth to surviving infants were at least five years old (Table 6–1). All females listed in Table 6–1 as having conceived during the study period had undergone at least one estrus cycle during this period and then did not cycle for at least four months prior to the end of this period. Sigg et al. (1982) report that hamadryas females at Erer Gota give birth to their first infant at an age of about six years (mean 6.1, range 5.5–7, N=8), suggesting that first conception in wild hamadryas occurs at an average age of about five and a half years, about a year after menarche. This is earlier than first conception in wild olive, yellow, and hybrid baboons, which occurs, on average, at least six months later (Altmann et al. 1981; Strum & Western 1982; Beehner 2003). In captivity, hamadryas females conceive at an even earlier age than in the wild: four females at the German Primate Center conceived at an age of three years and three months (though all their infants subsequently died; Kaumanns et al. 1989) and females at the Gumista Primate Reserve conceive at an average age of four and a half years (Caljan et al. 1987).

Ovarian Cycle Length

In baboons, ovarian cycles typically range from 30 to 40 days in length (Hendrickx & Kraemer 1969; Hausfater 1975; Gauthier 1999). At Filoha, the average length of all cycles observed across all females was 40.4 days

(N=39). Cycle lengths ranged from 23 to 60 days, but 36 of 39 cycles (92%) were between 31 and 51 days (Table 6–2). The only female for whom I have data on estrus cycles but who is not included in this average, Serena (SER), had two successive cycle lengths (between three estrus periods) of 60 and 32 days, respectively. As no other female showed such a marked difference between the lengths of two successive cycles (see below), I suspect that Serena conceived and then aborted between the first two estrus periods. I therefore did not include Serena in my calculations in order to be more certain that the cross-female average represented actual cycle length rather than other factors.

When females were examined individually, per female mean cycle lengths ranged from 31 to 52.5 days and the mean per female cycle length across all females was 39 days (N=17). The average cycle length of adult females was 38.5 days and the average cycle length of subadult or adolescent females was 40.7 days. With the exception of Serena (discussed above), females varied from 3 to 19 days in the difference between their shortest and their longest cycle. The two longest cycles of 52 and 60 days were both from the same female, Virgo (VIR), whose shortest cycle (47 days) was 8 days longer than the average cycle length for all females. The two shortest cycles of 23 days (HAZ) and 29 days (WHO) were both the first cycle of those females after their takeover by a new leader male (takeover #1 discussed in Chapter 5).

The mean cycle length at Filoha is slightly longer than the mean length of 36.9 days among the captive hamadryas at the Gumista Primate Reserve (Caljan et al. 1987). Whether cycle lengths at Filoha are similar to those of Erer Gota cannot be determined because Sigg et al. (1982) did not report them, but the mean cycle lengths at Filoha are within the range of wild populations of other baboon subspecies (median of 42 days for *P. h. anubis* at Gilgil, N=33, Smuts & Nicolson 1989; mean of 38.9 days for *P. h. cynocephalus* at Tana River, N=120, Bentley-Condit & Smith 1997; mean of 39.6 days for *P. h. anubis* – *P. h. hamadryas* hybrids in Awash, N=19, Beehner 2003).

Postpartum Amenorrhea

Lactational Amenorrhea.   As in other mammals, female baboons undergo a several-month period of lactational amenorrhea following the birth of a surviving infant, during which the suckling stimulus inhibits the resumption of regular cycling (Altmann & Altmann 1978; McNeilly et al. 1988; Lee 1996). Most females at Filoha either gave birth during the study period and did not come into estrus before the end of the study period or had their apparent first postpartum estrus during the study period but had given birth prior to the beginning of the study period. I was therefore unable to calculate lactational amenorrhea for most females in Group 1. Two females,

Table 6-2 Estrus Cycle Lengths

Name	Age Class	Cycle Lengths (days)[1] in Chronological Order	Average Cycle Length (days)	Difference between Shortest and Longest Cycle (days)	Total Number of Cycles Observed
KAJ	Subadult (4–5 yrs)	44, 41, 40, 38, 49, 47	43.2	9	6
KAY	Subadult (4–5 yrs)	41, 38, 31, 49, 34	38.6	18	5
PAT	Subadult (4–5 yrs)	43, 31, 50, 37	40.3	19	4
SYL	Young adult (5–6 yrs)	42, 41, 44, 59	46.5	18	3
URS	Young adult (5–6 yrs)	35, 41	38	6	2
ANA	Fully adult	33	33	N/A	1
BAR	Fully adult	31	31	N/A	1
CLE	Fully adult	51, 42	46.5	9	
HAZ	Fully adult	29	29	N/A	1
LIN	Fully adult	41	41	N/A	1
LOR	Fully adult	37	37	N/A	1
NAT	Fully adult	46	46	N/A	1
SER	Fully adult	60*, 32	*	28*	2
SOP	Fully adult	31	31	N/A	1
VIR	Fully adult	52, 60, 51, 47	52.5	13	4
WHO	Fully adult	23, 35	29	12	2
VER	Older adult	49, 40, 31	40	18	3
Mean values (st. dev.):		40.9 (8.3)	38.9 (7.0)	13.6 (4.9)	

[1]Cycle lengths measured from either the first day of maximal swelling to the day before the first day of maximal swelling in the following estrus period; or, in cases in which a female was not under observation during the first part of estrus, from the last day of full swelling to the day before the last day of full swelling during the next estrus period.

* The twofold difference between the length of the two cycles observed for SER suggested that she probably conceived and then spontaneously aborted during the first "cycle"; therefore, an average cycle length was not calculated for her and her cycle length of 60 days was not included in the overall averages.

139

however, conceived during the first observation season, had a black infant at the beginning of the second observation season, and then began estrus cycling again during the second observation season. For these two females, I was able to calculate approximate periods of lactational amenorrhea of 264 (VER) and 268 (FAN) days, or just under 9 months. This is shorter than at Erer Gota, where lactational amenorrhea after the birth of a surviving infant ranged from 10 to 16 months, with an average of 14 months (N=13; Sigg et al. 1982).

Resumption of Cycling after Infant Death.   At Filoha, the only known females whose infants died and who were observed thereafter, Beatrice and Marigold, resumed cycling within two weeks after the death of their infants (see section on takeovers in Chapter 5). At Erer Gota, infants of three known females died, and all three resumed cycling within one month after their infant's death (Sigg et al. 1982).

Number of Cycles to Conception

Because most females either started cycling before the beginning of the study period or had not yet conceived before the end of the study period, I was unable to calculate the number of cycles to conception for most of the females in Group 1. Two adult females, Beatrice and Fanny, had infants or yearlings at the beginning of the study period, began cycling, and then apparently conceived. Each of these two females conceived during their first estrus period. One of these females, Beatrice, was taken over by a new leader male (takeover #1, described in Chapter 5) during the study period, her infant died, she underwent one estrus period, and then she became pregnant. Two other females that were taken over by new leader males at the same time, Hazel and Whoopie, underwent two and three estrus periods, respectively, with their new leader males before conceiving. It is important to note, however, that I do not know how many cycles each of these females underwent with their previous leader males before being taken over so I cannot ascertain whether their number of cycles to conception after a takeover was statistically shorter than that during a stable period.

For the remainder of the females who were cycling during the study period, I calculated minimum numbers of cycles to conception based on how many cycles females underwent during the study period. The minimum number of cycles to conception varied from one to five cycles for adult females (mean: 2) and one to seven cycles (mean: 6) for subadult females. The only adult female that underwent five cycles during the study period, Virgo (VIR), had still not conceived by the end of the second observation season. She also had the longest cycle lengths of any female, ranging from 47 to 60 days and averaging 52.5 days. Although these two factors might indicate infertility, there was a small juvenile male associated with

Virgo's unit with whom she frequently groomed and who was probably her son. That wild hamadryas females sometimes undergo up to eight cycles before conceiving (mean 3.5 cycles, N=13) has been reported by Sigg et al. (1982) for the Erer Gota population. Up to five cycles to conception have been observed among captive hamadryas females at the German Primate Center (Kaumanns et al. 1989), and up to six cycles to conception have been observed in anubis–hamadryas hybrid baboons in Awash (Beehner 2003).

Interbirth Interval

Of the thirteen females in Group 1 at Filoha whom I could reliably identify from one observation season to the next, three had two infants between November 1996 and December 1998. Births after mid-September 1998 were inferred from estimated conception dates during the study period, based on cessation of cycling accompanied by pink perineal skin and/or obvious weight gain (see Chapter 3). Interbirth intervals for the above three females were 15.5 months (FAN), 19.5 months (VER), and 21.5 months (KAT). One female, Audrey (AUD), conceived during the first observation season, in late January 1997, and would presumably have given birth in late July 1997 but her infant was either aborted or did not otherwise survive. The interval between the presumed birth of her first infant and the actual birth of her next infant was 11 months, but this interval was presumably shorter than it would have been had her infant survived. Three other females—Anja (ANJ), Chiara (CHI), and Natalie (NAT)—had black infants at the beginning of the first observation season in November 1996 and then gave birth during the second observation season. Because I do not know when their first infants were born, I cannot estimate full interbirth intervals for these females. The minimum possible interbirth intervals for these females are 17 months (ANJ), 18 months (CHI), and 14 months (NAT).

The average of the three known interbirth intervals at Filoha, 18.8 months, is shorter than the average interbirth interval of 22 months (N=12) reported by Sigg et al. (1982) for the Erer Gota population. Two of the three Filoha females just noted, however, had not yet given birth by the end of the second observation season, so they may not have given birth to a second surviving infant and their actual interbirth interval may therefore be substantially longer.

Seasonality of Reproduction

Consistent with the lack of seasonality found for most other baboon populations (Bercovitch & Harding 1993), there was no obvious seasonal

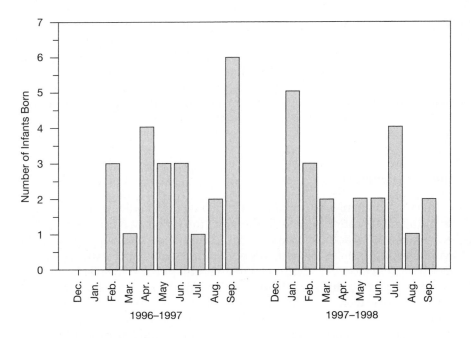

Figure 6–1 Distribution of Births over Both Observation Seasons

pattern to births at Filoha (Figure 6–1). Kummer (1968a) reported that the Erer Gota population showed two peaks of mating behavior and births, in May and June and then again in November and December. He suggested, though, that the timing of the birth and mating peaks varied among troops in the same area, as one troop showed a mating and birth peak two months later than another. Without data over at least a multiyear period, it is difficult to know for certain whether there is a seasonal pattern to births among wild hamadryas.

Captive hamadryas, on the other hand, may have seasonal birth peaks that vary depending on location. Hamadryas at the Gumista Primate Reserve in Georgia show a birth peak in February and March and again in September and October, with the fewest births in June and July (Chalyan et al. 1994b). In Georgia, natural foods are most available in April through June. Chalyan et al. (1994b) conclude that there is a relationship between food availability and reproductive seasonality in the temperate forested environment of Gumista, although no significant relationship was found between birth rate and food availability over a 15-year period except for a relationship between female fertility parameters and the harvest quality of beech and chestnut trees the preceding year.

Reproductive Synchrony

During the 1996–1998 study period, females in the Filoha population were not synchronized in their reproductive cycles. As discussed in Chapter 5, in the 4 two-female units from which data were collected, one female was pregnant and then gave birth to an infant during the study period, while the other female underwent one or more estrus cycles and then conceived during the study period. Most other units also consisted of females in varying stages of reproduction. Over both observation seasons, only five OMUs contained more than one female in the cycling phase of reproduction (i.e., not pregnant or lactating).

Of the five pairs of females who cycled simultaneously during the study period, each pair of females also overlapped significantly with one another in the swelling phase of their monthly estrus cycle. Two of these pairs, Audrey/Verena and Fiona/Sophia, each consisted of two adult females in a two-female unit and a nine-female unit, respectively. Each of these pairs underwent one synchronous estrus period, during which one of the females (Audrey and Fiona, respectively) conceived, after which the second female (Verena and Sophia) underwent several more nonconceptive cycles. Two other pairs of females with synchronized reproductive cycles, Belinda/Patsy and Sylvia/Kaja, each consisted of one adult female and one adolescent female in a four-female unit and a five-female unit, respectively. Each of these pairs underwent at least one synchronous estrus period, during which the adult female (Belinda and Sylvia) conceived, followed by continued nonconceptive cycling by the adolescent female (Patsy and Kaja). Finally, one of these pairs consisted of two adolescent females, Natasha and Sylvia, who had at least one synchronous cycle, after which Natasha conceived, followed by one more cycle and a conception by Sylvia.

The fact that four of the five pairs of females with synchronized reproductive cycles were in units of four or more females suggests that the likelihood of two females in the same OMU being in the same phase of reproduction increases with unit size. Although, in general, females at Filoha do not appear to have synchronized reproductive cycles, in larger units this most likely becomes statistically inevitable. When synchronization of reproductive cycles does occur, the females involved are also synchronized in their monthly cycles so that they are both swollen simultaneously. Adolescent females, it seems, are more flexible in their sexual cycles and are thus more likely to synchronize their cycles than are adult females. It is also likely that the onset of cycling in an adolescent female is induced in part by the sexual swellings of other females in her unit. Schwibbe et al. (1992) suggested that social facilitation plays a large role in menarche and first postpartum estrus in hamadryas females. Kummer (1968a) also reported that adolescent females who were in units with adult swollen females tended to be sexually swollen themselves.

Kummer and Kurt (Kummer 1968a), in their surveys of several hamadryas troops in the Erer Gota area, found that most OMUs with more than one female contained either all swollen females or all females who had black infants or were otherwise not swollen. In an examination of two-female units in particular, Kummer found that only 5% of these units consisted of one swollen female and one female who either had a black infant or was "otherwise sexually inactive" (Kummer 1968a, p. 177). By contrast, 27% of two-female units consisted of two swollen females, 5% consisted of two females with black infants, and 39% consisted solely of "otherwise sexually inactive" females. In the Filoha population, however, with only one exception during one week in December 1997, no two-female units ever contained two swollen females and all two-female units consisted of females that appeared to be at least six months apart in their reproductive cycles.

Kummer and Kurt's estimate of the percentage of units with "sexually inactive" females, however, was probably an overestimate, as they apparently had no way of distinguishing nonswollen cycling females (females who were between the swelling phases of their monthly cycle) from nonswollen noncycling females (i.e., females who were pregnant or who did not have a black infant but who had not yet resumed cycling). Depending on at which point in their sexual cycle females are sampled, two-female units might appear to consist of two females who are "otherwise sexually inactive" when, in reality, they consist of one "sexually inactive" (pregnant or lactating) female and one female who is between the swelling phases of her monthly cycle. Kummer and Kurt may therefore have easily mistaken nonswollen cycling females for females that were not cycling at all, may have assumed that all females in their units were not cycling, and may consequently have come to the conclusion that the females in those units were synchronous in their reproduction. The failure to distinguish these two categories of females, therefore, weakens Kummer and Kurt's (Kummer & Kurt 1963; Kummer 1968a) conclusions significantly. Their data are also problematical in that they represent only a single point in time, whereas data on reproductive cycles from Filoha were collected over a period of 14 months with repeated sampling of the same OMUs over time. Despite these criticisms, the fact that Kummer and Kurt observed such a high percentage (27%) of OMUs with all swollen females across several troops does suggest that there is a higher degree of synchrony among the females at Erer Gota than among those at Filoha and that there may be ecological factors distinguishing Erer Gota from Filoha that underlie these differences in reproductive synchrony.

Hamadryas females have also been reported to synchronize their reproductive cycles in captivity. At the German Primate Center, ovarian cycles of eight females over a 10-year period were more synchronous than would be expected by chance, and more synchrony was observed in the winter than during the summer (Schwibbe et al. 1992). Differences in the degree to which hamadryas females of various populations, both in the wild and in captivity, synchronize their reproduction may be related to differences in seasonal food availability. When food resources are more variably available (such as at Erer Gota, compared to at Filoha where doum palm fruits are available year-round), females might benefit from timing their births to coincide with seasonal peaks in food availability and might therefore be more synchronized in their reproduction as a result.

Post-Conception Swellings

Eight females at Filoha, while pregnant, showed small swellings that lasted from one to two days. These swellings resembled the "going up" phase of swelling development and most commonly occurred between day 46 and day 77 of gestation. In addition, four females had one-day swellings resembling the "going down" phase of the swelling, all occurring within the final two months of gestation. The only female who underwent post-conceptive swellings that did *not* fit this pattern was Dorothy, who was both sexually swollen and copulating with her leader male for at least two days when she was about 130 days pregnant. This occurred about one month after Dorothy was taken over from Sylvester by Felix. Two weeks after the takeover, Dorothy returned to Sylvester, and two weeks after her return to him she developed a sexual swelling (see Chapter 5 for details and Chapter 9 for further discussion).

SEXUAL BEHAVIOR

Copulations

During 1,731 minutes of continuous focal sampling of sexually swollen females between December 1997 and September 1998, I observed 27 copulations (defined here as mounts that included intromission and two or more thrusts). Copulations occurred about once an hour, on average, for a swollen female in Group 1. In addition to copulations that took place during focal samples, I observed 49 copulations by swollen females during ad libitum observations, totaling 76 observed copulations by swollen females. Of these, at least 20 included ejaculation, inferred from visible semen or a several-second pause at the end of the mount. On average, therefore, there were about four mounts per ejaculation. Of the eight sequences of two or more mounts in a row in which ejaculation did not take place before the last mount, the time interval between mounts averaged 5 minutes (range 1 to 17 minutes). Across all mounts observed, there was an average of 7.5 thrusts per mount. The number of thrusts did not differ between mounts that included ejaculation and mounts that did not include ejaculation. In the two cases where two successive ejaculations by the same male were observed

A female and her leader male copulating on the edge of the Wasaro cliff. *(Photo by the author)*

(and that male had been under constant observation between the two ejaculations so that the possibility of a third could be excluded), the intervals between these ejaculations were 10 minutes and 9.5 minutes, respectively.

Copulations with Non-Leader Males

I observed 15 copulations between females and males other than their leader (Table 6–3). Six of these were with medium juvenile males, five were with large juvenile males, and four were with subadult males (see Table 5–1 for age classes). Of the copulations with subadult males and young males (most of whom were probably capable of producing viable sperm), four occurred when the female involved had a sexual swelling and thus could have potentially led to conception. No multiple mounts with non-leader males were observed, but I cannot exclude the possibility that any of these copulations were part of a longer mount series, as each observation was brief and I did not see what occurred shortly beforehand or afterward. One copulation, involving a fully swollen adult female and a young male (aged 5 or 6), included an ejaculatory pause. Whether this male would have been capable of producing viable sperm is not known.

Table 6–3 Sexual Behavior with Non-Leader Males

Female	Estimated Age of Male*	Female's Reproductive Condition	Number of Thrusts	Vocalization during Copulation	Ejaculation	Location and Orientation of Female's Leader Male	Postcopulatory Behavior
ANA	Young male	Fully swollen	?	No	Yes	Walking away from them, facing opposite direction	Both continued traveling
AUD	Young male	Going up	3	No	No	<5 meters away and facing them	He groomed her
AUD	3–4	Going up	?	No	?	<5 meters away and facing them	?
BAR	Subadult	Fully swollen	?	No	?	10 meters away and facing in their general direction	She groomed him (see Chapter 9 for details)
BAR	3–4	Fully swollen	5	No	?	Not in view	Both looking furtively around during copulation
BEA	3–4	Fully swollen	?	No	?	?	?
BEA	3–4	Going down	?	No	?	?	?
KAT	Subadult	Pregnant	2	No	No	Traveling up cliff away from them, facing opposite	Both traveled up cliff
KAY	Young male	Flat	?	No	?	Walking away from them, facing opposite direction	Both continued traveling
KAY	Young male	Flat	3	No	No	Walking away from them, facing opposite direction	Both continued traveling
OPH	Subadult	Flat	3	No	?	Walking away from them, facing opposite direction	Both continued traveling
PAT	3–4	Going down	?	No	?	?	?
Unknown	Young male	Going down	?	No	?	?	?
Unknown	3–4	Going down	?	No	?	?	She groomed him
Unknown	Subadult	Flat	6	No	No	Walking away from them, facing opposite direction	She ran away from him toward her leader male

* Young male=large juvenile male (see Table 5–1)

147

Pre- and Postcopulatory Behavior

Of the 48 copulations for which the initiator of the copulation could be determined, 4 were female-initiated and 44 were male-initiated. Females initiated copulations by approaching and/or presenting to the male. Males initiated copulations by either approaching and mounting a standing female or approaching and touching the hip of a sitting female, to which the female reacted by standing and presenting, followed by a mount.

Of the 54 copulations by known individuals for which the immediate consequences were observed, 30 (56%) were followed by no social interaction. Sixteen (30%) were followed by the male grooming the female and six (11%) were followed by the female grooming the male. Whether a copulation included ejaculation did not appear to affect the likelihood of social interaction afterward. Females did not, "as a rule, groom" the male after ejaculation, as has been reported by Caljan et al. (1987, p. 184).

Copulation-Related Vocalizations

Copulations were sometimes accompanied by female vocalizations. During 6% of copulations, females kecked or grunted during intromission. During 37% of all observed copulations (23 out of 76), females gave a medium-frequency, groan-like call that was never given outside of a sexual context; this percentage does not represent the percentage of females who give calls, as it includes variable numbers of copulations per female. Such calls never accompanied copulations that occurred when females were not swollen or copulations that involved non-leader males, but were given exclusively by swollen females during copulations with their leader males. The call usually occurred during the last few thrusts of a mount, or sometimes during the entire mount. Copulation calls did not occur with any greater or lesser frequency during mounts that included ejaculation, nor did they appear to be associated with any particular type of pre- or postcopulatory social interaction. Rather, 4 of the 13 females (30%) in Group 1 that I observed in estrus—Audrey, Clea, Verena and Virgo—gave these calls, whereas other females did not. Females that gave calls varied from 16% to 75% in the percentage of their observed copulations that were accompanied by calls.

EFFECTS OF REPRODUCTION ON BEHAVIOR

Effects of Sexual Swellings on Female Behavior

Estrus is a behavioral state defined by increased attractivity, receptivity, and proceptivity of females (Beach 1976), and is therefore, by definition, also characterized by increased sexual behavior. The vast majority of

Females often remain closer to their leader male for about a month after giving birth, presumably due to the protective benefits he offers. *(Photo by the author)*

sexual behavior observed in the Filoha population occurred when females were in behavioral estrus (cf. Beach 1976; see Chapters 2 and 3) and had sexual swellings. Compared to 76 copulations observed when females were swollen, I observed only 9 copulations, none of which included multiple mounts or ejaculation, when females were not swollen.

A comparison of other behavior of adult females when they were swollen with that when they were not swollen revealed several other effects of estrus on a female's behavior. First, most females were, on average, closer to their leader male when swollen than when not swollen (Wilcoxon Signed Ranks Test, p=.023, N=13; see Table 6–4). No fully swollen adult female was observed more than 10 meters from her leader male, whereas seven out of nine adult females spent at least some of their time greater than 10 meters from their leader male when they were not swollen.

Another way in which sexual swellings appeared to affect female behavior was in the amount of grooming a female received from her leader male compared to from other females (see Table 6–5). Most adult females were groomed more often by their leader male when swollen than when not swollen. This difference was statistically significant for the nine adult females for whom I have scan sample data during both conditions (Wilcoxon Signed Ranks Test, p=.038, N=9). Correspondingly, most adult females were groomed more often by other females when they were *not*

Table 6–4 Mean Distance of Females to Their Leader Male When Swollen Compared to When Not Swollen (flat)

| Female | N | | | Estimated Age Class | Number of Females in OMU | Mean Distance to Leader Male (in meters) | | | Percentage of Scan Samples >10 Meters from Leader male | | |
| | Not Swollen | Going Up | Fully Swollen[1] | | | Not Swollen | Swollen[1] | | Not Swollen | Swollen[1] | |
							Going Up	Fully Swollen		Going Up	Fully Swollen
VIR	25	15	23	Fully adult	1	1.6	1.0	2.0	3	0	0
CLE	40	23	35	Fully adult	2	1.6	0.9	1.2	0	0	0
SER[2]	65	38	16	Fully adult	2–3	2.3	2.4	1.4	5	3	0
VER2	104	9	48	Older adult	2	1.3	0.9	0.6	2	0	0
NAT2	15	9	19	Older adult	3	1.1	4.4	1.3	0	18	0
BEL	85	10	14	Fully adult	4	0.8	0.6	1.0	3	0	0
JUD	39	0	15	Fully adult	4	3.7	16.3	0.5	14	75	0
ANA	23	7	25	Fully adult	5	5.4	0.8	2.2	19	0	0
SYL2	63	16	13	Young adult	5	2.5	0.6	0.9	1	0	0
KAJ	20	4	55	Subadult (4–5 yrs)	5	1.7	0.7	1.2	0	0	1
KAY	12	9	26	Subadult (4–5 yrs)	4	3.9	4.8	4.2	11	10	7
PAT	64	13	27	Subadult (4–5 yrs)	4	2.5	4.2	2.0	1	16	3

[1] "Going down" phase of estrus not included due to the small number of scan samples from this phase for most females.
[2] SER, SER2, and SER3 combined for this analysis.

Table 6–5 Percentage of Time Spent Being Groomed By the Leader Male versus Other Females When Swollen Compared to When Not Swollen

| | N | | | | % of Time Being Groomed By: | | | |
| | | | | | Leader Male | | Another Female | |
Female	Not Swollen	Swollen	Number of Females in OMU	Estimated Age Class	Not Swollen	Swollen	Not Swollen	Swollen
VIR	25	39	1	Fully adult	16	13	0	0
CLE	40	63	2	Fully adult	3	13	3	2
SER[1]	65	57	2–3	Fully adult	6	2	2	5
VER2	104	69	2	Older adult	19	35	0	0
NAT2	15	28	3	Older adult	0	11	0	0
BEL	85	33	4	Fully adult	0	6	4	0
JUD	39	15	4	Fully adult	3	20	18	7
ANA	23	38	5	Fully adult	0	5	22	3
SYL2	63	31	5	Young adult (5–6 yrs)	2	3	11	3
KAJ	20	76	5	Subadult (4–5 yrs)	15	5	5	8
KAY	12	46	4	Subadult (4–5 yrs)	0	0	0	17
PAT	64	42	4	Subadult (4–5 yrs)	0	0	3	2

[1]SER, SER2, and SER3 combined for this analysis.

swollen compared to when they were swollen. This difference, however, was not significant (Wilcoxon Signed Ranks Test, p=.075, N=9). As discussed in Chapter 5, females in two-female units who were undergoing estrus cycles (i.e., not pregnant or lactating) spent more time grooming or being groomed by their leader male than did females who were pregnant or lactating (see Table 5–6). It therefore appears that females who are cycling spend more time in grooming interactions with their leader male than do females who are pregnant or lactating, and that females who are actually in the swelling phase of their cycle receive more grooming from their leader males than they do when they are not swollen. No differences were found, however, in the overall amount of grooming females gave or received nor in the total amount of time they spent grooming between when they were swollen and when they were not swollen. There was also no consistent relationship between a female's reproductive state and her frequency of interaction with non-leader males. Finally, adolescent females showed no consistent pattern at all in their frequencies of interaction when swollen versus not swollen (see Tables 6–4 and 6–5).

According to Kummer (1968a, p. 43), estrous females, both in captivity and in the wild, "groom less and are less often groomed than" anestrous females (differences are statistically significant). At Filoha, I found that this pattern characterized grooming relationships among females but not between females and their leader males. In contrast to Kummer's results, data from Filoha suggest that most females stay closer to their leader males and engage more often in grooming interactions with their leader males when they have sexual swellings than they do when they are not swollen. That a leader males grooms his females more when they are swollen suggests additional motivation on his part to interact with a female during the swelling phase of her cycle compared to at other times. Ad libitum observations suggested that females were herded more frequently by their leader males when they were swollen and that it was therefore a change in male behavior, rather than a change in a female's own motivational state, that caused a female to stay closer to her leader male when she was swollen. That swollen females are herded more frequently than nonswollen females is also suggested by the finding of Zinner et al. (1994) that swollen females suffered nearly five times more injuries, all inflicted by their leader male, than did nonswollen females.

Effects of Parturition on Female Behavior

As shown in Table 6–6, females in Group 1 spent more time sitting close to other females after giving birth than they did when they were pregnant. All individual females for whom I had data during both conditions spent either an equal or higher percentage of time sitting close to other females when they had an infant compared to when they were pregnant, and this

Table 6–6 Percentage of Available Social Time Spent by Females Sitting Close to Other Females When Pregnant Compared to After the Birth of Their Infant

| | N | | | % Time Spent Sitting Close to Another Female | |
| | When Pregnant | After Birth of Infant | Number of Females in OMU | When pregnant | After birth of infant |
Female					
JUL	38	28	1	0	0
AUD2	163	52	2	0	3
MAR	93	30	2	6	14
VEN	21	97	2	0	4
KAT	13	37	3	0	0
IRI	20	22	4	11	38
ROS	7	35	4	0	12
ANJ2	15	107	5	0	39
CHI2	19	64	5	20	36
ISA	41	42	5	23	40

difference was statistically significant across all females (Wilcoxon Signed Ranks Test, p=.01, N=10).

The difference between the amount of time females spent sitting close to other females when pregnant compared to after giving birth can be explained by a general interest in infants on the part of all age-sex classes of individuals, including other females. Like other primates, female hamadryas often approach new mothers to peer at, touch, or smell newborn infants. Interest in infants did not vary by age or parity, as both adult multiparous females and adolescent nulliparous females interacted with newborn infants of other females in their unit. As will be discussed further in the next chapter, these interactions even motivated females to interact across OMU boundaries. Infant inspection was the primary context in which females left the spatial and social boundaries of their OMUs, risking aggression from their leader male, to interact with a female in another unit. This type of inter-unit behavior appeared to be more tolerated by leader males than other types of inter-unit interactions, as I never observed a leader male threaten or neckbite a female when the sole apparent reason she left her OMU was to inspect another female's infant. Kummer (1968a) also reported that "between females of different units short hesitant relationships arise motivated by an interest in small infants." (p. 50)

Another effect of parturition on female behavior was an observed tendency for females to remain closer to their leader male during the first month after the birth of an infant. As shown in Table 6–7, 7 of 10 females for whom I have data from the first and subsequent months after birth

Table 6–7 Average Proximity between Females and Their Leader Males Before and After the Birth of an Infant

	N		Average Distance to Leader Male			
Female	When Pregnant	After Birth of Infant	When Pregnant	During First Month After Birth	During Subsequent Months	After Birth of Infant TOTAL
JUL	38	28	1.9	1.1	1.3	1.2
AUD2	163	52	2.9	1.4	3.4	2.4
MAR	93	30	2.0	3.7	2.9	3.2
VEN	21	97	1.4	2.4	2.7	2.6
KAT	13	37	1.2	1.6	2.7	2.2
IRI	20	22	1.7	1.0	*	1.0
ROS	7	35	1.6	.0.9	1.1	1.0
RAQ	8	144	7.9	4.3	4.0	4.1
ANJ2	15	107	0.8	1.5	3.1	2.6
CHI2	19	64	4.0	1.5	2.3	1.9
ISA	41	42	5.2	2.8	2.7	2.8

* No data for more than one month afterward.

were closer, on average, to their leader male during the first month after birth compared to subsequent months. Of the 11 females for whom I have data from when they were pregnant and from the one-month period after they gave birth, 7 were, on average, closer to their leader male during the month after giving birth compared to when they were pregnant. These differences, however, were not statistically significant.

Overall, estrus and parturition appear to affect a hamadryas female's behavior in several ways. Most broadly, females spend more time with their leader males while estrous, more time with other females while anestrous, and more time near their leader males within the first month after giving birth to an infant. These differences make sense in light of the optimal reproductive strategies of both leader males and individual females: a leader male benefits from guarding his females from other males while she is most fertile, and a female benefits from remaining close to a protective leader male when her infant is most vulnerable.

7

Friendship among Females[1]

In most papionin monkeys, including geladas (*Theropithecus gelada*) and most populations of baboons (*Papio hamadryas* subspp.), affiliative and agonistic relationships among related, philopatric females form the basic organization of social groups (Altmann 1980; Melnick & Pearl 1987; Dunbar 1983). Relationships between females and males in these taxa are usually weaker and limited to particular individuals or to certain periods during the reproductive cycle (e.g., Seyfarth 1978; Smuts 1985; Palombit et al. 1997). Hamadryas baboons are an exception to this general pattern in that relationships between males and females are stronger and more enduring than those among females (Kummer 1968a; Abegglen 1984).

As noted in Chapter 5, previous research on hamadryas baboons, both in the wild and in captivity, has indicated that hamadryas one-male units are characterized by a star-shaped sociogram, wherein each female has a much stronger bond with her leader male than with any other adult member of her OMU. These bonds are expressed in the tendency of hamadryas females to groom and interact predominantly with their leader male, and, as reported by previous field studies, rarely with other females (Kummer 1968; Sigg 1980; Abegglen 1984). Kummer (1968a) noted that "this star-shaped pattern, the center of which is the male, keeps the unit together. In

[1]A portion of the text of this chapter and several figures therein were previously published in "Affiliation among Females in Wild Hamadryas Baboons (*Papio hamadryas hamadryas*)," *International Journal of Primatology 23*, no. 5 (2002): 1205–1226, and are reprinted with permission from Kluwer Academic/Plenum Publishers.

most of the units, other possible interactions, as those between the leader and juveniles, or between females and females, are not more frequent than contacts with strangers" (Kummer 1968a, pp. 80–81). In this model, there are only two major social strata of adult group members—a dominant individual (the leader male) and several relatively undifferentiated subordinates (the females)—and most interactions occur between the dominant individual and each subordinate rather than among the subordinates themselves. In captivity, when a group of hamadryas females is left alone to interact in the absence of a male, this same social organization resurfaces in a different form: one female assumes the dominant role of the leader male, all other females remain relatively undifferentiated, and most social interactions occur between the dominant female and each of the other females rather than among the other females (Stammbach 1978; Coelho et al. 1983; Pfeiffer et al. 1985). Because the star-shaped social organization persists even when males are removed, these authors have concluded that it is not simply imposed on the females by hamadryas males, but that hamadryas females must have an innate tendency to form social units that are oriented around a single central individual (Stammbach 1978; Coelho et al. 1983).

Byrne et al. (1989) proposed the term *cross-sex bonding* to describe such a social organization in which bonds between the sexes are stronger than those within each sex. Byrne et al. distinguished cross-bonding (as in hamadryas) from the "female bonding" (cf. Wrangham 1980) reported for most baboon populations, predominantly anubis (*P. h. anubis*) and yellow (*P. h. cynocephalus*) baboons (Seyfarth 1976; Altmann 1980; Dunbar 1983; Melnick & Pearl 1987; Saunders 1988; Barton et al. 1996; Silk et al. 1999). In particular, Byrne et al. suggested that mountain chacma baboons (*P. h. ursinus*) might be more accurately characterized as cross-bonded rather than female-bonded, and that this distinction would obviously apply to hamadryas baboons as well.

Whether a baboon population will be cross-bonded or female-bonded has often been attributed to patterns of food distribution and predator pressure, both of which have been argued to be primary determinants of the structure and patterning of social relationships among primate females (Wrangham 1980; van Schaik 1989; Isbell 1991; Barton et al. 1996; Sterck et al. 1997). When food is clumped and defensible, which promotes intragroup contest competition, females will remain in their natal groups and will form differentiated, kinship-based affiliative and agonistic relationships, that is, they will be female-bonded. When food is more evenly distributed and does not promote contest competition, females should not benefit from forming kin-based alliances; thus, they would not benefit as much from philopatry or female bonding and should therefore disperse from their natal groups and develop weak, if any, bonds with other females.

Traditionally, savanna baboons, including anubis, yellow, and some populations of chacmas, have been placed in the former category, whereas hamadryas have been placed in the latter (Wrangham 1980; Barton et al.

1996; Sterck et al. 1997). Among chacma baboons (*P. h. ursinus*), the degree of female-bonding relative to cross-bonding may vary depending on a number of factors, including food distribution, predator pressure, altitude, and group size (Byrne et al. 1989; Anderson 1990; Hamilton & Bulger 1992; Henzi et al. 1997; Henzi et al. 2000), and this may be the case for Guinea baboons (*P. h. papio*) as well (Dunbar & Nathan 1972; Boese 1975; Byrne 1981; Anderson & McGrew 1984). Within the context of this model, the weak affiliative and agonistic relationships among females that have been reported for wild hamadryas (Kummer 1968a; Sigg 1980; Abegglen 1984) can be easily explained by the scarcity and wide dispersion of food resources that typify hamadryas habitats (Wrangham 1980; Barton et al. 1996; Barton 2000).

Although relationships among hamadryas females in the wild have been reported to be relatively undeveloped and undifferentiated, no research on wild hamadryas prior to this study had focused specifically on social interactions among females. Captive hamadryas females, which have been studied extensively, exhibit both dominance and grooming relationships, especially in the absence of males (Stammbach 1978; Sigg 1980; Stammbach & Kummer 1982; Coelho et al. 1983; Chalyan et al. 1991; Gore 1991; Vervaecke et al. 1992; Colmenares et al. 1994; Gore 1994; Zaragoza et al. 1996; Leinfelder et al. 2001). Given that other aspects of hamadryas behavior, such as the one-male unit social structure and male herding behavior, are little modified by captivity (Kummer & Kurt 1965), the same is likely true of female behavior. If so, then the lack of evidence for differentiated relationships among females in wild hamadryas prior to this study may have been due to a lack of relevant data rather than to a lack of such relationships.

METHODS SPECIFIC TO THIS CHAPTER

One-male unit scan sample data (see Chapter 3) were used for the analyses reported in this chapter. As discussed in Chapter 6, sexually swollen females maintain closer proximity to, receive more grooming from, and are herded more by their leader males than nonswollen females. Swollen females are therefore more constrained by the behavior of their leader male and less likely to act on their own motivations than are nonswollen females. Because females spend most of their time pregnant or lactating (i.e., not swollen), and in order to control for the effects of sexual swellings on female behavior, for this analysis I used only data from scans during which females were not swollen, or anestrous. I compared the percentage of "available social time" scan samples (see Chapter 3) that each female spent sitting close to, grooming, or being groomed by her leader male with the percentage of such samples that she spent sitting close to, grooming, or being groomed by other females. All behavioral categories were mutually exclusive. I did not include scans during which a female was sitting close to both her leader male and another female, because in these cases it was not clear who was the female's primary social partner. I also did not include scans during which a female was interacting with an individual other than her leader male or another female (e.g., a follower male or a member of another OMU) because my primary purpose in this chapter is to compare patterns of behavior involving the leader male with those involving other females. I used nearest neighbor data to calculate patterns of proximity between focal females and other adult or subadult members of their OMU.

PATTERNS OF AFFILIATION AMONG FEMALES

Table 7–1 shows the percentage of available social time that anestrous females spent in various social activities and with the leader male or another female as their nearest neighbor. On average, anestrous females spent 9% of their social time sitting close to their leader male, 14% sitting close to other females, 11% grooming their leader male, 5% grooming other females, 4% being groomed by their leader male, and 5% being groomed by other females. A female's nearest neighbor was her leader male an average of 35% of the time and another female an average of 46% of the time.

Figure 7–1 is a graphical representation of the percentages listed in Table 7–1. While there was substantial variation among females in the percentage of time they spent with their leader male compared to other females, an average across females shows that they spent at least as much overall time sitting close to other females as they did sitting close to their leader male. While females spent more time, on average, grooming their

Females spend, on average, about as much time grooming other females in their unit as they spend grooming their leader male. *(Photo by the author)*

Table 7–1 Percentage of Available Social Time Spent by Anestrous Females with Leader Males Compared to Other Females

Name and Number of Scan Samples per Female		Sitting Close to		Grooming or Being Groomed by		Sitting Close to, Grooming, or Being Groomed TOTAL	
	Name	Number of Scan Samples	Leader Male	Another Female	Leader Male	Another Female	With Leader Male	With Another Female
Females in one-female units	URS	83	14	0	32	0	46	0
	JUL	66	14	0	36	0	50	0
	FAN	34	27	0	27	0	54	0
	VIR	30	40	0	36	0	76	0
	JUA	31	27	0	40	0	67	0
Females in two-female units	ANT	72	11	9	7	6	18	15
	LIN	72	8	8	22	4	30	12
	VER	124	16	0	40	0	56	0
	AUD	218	9	1	7	0	16	1
	VEN1	118	15	3	4	4	19	7
	SER	78	17	5	24	5	41	10
	CLE	46	3	8	16	3	19	11
	MAR	123	14	8	16	2	30	10
Females in three-female units	KAT	50	5	0	5	5	10	5
	OPH	50	13	4	10	0	23	4
	VEN2	39	6	9	0	23	6	32
Females in four-female units	BEL	108	9	13	13	11	22	24
	RAQ	152	4	25	3	14	7	39
	NET	86	2	21	5	26	7	47
	FAN2	81	5	13	13	25	18	38
	WHO	161	4	17	10	11	14	28
	IRI	42	0	25	15	11	15	36
	CLA	54	9	13	15	8	24	21
	ZEN	42	15	18	11	11	26	29
	VIO	42	15	11	7	4	22	15
	ROS	42	8	10	21	0	29	10
	JUD	63	3	33	13	36	16	69
	PAT	78	2	22	6	9	8	31
	SEL	56	6	0	16	12	22	12
	MIR	54	6	15	12	27	18	42
	TYN	55	0	19	0	23	0	42

(Continued)

Table 7–1 Continued

Name and Number of Scan Samples per Female		Number of Scan	Sitting Close to		Grooming or Being Groomed by		Sitting Close to, Grooming, or Being Groomed TOTAL	
	Name	Samples	Leader Male	Another Female	Leader Male	Another Female	With Leader Male	With Another Female
	ANJ	122	2	34	12	14	14	48
	ELE	121	8	33	13	18	21	51
	CHI	83	11	33	24	0	35	33
Females in	ROM	83	5	27	14	15	19	42
five-female	GIN	77	4	35	5	16	9	51
units	TON	117	1	18	0	19	1	37
	SYL	88	3	27	16	25	19	52
	ISA	83	3	32	3	19	6	51
Mean values:		80.1	9.3	14.1	14.6	10.4	23.9	24.5

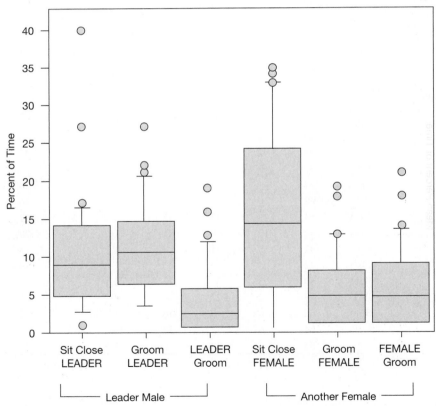

Figure 7–1 Percentage of Available Social Time Spent by Anestrous Females Sitting Close to, Grooming, or Being Groomed by the Leader Male versus Another Female

leader males than they spent grooming other females, they spent at least as much time, on average, being groomed by other females as they did being groomed by their leader male.

For purposes of comparison with Kummer's (1968a) findings, Figure 5–2 in Chapter 5 shows the distribution of grooming activity among the members of two OMUs: Leonardo's unit (LEO), which had five females, and Alexander's unit (ALE), which had four females. Each of these units remained stable in membership and relatively consistent in patterns of social interaction for the entire length of the second observation season.

Effect of the Number of Females in a One-Male Unit

An anestrous female's frequency of interaction with other females was primarily affected by the number of females in her unit. For Figure 7–2, I collapsed the measures "sit close," "groom," and "groomed by" into a single measure of "time spent with" the leader male versus with another female, and then broke the results down by size of unit. The resulting bar chart shows that as the size of the unit increases, the percentage of time

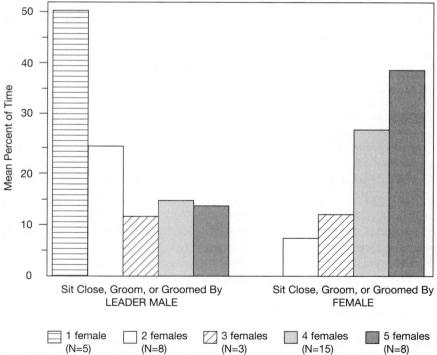

Figure 7–2 Mean Percentage of Time Spent by Anestrous Females Sitting Close to, Grooming, or Being Groomed by the Leader Male versus Another Female, by Size of Unit

spent with the leader male decreases and the percentage of time spent with other females increases. Females in one-female units (N=5) did not interact socially with any other adult females. Females in two-female units (N=8) spent an average of 8% of their available social time with the other female in their OMU and an average of 29% of their available social time with their leader male. On average, their leader male was their nearest neighbor 44% of the time and the other female in their OMU was their nearest neighbor 29% of the time. Females in three-female units (N=3) spent an average of 13% of their time with their leader male and an average of 14% of their time with another female. Their leader male was their nearest neighbor an average of 21% of the time and another female was their nearest neighbor an average of 25% of their time. Females in four-female units (N=15) spent an average of 17% of their time with their leader male compared to an average of 32% of their time with another female. For these females, their leader male was their nearest neighbor an average of 24% of the time and another female was their nearest neighbor an average of 62% of the time. Finally, females in five-female units (N=8) spent an average of 16% of their time with their leader male and an average of 46% of their time with another female. Their leader male was their nearest neighbor an average of 20% of the time, whereas another female was their nearest neighbor an average of 71% of the time.

Figure 7–3 shows the relationship between the number of females in an OMU and the percentage of time that an anestrous female spent (a) sitting close to another female, (b) grooming or being groomed by another female, (c) with another female as her nearest neighbor, (d) sitting close to her leader male, (e) grooming or being groomed by her leader male, and (f) with her leader male as her nearest neighbor. Overall, the number of females in an OMU was positively correlated with time spent sitting close to other females (Spearman Rank Correlation r_s=.882, p<.0001, n=39) and negatively correlated with time spent sitting close to leader males (r_s=−.575, p<.001, n=39). The number of females in an OMU was also positively correlated with time spent grooming or being groomed by other females (r_s=.684, p<.0001, n=39) and negatively correlated (albeit relatively weakly) with time spent grooming or being groomed by leader males (r_s=−.374, p=.021, n=39). Finally, the number of females in a unit was positively correlated with the likelihood of a female's nearest neighbor being another female (r_s=.847, p<.0001, n=39) and negatively correlated with the likelihood of a female's nearest neighbor being her leader male (r_s=−.590; p<.001, n=39).

Social Availability of Unit Members

To assess whether the likelihood of either the leader male or another female being a female's social partner was a function of simple social availability, I compared the percentage of scan samples that each female spent sitting

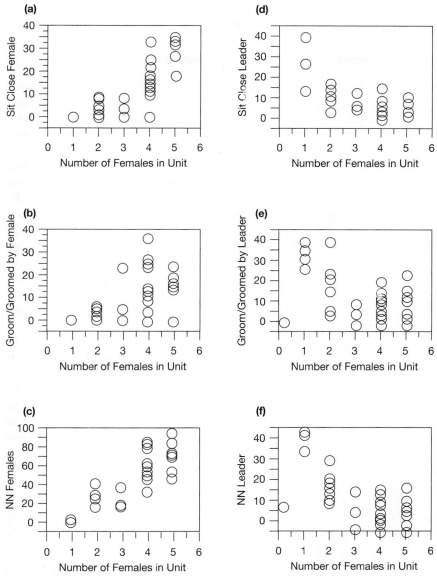

Figure 7–3 Relationship between the Number of Females in an OMU and the Percentage of Available Social Time That Anestrous Females Spent Sitting Close to, Grooming, or Being Groomed by Another Female versus the Leader Male or with Another Female versus the Leader Male as Their Nearest Neighbor

close to, grooming, or being groomed by the leader male or another female with the percentages that would be expected based on the number of other OMU members available to each female (Table 7–2). The leader male of the

Table 7–2 Observed versus Expected Percentages of Social Time (Calculated from Scan Samples) Spent Sitting Close to, Grooming, or Being Groomed by Leader Males and Other Females

Name	Number of Females in OMU	Number of Follower Males in OMU	Total # of Potential Adult or Subadult Social Partners in OMU	% of Available Social Time Spent Sitting Alone	Expected and Observed Percentages of Social Time Spent Sitting Close, Grooming, or Being Groomed by Leader Male				Expected and Observed Percentages of Social Time Spent Sitting Close, Grooming, or Being Groomed by Another Female			
					EXP[1]	OBS[2]	O>E	O<E	EXP[1]	OBS[2]	O>E	O<E
URS2	1	0	1	53	100	98			0	0		
JUL	1	0	1	30	100	71			0	0		
FAN	1	0	1	21	100	68			0	0		
VIR	1	0	1	16	100	90			0	0		
JUA	1	0	1	23	100	87			0	0		
CLE	2	0	2	53	50	40		✓	50	23		✓
ANT	2	0	2	51	50	37		✓	50	31		✓
VER2	2	0	2	42	50	97	✓		50	0		✓
VEN	2	1	3	48	33	37	✓		33	13		✓
SER	2	1	3	46	33	76	✓		33	19		✓
AUD2	2	0	2	58	50	38		✓	50	2		✓
LIN	2	0	2	39	50	49		✓	50	20		✓
MAR	2	0	2	48	50	58	✓		50	19		✓
KAT	3	1	4	49	25	20		✓	50	10		✓
OPH	3	1	4	54	25	50	✓		50	9		✓
VEN2	3	1	4	20	25	8		✓	50	40		✓
BEL	4	0	4	46	25	41	✓		75	44		✓

ID												
RAQ	4	0	4	45	25	13		✓	75	71		✓
NET	4	0	4	43	25	12		✓	75	82	✓	
FAN2	4	0	4	35	25	28	✓		75	58		✓
WHO3	4	0	4	42	25	24		✓	75	48		✓
IRI	4	0	4	33	25	22		✓	75	54		✓
CLA	4	2	6	46	17	44	✓		50	39		✓
ZEN	4	0	4	40	25	43	✓		75	48		✓
VIO	4	0	4	48	25	42	✓		75	29		✓
ROS	4	0	4	38	25	47	✓		75	16		✓
JUD	4	0	4	21	25	20		✓	75	87	✓	
PAT	4	0	4	44	25	14		✓	75	55		✓
SEL	4	2	6	43	17	39	✓		50	21		✓
MIR	4	2	6	21	17	23	✓		50	53	✓	
TYN	4	2	6	37	17	0		✓	50	67	✓	
ANJ2	5	0	5	29	20	20	✓		80	68		✓
ELE	5	0	5	26	20	28	✓		80	69		✓
CHI2	5	0	5	32	20	51	✓		80	49		✓
ROM2	5	0	5	38	20	31	✓		80	68		✓
GIN	5	0	5	36	20	14		✓	80	80		
TON	5	0	5	45	20	2		✓	80	67		✓
SYL2	5	0	5	30	20	27	✓		80	74		✓
ISA	5	0	5	33	20	9		✓	80	76		✓

[1] Calculated as a percentage, based on number of potential social partners in OMU.

[2] Calculated in the following way: (% time spent sitting close to, grooming, or being groomed by leader male or another female) / (100 – % available social time spent sitting alone) × 100.

OMU, adult and subadult females, and adult or subadult non-leader males that were consistent followers of the OMU were all included as OMU members. Other individuals that females interacted with occasionally, such as more transient follower males, juveniles, and members of other OMUs, were excluded from this analysis and did not contribute to the expected values. I also excluded from this analysis females that were in OMUs consisting solely of a leader male and one female (N=5), because these OMUs lacked the corresponding observed versus expected values for time spent with females (i.e., both were equal to zero). For all OMUs that consisted of at least two females (N=34), expected percentages were calculated based on the number of adult or subadult individuals in the OMU. For example, females in two-female units, when not sitting alone, should spend 50% of their social time with their leader male and 50% of their social time with the other female in their unit; females in three-female units should spend 33% of their social time with their leader male and 66% of their social time with other females (33% with each female); and females in OMUs with two females and one follower male should spent 25% of their social time with their leader male, 50% of their social time with other females (25% with each one), and 25% of their social time with the follower male. I compared these expected percentages to the observed percentages of scan samples during which females were sitting close to, grooming, or being groomed by either the leader male or another female (calculated as a percentage of total scans that females spent interacting socially, i.e., not sitting alone). Table 7–2 shows these comparisons.

A comparison of observed with expected percentages revealed that about half (17) of the females spent more time sitting close to, grooming, or being groomed by their leader male than expected, while the other half (16) spent less time sitting close to, grooming, or being groomed by their leader male than expected. One female, ANJ, spent about as much time as expected with her leader male. The vast majority of females (29), on the other hand, spent *less* time than expected sitting close to, grooming, or being groomed by other females, whereas only four females spent more time than expected with other females and one female spent about as much time as expected with other females. These results suggest that the likelihood of either the leader male or another female being a female's social partner was not a function of simple social availability.

Social Availability of the Leader Male

To investigate the possibility that females spend time sitting close to and grooming other females only when they do not have access to their leader male, I examined the availability of the leader male for social interaction during each scan sample in which a female was sitting within 10 cm of another female, grooming another female, or being groomed by another

Hamadryas females often appear to prefer to groom with one another rather than with their leader male. A leader male sitting nearby while his females are grooming, as shown here, is a common sight. *(Photo by the author)*

female (Table 7–3). I considered the leader male to be available for social interaction if he was sitting alone, at least 10 cm from any other individual, and not interacting socially with any other individual. Because females in one-female units were never observed to interact socially with other females and neither female in one of the two-female units (VER and

Table 7–3 Social Availability of Leader Male during Scans in Which Anestrous Females Were Sitting Close to, Grooming, or Being Groomed by Other Anestrous Females*

| | *Percentage of Time Leader Male Was:* | | | |
| | *Not Socially Engaged & Thus Available for Social Interaction* | *Socially Engaged With Others:* | | |
		Sitting Close to Another Individual	*Grooming or Being Groomed by Another Individual*	*Total*
Female sitting close to another female	41%	34%	26%	59%
Female grooming another female	52%	18%	31%	48%
Female social contact Total	48%	25%	27%	52%

* Percentages are averages across 11 one-male units and 32 females.

AUD) interacted socially with the other, only 11 OMUs—and 32 females—contributed to this analysis.

Of all samples in which a female was sitting within 10 cm of at least one other female, that female's leader male was available for social interaction an average of 41% of the time. Of all samples in which a female was grooming or being groomed by another female, that female's leader male was available for social interaction an average of 52% of the time, and in only 31% of these samples was that female's leader male actually grooming or being groomed by another individual.

If females simply interacted with other females in their unit when their leader male was socially engaged with another individual, then the interactions among females observed in this study could be interpreted as a second choice to their leader male. Females might prefer to socialize with their leader male but settle for socializing with other females instead if their leader male is not available. The above results show, however, that in half of the samples during which a female was grooming with another female, her leader male was sitting alone and not interacting with anyone at all (Table 7–3). If a female's leader male is sitting alone and yet she chooses to groom another female instead, then she might, in these cases, prefer to interact with the other female over her leader male.

A leader male need not even be alone to be considered "available" for social interaction. On at least 25 occasions, I observed two or more females grooming their leader male simultaneously. Even more frequent were instances in which one female was sitting close to her leader male while another female was grooming him, and two or more females sitting close to their leader male at the same time was commonplace. Given that females need not wait for their leader male to be alone to interact with him, the fact that females spent so much time with other females is all the more indicative of a high level of motivation to establish and maintain social contacts with other females.

Variation among Females

As shown in Table 7–1, females varied widely in the amount of time they spent with other females. Some females spent little or none of their time in grooming interactions with other females, but instead spent time exclusively with their leader male or, occasionally, their own offspring or a follower male. Other females, however, spent over 20%, even 30%, of their available social time in grooming interactions with other females. Figure 7–4 shows a frequency distribution of the percentage of available social time spent by females sitting close to, grooming, or being groomed by other females. Only females in units of two or more females are shown, as females in units of only one female never interacted with other females.

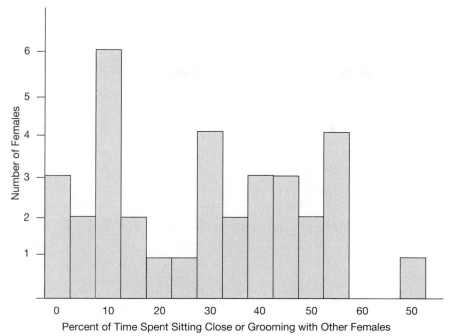

Figure 7–4 Frequency Distribution of Percentage of Time Spent by Anestrous Females Sitting Close to, Grooming, or Being Groomed by Other Females

Although females in larger units spent more time with other females than females in smaller units, females within OMU size categories were also not uniform in the amount of time they spent with other females. Figure 7–5 shows a frequency distribution of the percentage of time females spent with other females, broken down by size of unit.

As shown in Figure 7–5a, the 8 females in two-female units ranged from 0 to 15% in their amount of available social time spent sitting close to, grooming, or being groomed by another female. The 3 females in three-female units ranged from 4% to 32% (Fig. 7–5b), the 15 females in four-female units ranged from 10% to 69% (Fig. 7–5c), and the 8 females in five-female units ranged from 33% to 51% (Fig. 7–5d) in the amount of time females spent with other females. Of the females in units containing 2 or more females, 5 females (VER, AUD, OPH, ROS, and CHI) were never observed grooming or being groomed by another female, whereas 5 females (NET, FAN, JUD, MIR, and SYL) spent 25% or more of their available social time engaged in such interactions.

Of the seven females that spent over 20% of their available social time in grooming interactions with other females, three (NET, FAN2, and JUD) were members of one OMU in particular, Alexander's unit (shown sociographically in Figure 5–2, page 99). This unit consisted of four females,

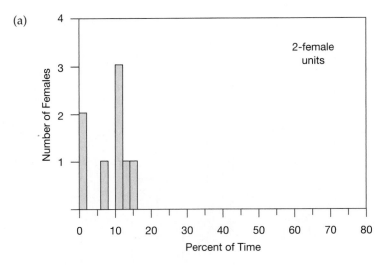

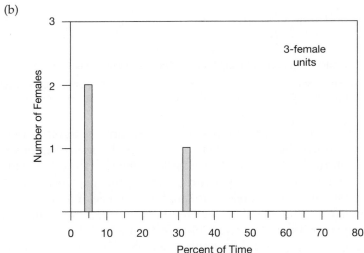

Figure 7–5 Frequency Distribution of Percentage of Time Spent by Anestrous Females Sitting Close to, Grooming, or Being Groomed by Other Females, by Size of Unit

each of whom spent at least 25% of her time in grooming interactions with other females. Of the six possible female-female dyads in this unit, all spent time in close proximity to one another and in grooming interactions with one another.

Of the remaining four females that spent over 20% of their time with other females, another two (MIR and TYN) were members of the same OMU, and many of their grooming interactions were with one another.

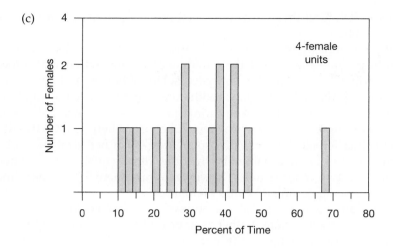

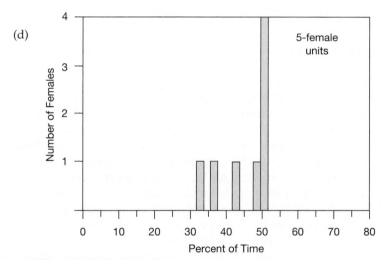

Figure 7–5 Continued

The remaining two females who spent over 20% of their time with other females were in two separate units, a three-female unit (VEN2) and a five-female unit (SYL).

By contrast, two of the five females that were *never* observed grooming or being groomed by other females (VER and AUD) were also in the same OMU, a two-female unit. These two females rarely sat near one another, and in each case their nearest neighbor was typically their leader male rather than one another. Also, one female (CHI) was never observed grooming or being groomed by another female despite the fact that there were four other females in her unit, three of whom (ROM, GIN, and ISA) spent at least 15% of their available social time in grooming interactions with one another.

Finally, the units of two females (FAN and VEN) changed in size during the study period, and so did their frequency of interaction with other females. When in an OMU that consisted solely of herself and her leader male, Fanny (FAN) did not interact with other females. When in an OMU with three other females, however, Fanny spent 24% of her available social time in grooming interactions with them. Likewise, when in an OMU with only one other female, Venus (VEN) spent only 4% of her available social time grooming or being groomed by the other female in her OMU. When in a unit with two other females, however, Venus spent 23% of her time grooming or being groomed by other females.

Variation among females did not appear to be related to female age, parity, or reproductive state. Rather, it appeared that certain females and dyads simply had a greater intrinsic motivation to develop and maintain female-female social relationships than did others, and that being in a larger OMU provided these females the opportunity to express these motivations.

Interactions across Units

This motivation to interact with other females occasionally extended across OMU boundaries. The threat of aggression from a female's leader male was real and constantly reinforced, and played a powerful role in conditioning females to stay within their OMU. Often, however, females left their OMU's spatial boundaries briefly to inspect another female's infant or to lip-smack to the female and/or the infant from a distance. On thirteen occasions during focal samples and ad libitum observations, I observed females leaving the spatial boundaries of their units to interact with a female in another OMU. Seven of these interactions were directed toward females with young infants. Individuals of all age-sex classes directed much attention toward infants, and adult females were no exception.

I also observed interunit affiliative interactions that did not involve infants. Three of these interactions consisted of a female from one unit approaching and sitting within 10 cm of a female from another OMU for at least 20 seconds, and another three of these interactions involved grooming between females from different units. Two of the latter cases involved the same pair of females, Katy (KAY) and Katrina (KAT) (shown in Figure 5–2, page 99), that were attempting to interact socially though opposed by at least one of their leader males. The first time I observed these two females grooming, the leader male of one of the females chased her and attempted to bite her neck, but she escaped into a tree. The second time I observed them grooming, however, neither leader male tried to prevent it, although both watched the over 20-minute long grooming session almost continuously as it took place. The third case of inter-OMU grooming involved two other females, one of whose leader male was over 30 meters away at the time, and the grooming bout lasted 15 minutes.

INTERPRETATIONS OF THESE FINDINGS

Although hamadryas bands are large, cohesive social groups analogous to those of other *Papio* baboons, the herding behavior of hamadryas males divides groups into smaller units and inhibits social contact between adult members of different units. Typically, females receive threats and neck bites from their leader males if they attempt to interact with individuals outside the unit, and leader males usually avoid interacting with outsiders as well. Thus, each adult individual's social options are essentially limited to other individuals within the OMU and the number of social options available to a female is therefore determined by the size of her unit. The results reported in this chapter show that the number of females in an OMU is positively correlated with each female's frequency of interaction with other females. It may be, therefore, that the more social options that are available to a female, the more social relationships she will develop and maintain.

Comparisons with Other Studies

These results contrast with previously published models of hamadryas social organization that have described a star-shaped sociogram, in which most interactions occur between the leader male and each female and very few interactions occur among the females themselves (Kummer 1968; Colmenares et al. 1994; see Figure 5–2). While no previous studies of wild hamadryas have focused specifically on female social behavior, the available data from other field studies suggest that females from other hamadryas populations do not spend as much social time with one another as do females at Filoha.

Kummer (1968a) found that hamadryas females near Erer Gota interacted socially with their leader males almost three times as much as with other females (on average, 19% versus 7% of total observation minutes). My results, on the other hand, indicate that females spent, on average, about the same amount of time interacting socially with their leader male as they did with other females (Figure 7–1). In his study of a hamadryas group near Awash Station, Nagel (1971) found that females spent about half as much time grooming other females as would be expected by chance, whereas they spent almost twice as much time grooming their leader males as would be expected by chance. Although females in the Filoha population also spent less time interacting with other females than would be expected by chance, on average they spent a greater percentage of their expected time interacting with one another than did Nagel's females, and only about half spent more time than expected interacting with their leader males, whereas half spent *less* time than expected interacting with their leader males (Table 7–2).

The results reported here do agree with those of Sigg (1980), whose study focused exclusively on several two-female OMUs, also near Erer Gota. Sigg found that most females spent over twice as much time in grooming interactions with their leader male as they did with the other female in their unit, though one female spent far more time grooming with the other female than she did with her leader male. Sigg's data also suggest that each female was, on average, closer in proximity to her leader male than to the other female in her OMU. Of the eight females in this study that were in two-female units and are thus comparable to Sigg's study animals, six spent over twice as much time in grooming interactions with their leader male as with other females and more time overall with their leader male, rather than another female, as their nearest neighbor (Table 7–1).

Kummer's findings from Erer Gota (Kummer 1968a) and Nagel's from Awash Station (Nagel 1971) differ from the results of this study with regard to female interactions with other females compared to leader males. The average number of females in each OMU in Kummer's and Nagel's study groups, however, was 2.3 and 2.2, respectively, as opposed to an average of 2.5 for Group 1 at Filoha (see Chapter 5). If females in larger units spend more time in female-female interactions than do females in smaller units, as the above results suggest, then social interactions among females would be less frequent in a population with smaller OMUs (e.g., Erer Gota and Awash Station) than in a population with larger units (e.g., Filoha). Differences in demographic structure may thus partially account for the differences between the results of this study and previous studies of wild hamadryas baboons with regard to social interactions among females.

Alternatively, there may be differences in food availability and distribution at each site, leading to differences in female competitive regimes, that may account for differences in affiliative interactions among females between sites. Consistent with previous studies of wild hamadryas, however, the Filoha females do not appear to compete directly over food (see Chapters 4 and 9). It thus seems unlikely that differences in affiliation among females are driven by differences in competitive regimes between Filoha, Erer Gota (Kummer 1968), and Awash Station (Nagel 1971).

The most likely factor contributing to the differences between these studies may be the fact that the research reported here was the first to focus specifically on female-female social interactions in wild hamadryas baboons. Female behavior in hamadryas society is far less obvious than that of males, and interactions among females may be easily overlooked if they are not the explicit focus of observations.

The Relative Importance of Bonds with Females versus Leader Males

Although females in the Filoha population interact with other females as well as with their leader males, they still do not interact with other females as much as would be predicted based on simple social availability. This only serves to emphasize that, while females may develop and maintain social relationships with one another, the bonds between hamadryas females and their leader males are, with little doubt, the most important relationships underlying hamadryas social organization. In Figure 7–3, the positive correlations between the number of females in an OMU and their frequency of interaction with other females were much stronger than the respective negative correlations between the number of females in an OMU and their frequency of interaction with their leader males. This suggests that, as unit size increases, females increase their frequency of interaction with other females but do not necessarily decrease their frequency of interaction with their leader male to the same degree. Also, Table 7–2 shows that females spent, on average, about as much time with their leader male but less time with other females than would be expected by chance. Thus, although females in the Filoha population spend more time with other females than would be expected based on the star-shaped model of hamadryas social organization, they still spend *less* time with other females than would be expected based on pure social availability.

The importance of relationships between females and their leader males compared to relationships among females is underscored by results of other studies as well. In a study of reconciliation in captive hamadryas and hybrid baboons at the Madrid Zoo, Zaragoza and Colmenares (1997) found a reconciliatory tendency of 16% for dyads of two females in the same unit, 40% for dyads of two males, and 59% for dyads consisting of a female and her leader male. If, as shown by Cords and Thurnheer (1993), dyads with more important or more valuable relationships reconcile with one another after conflicts more often than those with less important or less valuable relationships, then the findings of Zaragoza and Colmenares suggest that the bonds between leader males and their females are the most important relationships in hamadryas society, followed by bonds among males, and lastly bonds among females.

Social Relationships and Kinship

Differences among females in their motivation to interact socially with other females, as well as the relative strength of social bonds between various female dyads, may be a function of kinship. In other baboon populations, related females spend more time grooming one another than do unrelated females (Walters 1981; Saunders 1988; Silk et al. 1999). Among mountain gorillas, which, like hamadryas, live in one-male groups between which female transfers occur, maternally related females interact affiliatively more often and aggressively less often than do unrelated females (Watts 1994b). An association between social interaction and kinship characterizes many other primate taxa as well (Gouzoules & Gouzoules 1987).

Although data on genetic relatedness of females in Group 1 are not yet available (see Epilogue), microsatellite data from a nearby hamadryas population show a higher level of relatedness among females within each group than typically exists for the dispersing sex in other taxa (Woolley-Barker 1998, 1999). Hamadryas females, at least in the Filoha area, may therefore show higher levels of intragroup relatedness and lower frequencies of dispersal than has previously been assumed (see Chapter 8), and females who interact the most may do so because they are half siblings or mother-daughter pairs.

Although some of the females in the Filoha group transferred into their respective one-male units during the study period and thus were known to have been in separate units before that time, it is certainly possible that they were originally born into the same unit, were taken over and transferred into a new unit by a leader male, and then ended up the same unit as adults. This could occur through an expression of female choice on transfers of females between OMUs (Bachmann & Kummer 1980; Abegglen 1984; Swedell 2000; see Chapter 9), through a regular transfer of females between specific OMUs due to a relationship between their leader males (cf. Abegglen 1984), or simply by chance. That females often end up in the same unit with familiar adult or juvenile females from their original unit has been reported for the hamadryas baboon population at Erer Gota (Sigg et al. 1982), and female relatedness reportedly influences unit membership among the free-ranging hamadryas of the Gumista Primate Reserve in Georgia as well (Chalyan et al. 1994a). Because of the forced transfer of females between OMUs and the rarity of social interaction between them, long-term relationships among hamadryas females, whether or not they are based on kinship, cannot develop to the extent that they do in other baboons. These relationships, however, especially if they *are* based on kinship, may be strong enough to endure periods of separation and to be continued when two females are reunited in the same OMU after having been in different ones for lengthy periods of time.

If related females do not end up in the same OMU, they may cross unit boundaries to interact. Chalyan et al. (1994a) found that most free-ranging hamadryas females who crossed unit boundaries to groom one another were relatives, and Abegglen's (1984) observations also suggest that females attempt to interact with female relatives from whom they have been separated by OMU transfers. This may also be the case for the instances of interunit grooming observed at Filoha. A readiness to cross OMU boundaries to interact with other females would suggest that the importance of female-female social relationships to female hamadryas baboons may sometimes outweigh the potential risk of aggression from a female's leader male for leaving the socio-spatial boundaries of their one-male units.

Benefits of Hamadryas Female Social Relationships

Whether or not grooming relationships among hamadryas females are based on kinship, how might females benefit from these relationships? Models of social relationships among female primates have suggested that female grooming relationships serve to strengthen bonds that come into play in the form of agonistic support or coalitions against other females or against males (Seyfarth 1977; Seyfarth & Cheney 1984; Dunbar & Sharman 1984). Friendships between unrelated individuals can presumably be beneficial when both individuals share certain social goals and can cooperate to achieve those goals, such as the defeat of a more powerful individual (de Waal 1982; Goldberg & Wrangham 1997). Female hamadryas, however, do not typically compete with one another (with the exception of Arabian populations: Kummer et al. 1981), nor do they form coalitions against other individuals (Kummer 1968a; Sigg 1980; this study).

Another benefit of grooming relationships to females may be increased tolerance of one another at limited resources (Cords 1997; Henzi & Barrett 1999). However, as hamadryas females do not typically experience feeding competition with one another (Kummer 1968a; also see Chapters 4 and 9), this function of grooming relationships is unlikely to be relevant. Hamadryas females do, however, compete over grooming access or close proximity to their leader male (Kummer 1968a; Sigg 1980; Vervaecke et al. 1992), and when fights do occur among females, they typically occur when two or more females are grooming the leader male simultaneously (Kummer 1968a; Abegglen 1984; see Chapter 9). Grooming bonds among females, therefore, may increase tolerance among females around the leader male, a limited resource for hamadryas females.

Grooming may also be important to hamadryas females in its own right. Recent models of grooming in female primates have suggested that grooming is a commodity that may be traded, either for benefits that one of the participants can offer the other (such as tolerance at resources or aid in agonistic interactions) or for additional grooming in return (Barrett et al. 1999; Henzi & Barrett 1999). In hamadryas baboons, females would be most likely to exchange grooming reciprocally, as there is typically no power differential between females and thus neither female can offer to the other any services besides grooming in return. If grooming is indeed traded for itself, then its value must lie in its direct, immediate benefits in the removal of debris and ectoparasites (Hutchins & Barash 1976; Barton 1985) and the release of endogenous opioids (Keverne et al. 1989).

Finally, the possibility remains that sociality in itself is adaptively beneficial to hamadryas females. Silk et al. (2003) found that female yellow baboons (*P. h. cynocephalus*) who spent more time in close proximity to, grooming, or being groomed by other adult members of their group experienced greater short-term reproductive success (measured in terms of infant survival to one year) than less socially active females. Silk et al. suggest that increased social contact reduces stress levels, which may result in lower levels of stress hormones, greater immune system responsiveness, and consequent health and reproductive benefits for females. It is quite possible that hamadryas females may benefit from social contact in general—and the development and maintenance of social relationships with other females—in a similar way.

CHAPTER SUMMARY AND CONCLUSIONS

The results reported in this chapter suggest that bonds among hamadryas females, at least in the Filoha population, are stronger than has been reported by previous studies of wild hamadryas baboons. In contrast to the star-shaped sociogram previously described for hamadryas one-male units, most females at Filoha spent about as much social time with other females as they did with their leader male and some females even crossed unit boundaries to interact with one another. Moreover, females were equally likely to spend social time with other females whether or not their leader male was available for social interaction at the time, suggesting that they may, in some cases, prefer to socialize with other females over their leader male. Females varied widely, however, in the amount of time spent with other females. Much of this variation was attributable to the size of a female's unit—in that females in larger units interacted with other females more than females in smaller units—but there were also substantial differences among individual females in their apparent motivation to interact with other females. Although kin relationships among females are not yet known for the Filoha population, variation among females in their interactions with other females may in fact reflect differences in relatedness among female dyads. Regardless of whether individual pairs of females are related, there are likely adaptive benefits to social relationships among hamadryas females. Overall, while the results discussed in this chapter do not diminish the importance of the relationships between a hamadryas female and her leader male, they do suggest that relationships among females are more important to hamadryas social organization than has previously been assumed.

8

Dispersal and Philopatry in Hamadryas Baboons

Migration between groups imposes costs to individual primates. Not only does it increase stress levels (Sapolsky 1983, 1996) but it increases one's risk of predation as well (Alberts & Altmann 1995a) and may also decrease one's possibility of finding mates. The fact that dispersal occurs so widely, therefore, suggests that it is adaptively beneficial.

DISPERSAL AS A REPRODUCTIVE STRATEGY

Leaving one's natal group is commonly thought to be necessary to prevent inbreeding among conspecifics (Packer 1979, 1985; Pusey & Packer 1987). In theory, inbred offspring have a lower probability of survival and reproduction than outbred offspring. That dispersal functions to avoid such inbreeding is suggested by a pattern of decreased survival in offspring of close relatives among many primate species (Packer 1979; Ralls & Ballou 1982; Ralls et al. 1986; Smith 1986; Miller & Hedrick 1993; Alberts & Altmann 1995a; but see Shields 1982) and the fact that close maternal relatives avoid inbreeding even when residing in the same group (Sade 1968; Pusey 1980; Paul & Kuester 1985; Smith 1986; Kuester et al. 1994; but see Missakian 1973). Females also often prefer newly transferred males over males that have been resident in a group for longer periods of time (Packer 1979; Wolfe 1986; Bercovitch 1991a; Pereira & Weiss 1991; Berard 1993), and such a lack of sexual interest in individuals with whom an individual has been familiar from a young age may be a proximate mechanism by which inbreeding avoidance occurs (Sade 1968; Kuester et al. 1994). Paul and Kuester (1985) suggest that behavioral inhibition of mating between close relatives has been selected for—and is thus more prevalent—in species in which dispersal patterns do not necessarily prevent inbreeding (e.g., in species in which males do not necessarily leave their natal group before sexual maturity, such as Barbary macaques, *Macaca sylvanus*).

Alternatively, or additionally, dispersal may function to improve reproductive opportunities (Drickamer & Vessey 1973; Moore 1984, 1993; Crockett 1984; Watts 1990; Alberts & Altmann 1995a; Berard 1991, 1993, 1999; Berard et al. 1993). Individuals who leave their natal group may gain access to more mates and reproduce more successfully than those who do not. Male yellow baboons (*P. h. cynocephalus*) are more likely to transfer from groups with high numbers of excess males into groups with low numbers of excess males. Residence lengths of males also depend on their mating success: successful male baboons stay in groups longer than unsuccessful males (Alberts & Altmann 1995). In some species, most notably rhesus macaques (*Macaca mulatta*), it appears that an enhancement of one's mating success is indeed a consequence of dispersal to new groups (Lindburg 1969; Berard 1999).

FEMALE DISPERSAL

In many primates, females regularly migrate between groups instead of, or in addition to, males (Moore 1984; Pusey & Packer 1987). Both female and male dispersal occurs regularly in mountain gorillas (*Gorilla gorilla:* Harcourt 1978; Sicotte 1993; Robbins 1995), purple-faced langurs (*Presbytis senex:* Rudran 1973), Thomas's langurs (*Presbytis thomasi:* Sterck 1997), and howler monkeys (red howlers, *Alouatta seniculus:* Sekulic 1982, Crockett 1984; mantled howlers, *A. palliata:* Glander 1980, 1992). Female dispersal with male philopatry occurs in chimpanzees (*Pan troglodytes:* Wrangham 1979b, Pusey 1980), bonobos (*Panpaniscus:* White 1996), and the atelines (Strier 1999a), and female dispersal with limited male dispersal occurs in red colobus monkeys (*Colobus badius:* Struhsaker 1975; Struhsaker & Leland 1987).

As discussed in Chapter 2, female dispersal in many of these species probably functions ultimately to prevent inbreeding (Pusey 1980; Pusey & Packer 1987; Stewart & Harcourt 1987). Avoiding inbreeding in this way might be particularly important in species characterized by male philopatry or in polygynous species with long periods of male residency, as females who remain in such groups may be likely to mate with their fathers. Females may also transfer between groups to reduce feeding and/or mating competition with other females or to otherwise improve their reproductive opportunities (Glander 1980; Crockett 1984; Moore & Ali 1984; Anderson 1987; Stewart & Harcourt 1987; Watts 1990; Glander 1992). Another function of female transfer may be the avoidance of infanticide (Stewart & Harcourt 1987; Smuts & Smuts 1993). Females might transfer out of a group to avoid a potentially infanticidal immigrant male or transfer into a group to gain protection from infanticide from the evicted father of their infant or another noninfanticidal male (Rudran 1973; Wrangham 1982; Watts 1989; Smuts & Smuts 1993; Sterck 1997).

DISPERSAL IN HAMADRYAS BABOONS

Hamadryas baboons have traditionally been classified as a species characterized by female dispersal and male philopatry (Pusey & Packer 1987; Stammbach 1987). However, the notion of female dispersal in hamadryas is misleading in two ways. First, hamadryas females do not necessarily transfer between *bands*, which are the groupings analogous to "troops" or groups of non-hamadryas baboons and most other primate taxa. Rather, it appears that most female transfers occur between one-male units within the same band. Transfer between OMUs within a band is *not* analogous to female dispersal in other female-dispersing taxa or to the male dispersal that characterizes other papionins, as it simply rearranges females within a group rather than dispersing them to other groups.

Hamadryas males are thought to be philopatric, in that they remain in their natal band for most of their lives. Most likely because they are close relatives, hamadryas males enjoy closer social relationships with one another than males of other baboon subspecies and are often seen grooming. Such grooming relationships usually diminish, however, once males obtain females and begin reproducing. *(Photo by the author)*

Secondly, female dispersal in hamadryas occurs neither through eviction of females from their natal group by other females, as occurs in howler monkeys (Glander 1980; Crockett 1984), nor through self-motivated migration by females, as occurs in most other female-dispersing taxa (Watts 1996; Pusey 1980; Sterck 1997; Strier 1999b). Rather, hamadryas females are transferred *by males*, who herd them forcibly out of their natal OMU and into a new unit.

Male versus Female Dispersal

The original assumption that hamadryas baboons are characterized by female dispersal and male philopatry was largely based on the observation that hamadryas males appeared to have relatively strong, apparently kinship-based, bonds with other males (Kummer 1968a). As discussed in Chapter 7, however, same-sex affiliative relationships also likely characterize hamadryas females, which might, with equal validity, suggest that females are philopatric as well. As Moore (1984, p. 539) points out, however, "inferred nepotism cannot be invoked to explain behavior," so we must look for actual evidence of philopatry and dispersal by each sex. Unfortunately, we have very little behavioral evidence with which to examine this question, but we can make some preliminary conclusions with the data available so far.

Sigg et al. (1982), in their summary of five and a half years of reproductive data from Band I at Cone Rock, reported that hamadryas males leave their natal one-male unit when they are about two years of age and spend the next several years in loose temporary associations with OMUs both in and outside of their natal clan and band. Of the seven males whose origin was known, all had returned to their presumed natal clans when adult. As these data span only five and a half years, however (and as male baboons do not begin reproducing until they are about 10 years of age), it is not known whether these males ended up reproducing in their natal clans. The fact that a few males were observed following other bands for periods of several weeks or months at a time (over a year in one case) shows that males are attracted to other bands and suggests that at least some males may transfer permanently. The appearance of adult and juvenile hamadryas males in anubis and hybrid groups along the Awash River confirms that at least some hamadryas males do disperse and remain in their new groups for periods of five years or more (Phillips-Conroy et al. 1991, 1992). Phillips-Conroy and Jolly (2004) suggest that these cross-migrants are attracted to anubis groups by the apparent high availability of unattached females compared to hamadryas groups. In addition to the evidence from the Awash hybrid zone, recent observations at Filoha have confirmed the transfer between bands of one of four males that were fitted with radio collars in 1998.

Relationships among hamadryas males begin early in life. Juvenile and subadult males of all ages groom, play with, and carry infant and juvenile males and maintain those relationships through adulthood. Whether male "friends," such as the two juveniles in this photo, are related to one another is not known. *(Photo by the author)*

Compared to male transfer in hamadryas, female transfer is suggested by Sigg et al. (1982) to be more frequent and more permanent. Of the 16 females at Erer Gota whose natal OMUs were known, all but one transferred out of their natal unit. Six transferred to other units within the same clan, seven transferred to other clans, and five transferred to another band.

Abegglen (1984) reported that of the three individuals who immigrated into Band I at Cone Rock between May 1971 and February 1974, two were adult males and only one was an adult female, though of the nine adult or subadult individuals that died or emigrated from Band I during that time, three were males and six were females. Abegglen also reported, however, that juvenile males interacted across bands more than did juvenile females and that, among adults, only males interacted across bands (these interactions usually consisted of "notifying" behavior). These observations suggest that male transfers are motivated by attraction to other bands, whereas females would probably stay in their natal band (or unit or clan) if they were not forcibly transferred by males. That Abegglen does not specify whether individuals died or emigrated reinforces the point that the disappearance of an individual cannot be simply assumed to be either death or migration based on what might previously have been known (or assumed) about sex-biased dispersal in that species (Moore 1984).

In a study of free-ranging hamadryas baboons in the Gumista Primate Reserve in Georgia, Chalyan et al. (1994a) found that kinship among females appeared to influence the composition of OMUs and that kinship among males appeared to influence other levels of social structure such as bands and clans. These results suggest that both male and female hamadryas attempt to remain with their relatives.

Units of Transfer

In taxa in which there is only one level of social structure—the social group or troop—it is those units between which transfer occurs. In hamadryas, however, individuals may transfer between one-male units, between clans, between bands, or even between troops. Distinguishing at which level transfer occurs is crucial in determining patterns of dispersal and philopatry and how they affect the genetic structure of hamadryas populations. Sigg et al. (1982) appear to have focused on female transfer between *one-male units*, whereas they focused on the *lack* of male transfer between *clans*. The relevant units between which individuals transfer are the breeding units, that is, the units between which reproductive behavior typically does not occur (e.g., the hamadryas OMU). If this level—the one-male unit—is used as the unit of transfer for hamadryas, then the results of Sigg et al. (1982), as well as my own observations, suggest that virtually *all* individuals, both males and females, disperse from their natal groups before puberty. If, on the other hand, the *band* (the ecological unit for all group members and the social unit for solitary males) is used as the unit of transfer, then Sigg et al.'s results suggest that about one-fourth to one-third of adult females disperse from their natal groups, whereas adult males disperse only rarely, if at all. When Abegglen's (1984) and Phillips-Conroy et al.'s (1992) observations are considered as well, though, it appears that both some males and some females disperse from their natal band and that the level of male dispersal between bands may in fact be similar to that of females.

How Much Dispersal Occurs in Hamadryas Baboons?

Between May 1971 and February 1974, Abegglen (1984) observed very few permanent inter-band transfers and concluded that "leaving a band is not common in hamadryas" (p. 49). Abegglen suggested that the two most common classes of individuals to change bands are (1) females that are taken over by males of other bands and (2) adult males who have lost their females. In terms of genetic exchange between bands, Abegglen suggested that this occurs mainly via the few females that are forcibly transferred between bands by males, but that even females do not transfer between bands very often. Overall, Abegglen's observations, as well as those of

Sigg et al. (1982)—which include data from Abegglen's study—suggest that the composition of hamadryas bands is quite stable over time and that very little gene flow occurs between them.

So far, the genetic data that we have to address this question are, unfortunately, somewhat contradictory. On the one hand, the results of Woolley-Barker (1999) suggest that hamadryas bands are much more inbred than other baboon groups. Microsatellite data from both the Filoha population and a hamadryas band about 20 km southeast of Filoha show very high levels of relatedness (r=.2) among both males and females, as well as high levels of inbreeding overall (coefficient of inbreeding=.16). Woolley-Barker (1999) interpreted these results as suggesting that neither hamadryas males nor females regularly transfer from their natal groups.

The results of Hapke et al. (2001), on the other hand, suggest that hamadryas females do regularly transfer from their natal groups. In a comparison of mitochondrial DNA variation among 10 hamadryas troops and 2 anubis troops in Eritrea, Hapke and colleagues found the pattern of genetic variation among the hamadryas troops, but not the anubis troops, to be consistent with the idea that gene flow is mediated by dispersal of females. Because their study focused on mitochondrial DNA, however, it did not address the possibility of migration by males as well.

Based on genetic evidence, therefore, it appears that hamadryas females do transfer between hamadryas bands to at least some degree. Based on behavioral evidence, it appears that males transfer to at least a limited degree as well. It seems clear, however, that neither sex disperses as much as a male anubis baboon, for example, or an individual of the dispersing sex in a species with sex-specific dispersal pattern. Overall, it seems that the ancestral "savanna baboon" social system of female philopatry and male dispersal has evolved in hamadryas baboons into a system in which neither males nor females willingly or regularly transfer between groups, but rather females are transferred on occasion by males and males migrate on occasion to find females.

IMPLICATIONS FOR PATTERNS OF KINSHIP AND FEMALE RELATIONSHIPS

Several lines of evidence suggest that hamadryas females pay more attention to relationships with other females than has previously been assumed (e.g., Kummer 1968a; Stammbach 1987) and that social relationships among hamadryas females may be based on kinship. As mentioned in Chapter 7, it has been shown for other taxa, including non-hamadryas baboons, that related females engage in more affiliative behavior than do unrelated females (Walters 1981; Gouzoules & Gouzoules 1987; Silk et al. 1999). The marked variation in levels of affiliative behavior among females at Filoha, combined with genetic data showing high levels of relatedness among females in this population (Woolley-Barker 1999), suggest the possibility that females at Filoha who interact the most may do so because they are close relatives.

Evidence from other studies suggests that hamadryas females attempt, when possible, to remain with their female relatives. Sigg et al. (1982) reported that most females at Erer Gota who transferred between one-male units transferred into new OMUs that already contained females from their natal unit. Similarly, Chalyan et al. (1994) found that kinship among females at the Gumista Primate Reserve in Georgia appeared to influence the composition of OMUs, suggesting again that females may attempt to remain with their female relatives when they are transferred to a new unit. Hamadryas females, in general, may prefer to remain with their relatives, but the aggressive herding behavior of hamadryas males clearly limits their ability to do so.

As discussed in Chapter 7, previous models of the relationship between ecology and female social relationships have concluded that intergroup competition over food resources should lead to female philopatry, kinship bonds, and dominance relationships, whereas in an absence of food competition females should have no reason to develop differentiated relationships or to be philopatric (Wrangham 1980; van Schaik 1989; Isbell 1991; Barton et al. 1996; Sterck et al. 1997). Moreover, it is commonly thought that in species in which females transfer between groups, relationships among females are weak and undifferentiated due to a lack of relatedness among them (e.g., Wrangham 1980, 1987). Even in mountain gorillas, however, in which females transfer between groups and have weak bonds with one another relative to those with males, females still form differentiated relationships: related females engage in more affiliative interactions and fewer aggressive interactions with one another than do unrelated females, and some pairs of females form long-term friendships, whereas others do not (Watts 1994b). Like mountain gorillas, hamadryas females have traditionally been assumed to both regularly transfer between groups and have weak, undifferentiated relationships with one another. For hamadryas, however, neither of these assumptions may actually be true.

The savanna baboon pattern of female bonding (Wrangham 1980), presumably the ancestral condition for all *Papio* baboons, is typically assumed to have been replaced by a pattern of male philopatry and female dispersal during the evolution of hamadryas social organization (Kummer 1968b, 1990, 1995). I would agree with Abegglen (1984), however, in suggesting that not only do female hamadryas often remain with their female relatives, but the ability and motivation of hamadryas females to establish and maintain differentiated affiliative relationships with one another—though constrained by the herding behavior of hamadryas males and the evolution of the OMU social structure—was not entirely lost during the evolution of hamadryas baboons from their female-bonded ancestors.

9

Female Strategies in a Male-Dominated World

In this chapter, I will attempt to draw some general conclusions about hamadryas female reproductive strategies in the context of evolutionary theory and data from other primate taxa. The reader may wish to refer to Chapter 2 for theoretical perspectives on reproductive strategies in primates, including infanticide, female choice, and competition among females as selective forces in the evolution of female reproductive strategies. In this chapter, I will discuss each topic, respectively, in the context of hamadryas baboon behavior and evidence from my own research as of the writing of this book. I will conclude the chapter by proposing, based on evidence from this and other studies of hamadryas baboons, some general conclusions about the reproductive strategies of female hamadryas baboons.

INFANT MORTALITY AND INFANTICIDE

Infanticide in Hamadryas Baboons

Prior to this study, infanticide in hamadryas baboons had been observed only in captivity (Angst & Thommen 1977; Rijksen 1981; Gomendio & Colmenares 1989; Kaumanns et al. 1989; Chalyan & Meishvili 1990; Zinner et al. 1993) and under experimental conditions in the wild (Kummer et al. 1974). As a result of Kummer et al.'s (1974) experiments, two mothers with infants were transferred into new one-male units. One infant was missing a day later, and the other was seen dead with large canine-inflicted wounds on its skull and thighs. While it is possible that these infants were killed by their mothers' new leader males (though not certain, as this is only circumstantial evidence), it could have been a pathological behavior induced by the stress of the experimental situation, especially as these females changed units by artificial means. Likewise, the numerous incidents of infanticide among captive hamadryas might also be pathological in some way. Infanticide by hamadryas males in captivity is *not* usually associated with group takeovers, and in captivity infanticidal males often kill their *own* infants (Kaumanns et al. 1989; Zinner et al. 1993). Infanticide in captive and experimentally manipulated hamadryas could, therefore, be a maladaptive or pathological behavior induced by social stress or the stress of captivity and experimental conditions (Angst & Thommen 1977; Rijksen 1981; Zinner et al. 1993).

Gomendio and Colmenares (1989) suggest that infanticide does not typically occur in wild hamadryas because unit takeovers are a gradual process whereby the new leader male, having previously been a follower male to the group, is typically already familiar with the group's females. This stands in contrast to group takeovers in other species that live in one-male groups, such as langurs, where a new male may suddenly and aggressively take over a group of unfamiliar females. If male infanticide is stimulated proximately by a short period of social upheaval and the unfamiliarity of a new group of females, then the nature of group takeovers in hamadryas would not provide a proximate mechanism for infanticide to occur. Ultimately, infanticide in hamadryas may not be adaptive because leader males and the follower males who take over their units may be related (Abegglen 1984), and males may thus actually gain inclusive fitness by investing in, rather than killing, infants sired by the previous leader male.

Evidence from my research on the Filoha population, however, suggests otherwise. As outlined in Chapter 5, the consequences of four takeovers of known females with black infants have been witnessed to date at Filoha. After the first takeover, the infant disappeared and its mother developed a sexual swelling and copulated with the new leader male within 11 days of the takeover (Swedell 2000). After the second takeover, the infant was kidnapped by a subadult male for over an hour and a half with no attempt by the female's new leader male to retrieve the infant despite the female's obvious distress (Swedell 2000). After the third takeover, the infant disappeared within two weeks of the takeover, and after the fourth takeover, the new leader male repeatedly attacked the three-week-old infant, who subsequently died (Swedell & Tesfaye 2003; see Chapter 5). A fifth takeover of a known female in October 2003 (though the takeover itself was not actually witnessed) was followed by the disappearance of the six-month-old infant of the female involved. Overall, observations to date suggest that no black infant (i.e., younger than 8–10 months; see age classes in Table 5–1) of a female involved in a takeover has survived longer than two weeks after the takeover. Whether all of these infants were deliberately killed, however, is not known.

Infanticide after takeovers may reasonably be interpreted as a simple by-product of the generalized aggression that surrounds these events (cf. Bartlett et al. 1993; see Chapter 2 for details). I believe it to be unlikely, however, that such an interpretation explains infanticide in hamadryas baboons. Fights, chases, and threats among hamadryas males, whether among solitary males or between solitary and leader males, are a common occurrence in hamadryas society. While such episodes often result in visible wounds on males, I have never seen an infant wounded or killed at these times. Likewise, hamadryas leader males routinely herd their females by forcefully biting their neck. While neck bites increase in frequency and intensity after takeovers, they are a common element of life for hamadryas females during nontakeover periods as well. Moreover, I have never observed an infant harmed during such aggression, even when the infant is being carried by the female at the time. Furthermore, the fourth takeover discussed in Chapter 5 involved aggression that appeared to be directed exclusively at the infant itself, suggesting that the infant's death was not simply an indirect consequence of aggression directed at the mother.

Early Return to Reproductive Condition.   As discussed in Chapter 5, female hamadryas respond to male takeovers and infant death by returning to reproductive condition earlier than normal. The two shortest cycles observed among Filoha females as a whole were the first cycles of Whoopie and Hazel after their takeovers (see Chapter 6). Also, after two of the takeovers discussed in Chapter 5, the two mothers who were observed on days subsequent to the takeover (Beatrice and Marigold) developed sexual swellings within two weeks, after their infants died. In the one case where the infant's age was known, its mother (Marigold) resumed cycling 36 days after the infant's birth and 10 days after its death. Data from Filoha and Erer Gota on female cycle lengths (see Chapter 6) suggest that this would have been an 8- to 15-month acceleration in Marigold's reproduction as a result of her infant's death. Even for the female whose infant's age was not known (Beatrice), it is likely that she conceived sooner than she would have otherwise, as she not only came into estrus within two weeks of the takeover (and her infant's death) but then conceived during that first estrus period and gave birth six months later.

Overall, the consequences of the takeovers observed at Filoha strongly suggest that female ovarian cycles are accelerated in response to takeovers by new males and/or death of their infants. A return to reproductive condition within a similar time frame after takeovers has also been reported for captive hamadryas females at both the Madrid Zoo and the German Primate Center (Colmenares & Gomendio 1988; Zinner & Deschner 2000). Such an acceleration in reproduction gives new leader males an earlier chance of siring offspring with females than they would have had otherwise, and, if this is the case for most females, then infanticide by new leader males after takeovers should be selected for. An alternate explanation is that the sexual swellings observed after the takeovers at Filoha were failed (and belated) attempts by the females to *prevent* infanticide, as this may signal to the new leader male that a female is sexually receptive and may thus inhibit his infanticidal attacks. Such a scenario has been suggested by Zinner and Deschner (2000) for the hamadryas females at the German Primate Center.

Post-Conception Estrus.   In addition to an early return to reproductive condition on the part of mothers who lost their infants, I also observed one example of post-conception estrus after a takeover in the Filoha hamadryas population. As described in Chapter 5, the takeover of three of Sylvester's females by Felix was followed by the return of Dorothy to Sylvester within two weeks after the takeover. Dorothy then came into behavioral estrus and had a small sexual swelling two weeks after she returned to Sylvester. She was about 130 days pregnant at the time.

   Post-conception estrus has been proposed to benefit females in several ways, including developing and maintaining male-female social relationships (Wallis 1982; Small 1983; Andelman 1987; Cords 1988) and inhibiting male-female aggression (Wallis 1982). In hamadryas, aggression from a female's leader male is more likely to occur when a female is swollen than when she is not swollen (see Chapter 6), so reduced aggression is probably not a benefit of a post-conception swelling for a hamadryas female. Reestablishing her relationship with Sylvester, however, may have been an important function of the post-conception estrus shown by Dorothy in January 1997.

Infants and Non-Leader Males

The interest shown in infants by hamadryas non-leader males is an important factor in the reproductive strategies of hamadryas females in that it can adversely affect offspring survival. As discussed in Chapter 5, solitary and follower males are quite interested in female infants in particular and appear to preferentially associate with one-male units that contain female infants. This may be a means to establish a relationship with both the mother and the female infant herself so that the follower male can eventually disassociate the young female from her natal unit and begin a one-male unit of his own. Such a process is indeed apparently how many males form their own initial units (Kummer 1968a; Abegglen 1984).

   Probably as a consequence of this reproductive interest in young females, non-leader males at Filoha often attempt to kidnap infants from their mothers and sometimes succeed in these attempts. Once a non-leader male has obtained a female's infant, she is usually unable to

Non-leader males, whether they are followers or solitary, typically develop social relationships with infants and young juveniles of both sexes. *(Photo by the author)*

retrieve it unless aided by her leader male. As discussed later, leader males do typically intervene and retrieve infants from non-leader (usually follower) males. On the few occasions I witnessed when a female's leader male did not intervene, non-leader males succeeded in keeping infants from their mothers for periods of a half hour or more. Kummer (1968a) also reported kidnapping of black infants from mothers by subadult and young adult males for periods of up to 30 minutes at a time. He also observed adoption of infants and young juveniles by young adult males when the former were released into foreign troops and concluded from this that "when a hamadryas mother dies leaving an infant, it is probably not the unit leader or another female who takes care of such an orphan, but one of the young males" (Kummer 1968a, pp. 61–63).

I never observed a non-leader male attempt to harm an infant, but I often observed such males playing roughly with infants and holding them down to the ground or against themselves when the infants tried to leave. Such rough handling can lead to injury, and extended periods of separation of infants from their mothers can lead to starvation or dehydration. Thus, while the behavior of non-leader males toward infants is probably motivated by affiliative rather than aggressive tendencies, it has the potential, if unchecked, to lead to injury or death.

As discussed in Chapter 5, within hours of takeover #2, Ralaine's infant was kidnapped by a subadult male, who kept it from her for at least an hour and a half. Ralaine's new leader male, Jupiter, neither defended the infant nor tried to retrieve it, as leader males typically do (see next section). The infant probably died, not as a result of infanticide, but from death due to dehydration, indirectly caused by Jupiter's lack of protection of the infant and Ralaine's inability to retrieve the infant on her own. This observation suggests that infants of females who are taken over by new leader males are particularly vulnerable and may die from dehydration or injury if the new leader male does not help defend them from other individuals, especially non-leader males.

The Leader Male as a Female's Protector

Protection for Herself. As noted in Chapter 5, a female's leader male is her main protector from aggression (Kummer 1968a, 1995). When a threatening individual or potential predator comes near, females invariably move closer to their leader male. If a fight or chase moves past a female's unit, she temporarily moves closer to or behind her leader male to avoid it, then moves away again after the fight or chase has subsided. When Afar nomads are nearby, females move closer to their leader male and stay there until the Afar are no longer visible. As mentioned in Chapter 5, after a female is involved in a conflict, she usually runs to her leader male and grooms him for several minutes, suggesting that he provides some degree of reassurance and/or protection in such situations.

Colmenares (1992) found that, among the colony of hamadryas and hybrid baboons at the Madrid Zoo, the females who associated the most with their leader male and groomed him the most also received the most protection from him. These females were also the most loyal to him in their mating behavior, which conferred on him greater reproductive success (Colmenares 1992). In addition, Colmenares (1997) found evidence of grooming in exchange for protection (supporting the loser in agonistic interactions) in both male and female baboons; this could also apply to the relationship between the leader male and his females, in that they groom him in exchange for his protection of them and their offspring. A female grooming her leader male after a conflict may serve a dual purpose: she may be reassured because she is in contact with him *and* he may be more likely to protect her *because* she is grooming him.

A female's leader male is her main protector from aggression. Evidence from captivity suggests that higher levels of grooming between a female and her leader male are associated with higher levels of such protection. *(Photo by the author)*

Protection for Her Offspring. In addition to supporting their females, leader males also defend the infants born into their unit. On many occasions, I observed a leader male threaten and/or retrieve an infant from a non-leader male that had kidnapped the infant from his unit. The following two descriptions exemplify the general pattern:

June 27, 1998, 5:06 P.M. Raquel was sitting 6 meters away from Ike [her leader male], and Raquel's two-month-old male infant was playing between them. Suddenly, a fight erupted about 20 meters away. Ike immediately grabbed Raquel's infant and held it to his chest until the fight stopped. Ike watched the fight continuously as he was holding the infant.

July 14, 1998, 4:20 P.M. A subadult male was 1 meter from Nick [a leader male] and Cassie [his only female] and was playing with Cassie's six-week-old female infant. The infant suddenly screamed. Both Nick and Cassie immediately ran to it and both tried to grab it away from the subadult male, who backed off and ran to 2 meters away. Nick embraced the infant, both Nick and Cassie grunted several times, and then Cassie groomed Nick.

I observed only two cases of kidnapping of infants by non-leader males in which the non-leader male kept the infant from its mother for more than a half hour and yet the leader male did *not* defend or retrieve the infant. One of these instances involved the new leader male Jupiter's takeover of Ralaine, whose infant was almost certainly not his (takeover #2 described in Chapter 5). The other instance involved Hera, one of two females of Zeus:

> *April 23, 1998, 2:42 P.M. Ulysses* [a subadult male follower of Zeus] *is carrying around Hera's female infant. Hera screamed at Ulysses once and received no reaction from anybody. She then screamed again, and Zeus reacted by chasing her (while she continued screaming) into the water and back out again (but he did not neckbite her). After that, Hera did not scream any more, but watched Ulysses continuously as he played with her infant and forcibly kept it from leaving him. Ulysses kept Hera's infant until at least 3:50 P.M., at which point the group began traveling and Ulysses was carrying the infant. At 5:00 P.M. the same day, Ulysses had the infant again (or still?) and Hera was watching him from 1 meter away.*

> *April 24, 1998, 8:22 A.M. Ulysses is in a palm tree with Hera's infant. Hera is in another branch of the same tree, about 4 meters away. The infant keeps kecking and Hera keeps looking at them, but she is not watching them continuously as she was yesterday. She seems to have resigned herself to not being able to get back her infant from Ulysses. Ulysses occasionally glances at Hera.*

Hera did eventually retrieve her infant, and the infant did not die. Zeus, however, neither defended it nor tried to retrieve it. I never observed such a complete lack of infant defense by a leader male except in a situation in which the leader male was probably not the father of the infant (in Ralaine's case). Lack of paternity *may* also have been the case for Zeus and Hera. However, I have no way of knowing if Zeus was the likely father of Hera's infant; I had only known them individually for two months when the kidnapping occurred and do not know if Hera was in Zeus's unit when her infant was conceived.

Of course, lack of infant protection in cases in which paternity is uncertain in no way implies conscious strategizing on the part of a leader male, nor does it imply recognition and preferential treatment of one's own offspring (cf. Buchan et al. 2003). Rather, a leader male may simply be more likely to protect infants whose mothers have been in his unit for a sufficient period of time to have developed a strong social bond him, and this period of time may correspond generally to the length of time it takes for a female to undergo gestation. The strength of the bond between a leader male and each of his females may thus serve as the proximate mechanism leading to protection, or lack thereof, of the infants born into his unit.

That a leader male provides protection for a female's offspring is suggested by the tendency of females to remain closer to their leader male during the first month after the birth of an infant, when the infant is most vulnerable, compared to their distance to him in subsequent months or when pregnant (see Chapter 6). Although these differences in proximity did not characterize all females and were not statistically significant, my subjective impression from ad libitum observations was that females with newborn infants who normally spent more time farther away from their leader males (than other females) stayed closer to their leader male than usual after giving birth. This difference in proximity did not characterize all females and probably did not emerge as a general pattern because some females already spent more time closer to their leader male than did other females. These females, therefore, did not change their proximity to their leader male when they gave birth because they were apparently already sufficiently close to him. Those females who were normally farther away from their leader male (e.g., RAQ, CHI2, and ISA; see Table 6–7), however, appeared to noticeably decrease their distance to their leader male after giving birth.

Rohrhuber (1987 [in German], cited in Kaumanns et al. 1989) found that a high rate of grooming as well as close proximity between a female and her leader male was associated with a lower risk of infanticide for her offspring. Sigg et al. (1982) pointed out that infant survival is higher in hamadryas than in other baboons and suggested that the one-male unit social structure might provide a safer environment for infants and juveniles than the multi-male, multi-female social structure of yellow or anubis baboons. This suggests that a female's leader male plays a large role in protecting the infants in his unit and that his presence largely accounts for the higher rates of infant survival in hamadryas compared to other baboons.

Protection of both females and their infants from harm is probably, from the perspective of a female's own reproductive strategies, the main function of a hamadryas leader male (besides providing sperm, which would probably not be difficult to obtain in his absence). In particular, leader males protect infants that are born into their units from non-leader males that may, as a result of a high motivation to interact with infants, inadvertently or indirectly cause an infant's death. In most cases, leader males are probably protecting their own offspring, and are thus contributing to their own fitness as well as that of the infant's mother. When paternity is uncertain or unlikely, however, leader males may withhold this protection and "let" the infant die by not protecting it. Again, this can be explained proximately by a lack of long-term familiarity with the infant's mother, leading to a disinterest in protecting the infant from harm. Such behavior can be considered to be an indirect form of infanticide, as the frequency with which non-leader males interact with young infants probably necessitates protection of infants by leader males simply in order to keep them alive.

Infant Mortality and Hamadryas Female Reproductive Strategies

Regardless of how one interprets infant death from the male perspective, hamadryas infants are clearly at an increased risk of death after takeovers of one-male units. This may be due to either direct infanticide or kidnapping leading to starvation or dehydration. Kidnapping may be more dangerous for hamadryas infants than for infants of other baboon subspecies due to the hot and dry climate of hamadryas habitats, including the Filoha region, which would lead to an increased risk of dehydration if infants are separated from their mothers for long periods.

Van Schaik et al. (1999) suggest that in all "non-communally breeding infant-carrying primates [some lemuroids, some ceboids, and all cercopithecoids and hominoids], the risk of male infanticide should have selected for female counterstrategies" (p. 206). As discussed in Chapter 2, female counterstrategies to infanticide may include minimizing one's losses (through abortion, premature birth or weaning, or an otherwise earlier return to reproductive condition) or manipulation of paternity assessment (through pseudoestrus, including post-conception estrus). In the longer term, a female might also lower her risk of infanticide by establishing and maintaining a social relationship with the likely father of her infants in order to gain protection for them. Van Schaik et al. (1999) hypothesize that "female sexuality in species vulnerable to male infanticide has been molded by the dual need for paternity concentration and confusion: concentration in order to elicit infant protection from the likely father, confusion in order to prevent infanticide from non-likely fathers" (p. 207). Female hamadryas appear to use, or have been forced into, a paternity concentration strategy. Leader males probably sire most, if not all, of the infants born into their units, and the fact that leader males appear to play such an important role in infant survival suggests that a female benefits from associating with and copulating exclusively with a protective leader male. Paternity certainty is probably quite high among hamadryas leader males, and protective behavior of infants born into their unit has probably been selected for.

Overall, hamadryas females may use a paternity concentration strategy to such a degree that it obviates the need for a paternity confusion strategy. This does not mean, however, that female hamadryas do not have preferences for some males over others. Whether hamadryas females have such preferences, whether they attempt to exert them, and whether females attempt to use a paternity confusion strategy against infanticide by mating with males other than their leader will be addressed in the next section.

FEMALE MATE CHOICE

The control that hamadryas males exert over females leaves little opportunity for female expression of any strategies that might conflict with those of their leaders. As discussed above, a female hamadryas baboon may in fact have little option but to associate closely with a leader male in order to gain protection for her offspring, and, if so, a female's reproductive interests would coincide with those of her leader male. Females might have preferences for some males over others, however, or might benefit from interacting with males that might be likely to take over their OMU in the near future so as to elicit protection from a potential future leader male. Females in the Filoha population did show some indications that they might have preferences for some males over others and that, in general, their own reproductive strategies might sometimes conflict with those of their leader males.

Like all female primates, hamadryas baboons would benefit from selecting high-quality mates and choosing mates (or multiple mates) in a way that promotes offspring survival. Like all females in one-male groups, hamadryas females may be at risk of infanticide when male residency changes. As previously discussed, infanticide by hamadryas males has occurred in captivity, under experimental conditions in the wild, and in at least one instance at Filoha. To the extent that infanticide is a risk to her offspring, a hamadryas female might be expected to choose mates or to mate with males other than her leader male in order to minimize this risk.

Occurrence of Copulations with Non-Leader Males

Kummer (1968a) maintained that "as a rule, there is no contact between adult females and strange adult males" (p. 50). Likewise, Sigg et al. (1982) reported that "no complete copulation was observed between a female and a male other than her leader" (p. 478). In Kummer's (1968a) study group, however, females did "attempt to copulate with young males in the immediate neighborhood but behind the backs of their leaders" (p. 41), even though the leader usually attacked the female (not the male) if the couple was discovered. In one Saudi Arabian population, in fact, females interacted with males other than their leader quite often, "spontaneous[ly] shifting" between them (Kummer et al. 1985; Kummer 1995).

Biquand et al. (1994a), in an attempt to curtail the growth of a commensal population of hamadryas baboons in Saudi Arabia, vasectomized the leader males of four OMUs in an isolated group of five OMUs. During the subsequent four-year period, none of the females in units with vasectomized leader males reproduced. The authors argued that these results show "the very specific link between male leaders and females in the hamadryas social system, where the male can effectively prevent mating by females within his unit with other males" (Biquand et al. 1994b, p. 220). This particular group of hamadryas baboons, however, was unusual in that there was only one non-leader male (a subadult male) in the entire group, and this male died shortly after the four leader males were vasectomized. Thus, the only mating options for a female other than her leader male were *other* leader males. It seems highly unlikely that females in this experimental situation would mate with other leader males, given that leader males have strong bonds with one another (and with their females) and are socially inhibited from interacting with females other than their own, and that social interaction between a hamadryas leader male and a female other than his own has never been observed in the wild (Kummer 1971a; Kummer et al. 1974; Abegglen 1984; this study). As there were no actual follower males and only one other non-leader male available (and for only part of the study period), this "experiment" may not have been a very good test of a leader male's ability to prevent his females from mating with males outside of his unit.

As reported in Chapter 6, at Filoha I observed 15 copulations between females and males other than their leaders. Of these, six were with medium juvenile males, five were with large juvenile males, and four were with subadult males (see Table 5–1 for age classes). Four took place when the female involved had a sexual swelling and thus could potentially have led to conception. One copulation, between a swollen female and a large juvenile male, included an ejaculatory pause.

Significance of Copulations with Non-Leader Males

Kummer (1968a) judged female copulations with non-leader males to be reproductively insignificant, because (1) a long series of mountings resulting in ejaculation "is almost impossible in the vicinity of the unit leader," and (2) these young males are probably not yet sexually mature, so "such copulations may seldom result in pregnancy" (p. 41). Multiple mountings, however, are not necessary for ejaculation in hamadryas (Nystrom 1992), and age at first reproduction in male baboons is variable and dependent on many factors, so that males may be capable of inseminating females well before they reach adult size (Walters 1987; Alberts & Altmann 1995b). In wild hamadryas baboons, males are probably fertile by the age of five years (Jolly & Phillips-Conroy 2003), so all copulations with large juvenile males (i.e., those aged five to six years; see Table 5–1) may have had the potential to result in conception.

Whether or not copulations between hamadryas females and non-leader males have immediate reproductive potential, their occurrence suggests that females possess mating strategies that are not entirely contingent on those of their leader males. Even if no copulations with non-leader males resulted in conception, their occurrence could still function to confuse paternity and inhibit infanticide or elicit protection of infants by non-leader males.

Other Expressions of Female Preference

As discussed in Chapter 5, females at Filoha vary widely in their apparent motivation to be close to and interact with their leader male. Some females appear to prefer to interact with males other than, or in addition to, their leader, but do not express those preferences in front of him. Of the nine observed copulations with non-leader males that were probably at least six years old (and thus probably fertile), six took place when the female's leader male was walking away from the copulating pair, facing the opposite direction (see Table 6–3). This suggests that the female and her partner waited until that precise moment so as to mate surreptitiously and avoid detection by the female's leader. I also occasionally observed females sexually presenting to non-leader males, and most of these also occurred when the female's leader male was moving away from the female or otherwise not facing in her direction.

A few females in particular not only appeared to prefer to interact with males other than their leader, but actually expressed those preferences in front of him. Two of the copulations with non-leader males that I observed took place in full view of the female's leader male. One of these in particular, a copulation between Barbie and Skip, a follower male in her unit, did not appear to be well received by Ken, Barbie's leader male:

> *July 15, 1998, 7:15 A.M. Caught the end of a copulation between Barbie and Skip, Ken's follower male. Ken was sitting about 10 meters away, facing in their general direction. After the copulation, Barbie looked at Ken and moved toward him and away from Skip. Ken moved toward Barbie and Barbie looked at Ken again. Barbie then turned around, moved back toward Skip and began grooming Skip. Ken then approached them both, looked intently at Barbie (he had to stick his head almost between Barbie and Skip in order to do so), and then poked his muzzle under her arm, near her nipple, as if nudging her to stand up. She stood up and presented to Ken, he inspected her genitals, and then she sat back down again and returned to grooming Skip. Ken sat down just under a meter away.*

It is clear from this interaction that Ken either saw or suspected the copulation between Barbie and Ken and yet did not punish Barbie for it. It is possible that this was one event in a gradual transfer of leadership from Ken to Skip, who may have been related to one another. Takeovers among hamadryas often involve a long, gradual process whereby a leader male voluntarily relinquishes control of his females to a younger, related male (Abegglen 1984; Gomendio & Colmenares 1989), and such a transfer may have been taking place between Ken and Skip at the time of my observation. Alternatively, Ken might simply have been unable to condition his females to refrain from copulating with other males (or to at least only do so when he was not in view). In any case, Barbie apparently preferred Skip over Ken as a mate, at least at that moment, and also apparently preferred Skip as a grooming partner as well, as evidenced by this incident and other ad libitum observations of Barbie and Skip in grooming interactions.

Female preference may also be expressed in the context of takeovers of OMUs. Bachmann & Kummer (1980) used experimental choice tests to assess the relative preference of captive hamadryas females for each of several possible males. These tests showed that the degree to which a female preferred her leader male was positively correlated with the degree of "respect" shown by a rival male for the leader's "possession" of that female. Bachmann and Kummer's results suggest that females have preferences for some males over others and that rival males are able to assess those preferences and use that information to decide whether to challenge a leader for possession of his female(s).

While I have no evidence to suggest that follower or solitary males can assess a female's preferences and act accordingly, the events surrounding the takeover in December 1996 (described in Chapter 5) suggest that female choice may have played a role. A full day before the takeover, a day after Sylvester sustained his injury, Dorothy was already sitting within Felix's OMU. Dorothy was not yet, however, interacting with Felix or any of his females, suggesting that she had not yet been taken over by Felix but was sitting in Felix's unit on her own accord. An older and presumably experienced female, Dorothy may have chosen to associate with Felix because Sylvester was showing signs of weakness and would probably have been incapable of defending her (or her offspring) if the weakness had continued (or if he had subsequently died). Dorothy may have associated with Felix's unit in particular as a way of expressing her preference as to which unit she would like to transfer to should Sylvester not recover. The next day, when the takeover occurred, Felix did indeed acquire Dorothy and two of Sylvester's other females. Two weeks after the takeover, however, after Sylvester appeared to have regained his health, Dorothy returned to him. Because I observed no agonism between Felix and Sylvester nor between Dorothy and either leader male, I assumed Dorothy returned to Sylvester on her own accord. Such a reacquisition of a female by a defeated leader male has not been previously reported for hamadryas baboons. In Dorothy's case, her return to Sylvester may have reflected her underlying preference for him over Felix. Once Sylvester had apparently recovered from his injury, Dorothy may have been once again able to express her preference for him without potentially sacrificing her own protection or the survival of her unborn infant. Because Dorothy was pregnant at the time of the takeover, her return to Sylvester after his recovery can be interpreted evolutionarily as a means to ensure Sylvester's contribution to her unborn infant's protection and survival.

I have no direct evidence to suggest that female choice played a role in the takeover of Beatrice and Hazel, the other two females of Sylvester who were taken over by Felix. However, the fact that no aggression between Felix and Sylvester was observed at any time, either before or after the takeover, coupled with the fact that I never observed Felix neckbiting Beatrice and Hazel after the takeover (probably because they followed him closely enough on their own), suggests that Beatrice and Hazel may have preferred to transfer to Felix's unit rather than to be taken over by another male. Whoopie (Sylvester's fourth female), on the other hand, was neckbitten frequently by her new leader male, Ike, and proved to be quite difficult for him to control. It appears, therefore, that Whoopie probably would have preferred to be with a male other than Ike, but was unable to exert her preference and was eventually conditioned by Ike to stay with him.

The Role of Female Choice in Hamadryas Social Organization

The aggressive herding behavior of hamadryas males limits the extent to which hamadryas females can express their mating preferences, thereby imposing a limit on the amount of female choice that can occur. Female hamadryas do appear to have preferences, though, and do express them under some conditions. Overall, hamadryas females may be attempting to balance the protective benefits of strong bonds with their leader males with the potential benefits of pursuing social and/or sexual relationships with non-leader males. A sexual relationship with a non-leader male might benefit a female, by confusing paternity and inhibiting infanticide (or eliciting paternal care), if that male is likely to take over a female from her current leader in the near future. Even if such a takeover does not happen, a female may otherwise benefit from such a relationship in that a non-leader male might be less likely to harm or more likely to help protect a female's future offspring if he is a potential sire. A sexual relationship with a non-leader male may also be a strategy to ensure conception, as hamadryas testes are smaller than those of other baboons (Jolly & Phillips-Conroy 2003) and a hamadryas leader male's sperm supply may thus be limited (cf. Small 1988).

A *social* relationship with a non-leader male might also benefit a hamadryas female. A non-leader male may be more likely to protect or defend a female with whom he has an established relationship than a female with whom he has no such relationship, and this tolerance and/or protection might extend to her offspring as well. A non-leader male could therefore potentially be a second source of protection to a female in addition to her leader male.

The development of social relationships with preferred non-leader males may also be a way for a female to eventually gain sexual access to those males, in that the mere existence of such relationships may influence future takeovers. A non-leader male is probably more likely, and certainly better able, to take over a one-male unit whose females he is familiar with than a unit composed of unfamiliar females. As shown by the differences among Sylvester's females in their amount of resistance to their new leader males, a non-leader male would benefit from selectively attempting to take over females with whom he has an established relationship and who might be least likely to resist the takeover (and may even promote it). Bachmann and Kummer's (1980) experiments, discussed earlier, certainly suggest that non-leader males are able to assess a female's social prefer-ences in advance of an attempted takeover. Alternatively, even if female preferences are not involved, a female may be able to assess the probabil-ity that a non-leader male will attempt to take over her unit in the near future and cultivate a social and/or sexual relationship with that male well in advance so that he will be more likely to protect her and her off-spring once he becomes her new leader male. It is unclear whether female preferences and relationships between females and non-leader males actually do influence the occurrence and consequences of takeovers at Filoha, but the circumstances surrounding Dorothy's takeover and subse-quent return to her leader male suggest that female choice may have played a role in that takeover and may play a role in others as well.

Both social and sexual relationships with non-leader males, therefore, may benefit females in terms of protection from harm, inhibition of infan-ticide, and the potential ability to influence unit membership. In most cases, however, it appears that females must pursue relationships with non-leader males surreptitiously so as to not compromise their relation-ship with their leader male and lose the protective benefits that it offers.

FEMALE-FEMALE COMPETITION

As outlined in Chapter 2, female primates compete in many ways, all of which may lead to differential reproductive success. They may compete over access to food resources, mates, social partners, or advantageous spa-tial positions (e.g., Seyfarth 1976; Whitten 1983a; Whitten 1984; Barton & Whiten 1993; Barton 1993). They may also use strategies to lower one another's fertility, such as harassment at specific times during the repro-ductive cycle (e.g., Dunbar & Dunbar 1977; Keverne 1979; Wasser 1983; McCann 1995). In addition, they may compete by kidnapping or harming one another's offspring (e.g., Silk 1980; Hiraiwa 1981; Sommer 1989a; Maestripieri 1994a, 1994b). That success in female-female competition enhances fitness is usually inferred from correlations between dominance rank and access to resources, nutritional status, fertility, access to mates, or other measures of reproductive success (e.g., Silk et al. 1980, 1981; Small 1981; Whitten 1983a; Fairbanks & McGuire 1984; Wallen & Winston 1984; Altmann et al. 1988, 1990; Linn et al. 1991; McCann 1995).

Competition among Hamadryas Females in the Wild

Among females in the Filoha population, I found no evidence of dominance relationships and very little evidence of competition among females (see Chapter 4). The only "resource" over which females appeared to compete was grooming access to the leader male. Sometimes, when two or more females attempted to groom their leader male at the same time, one or both (or all three) females would stare threaten, eyebrow raise, grab at, or hit the other(s) repeatedly with one hand while continuing to groom the leader male with the other hand. Such agonistic interactions did not typically result in the departure of one of the females, but usually gradually dissipated as both females continued to groom the leader male on either side of him. These interactions were usually undecided in that there was no discernable "winner" or "loser," nor did one female display submissive gestures to the other (such as crouching, which female hamadryas do when they receive aggression from males). Rather, the initial target of the aggression would either ignore it (and continue grooming the leader male) or return it (with threats, while continuing to grooming the male). Competition for social access to the leader male accompanied by a lack of resolution to agonistic interactions has also been described for female mountain gorillas, who, like hamadryas, live in one-male groups and are dependent on males, rather than females, for protection and support (Watts 1996). Watts (1994a, 1994b) suggests that, in gorillas, the fitness benefits of bonds with males outweigh the fitness benefits of food competition with other females. This may be the case for hamadryas baboons as well.

As grooming the leader male seems to provide reassurance and protection for a hamadryas female, competition for exclusive grooming access to the leader male may be interpreted as competition for his protection. The competitive interactions described above usually occurred shortly after a conflict involving one of the females and a third individual or during periods of anxiety, that is, situations in which two or more females sought reassurance from their leader male at the same time. Kummer (1967, 1968a) described this competition for protection as "the fundamental form of aggressive encounter between adult hamadryas females" (Kummer 1967, p. 65). This competition for exclusive grooming access to the leader male sometimes extended to juveniles and young males as well, who sometimes competed with females for grooming access to the leader male.

As discussed in Chapters 5 and 6, Sigg (1980) found a distinction in two-female units between "central" females, who were consistently closer to the center of a triangle formed by the two females and the leader male, and "peripheral" females, who were consistently further away from the center of this triangle. Central females were older than peripheral females, and field experiments showed that, among three OMUs that were kept in enclosures, the central females were also dominant to the peripheral females. Moreover, when given the opportunity, peripheral females maintained a closer distance to the leader male and therefore seemed to prefer a position closer to him. Sigg concluded that females in two-female units compete for a position in the unit closer to the leader male and suggested (though did not provide evidence) that central females may have greater reproductive success than peripheral females. Kummer (1968a) and Sigg (1980) propose, therefore, that females not only compete for grooming access to and protection from the leader male but that they also generally prefer and compete for a position in the unit close to the leader male (Kummer 1967, 1968a, 1995; Sigg 1980). I saw no indications of competition over proximity to the leader male in the Filoha population, however, as females at Filoha did not appear to compete to be *closer* to the leader male; they only competed to *groom* the leader male when they were already sitting close to him. As discussed in Chapter 5, some females simply stayed further away from their leader male and others remained closer. These differences in proximity did not appear to be associated with any direct agonistic interactions on the part of the females themselves, but appeared to result from individual differences among females and/or the stage of a female's reproductive cycle (see Chapters 5 and 6).

Under some circumstances in the wild, females may benefit from maintaining a close position to their leader male. During the 1997 trapping season at Filoha by the ANPBRP (see Chapter 3), corn was used as bait, and hamadryas males competed for and monopolized clumps of corn. Because hamadryas males, unlike anubis males, allow females to forage next to them, females that stayed closest to their leader males gained access to more corn than did females who stayed farther away from their leader males (Jolly and Phillips-Conroy, unpublished observations). A hamadryas female, therefore, may be able to benefit from a close position to her leader male by obtaining more food, at least when it is clumped in distribution (see following section for similar evidence from captivity). The presence of such a clumped and abundant food item as corn is unusual for hamadryas baboons, however, and such a circumstance in which a female would benefit ecologically from a close position to the leader male does not, from my observations, typically occur outside of the context of trapping.

Competition among Hamadryas Females in Captivity

In contrast to reports from the wild (Kummer 1968a; Sigg 1980; this study), studies from captivity have indicated that hamadryas females show linear dominance hierarchies and may compete with one another over food acquisition and/or some aspects of reproduction. Relative dominance rank in captivity, however, is often inferred from proximity to the leader male, which assumes a priori that females compete over proximity to the leader male and that females who are closer to him are therefore higher ranking. Relative dominance rank measured in this way has been correlated with various indicators of female reproductive success to infer competition among females.

Kaumanns et al. (1987) found that in a captive group of nine adult females, one adult leader male, and seven subadults and juveniles, individuals whose average distance to the leader male was lower, as well as individuals who had a higher frequency of affiliative contact with the leader male, were able to drink significantly more liquid food per amount of time, drank more often (had more drinking events), and had a better position in the drinking order than individuals whose average distance to the leader male was lower and who had a lower frequency of affiliative contact with the leader male. Females who spent more time near the leader male, consequently, had greater access to food than females who spent less time near the leader male. Similarly, Gil-Burmann & Peláez (1997) found that one-male units were more cohesive and females followed their leader males more in situations when food was clumped than when food was dispersed, suggesting that females are more likely to remain close to the male when he can provide food resources for them. Gore (1993), however, in an experimental comparison of captive hamadryas baboons and rhesus macaques, found no difference in time spent foraging between females within hamadryas OMUs. She concluded that "dominance appears to be related to greater [foraging] success in rhesus monkeys but not in hamadryas baboons" (p. 785).

Chalyan et al. (1991) found a positive correlation between female dominance rank and infant survival in captive hamadryas. A similar pattern was observed by Vervaecke et al. (1992), who suggested that females compete over proximity to the leader male to ensure protection of their infants from harassment by other group members. According to Colmenares and Gomendio (1988), females may seek interactions with the leader male to receive coalitionary support against other *females* in particular. Thus, higher-ranking hamadryas females in captivity, by achieving the most proximity to and protection from the leader male, may compete more effectively against other females, gain greater access to food resources, and raise more surviving infants than lower-ranking females.

Among captive hamadryas females at the German Primate Center, the degree of estrus synchrony within OMUs is lower during estrus cycles that result in conception than during nonconceptive cycles (Zinner et al. 1994). In this captive population, therefore, it appears that if more females are simultaneously in estrus, fewer of them will actually conceive. These results suggest that the leader's sperm supply is limited and may be monopolized by some females, to the detriment of others, when estrus is synchronized. Although Kummer (1968a) found estrus synchrony among the hamadryas population near Erer Gota, I did not observe estrus synchrony and so any disadvantage of synchrony with regard to female fertility is unlikely to be relevant for the Filoha population.

Female Competition and Hamadryas Female Reproductive Strategies

Overall, female-female competition does not appear to play a large role in patterns of social behavior among wild hamadryas. Females sometimes compete with one another over grooming access to the leader male, but they do not appear to compete over access to any other resource nor do they show evidence of dominance relationships with one another. Kummer (1992) points out that female hamadryas do not form coalitions, do not cooperate with other females against males, and recruit the male rather than other females as allies. He suggests that such behaviors can be attributed to the fact that hamadryas females are essentially dependent on their leader males because they have been socialized by leader males from an early age. Leader males, for females, thus function as "permanently restrictive mother-substitutes" and contribute greatly to a hamadryas female's lack of competitive and coalitionary relationships with other females.

CONCLUSIONS AND INTERPRETATIONS

Hamadryas Female Reproductive Strategies: Summary

Overall, a hamadryas female's main reproductive strategy may be to gain protection for herself and her offspring by associating with a leader male that is able to provide such protection. Hamadryas males are particularly interested in infants and young juveniles, especially females, probably as a consequence of their motivation to start acquiring females at an early age for their own one-male unit. This interest in a female's infants by males outside of her OMU can threaten the survival of her offspring if her leader male does not intervene to protect them, and this contribution of a female's leader male to offspring survival is probably the main function of a hamadryas leader male for his females.

Hamadryas females do not appear to be exclusively interested in their relationship with their leader male, however. Evidence from my research suggests that females are motivated to interact with non-leader males in addition to their leader males, and that at least some females have preferences for some males over others. Although the threat of aggression from leader males limits a female's ability to choose mates, females do, on rare occasions, exert their preferences. Whether these preferences are based on qualities of males that might lead to a male being more or less likely to protect a female and her offspring, or more or less likely to take over her OMU in the future, is unclear; if they are, then a female may be able to assess a male's future protective abilities and influence takeovers of OMUs accordingly. Females may mate with other males in addition to their leader in order to supplement a paternity concentration strategy with a paternity confusion strategy to garner additional protection for their offspring (cf. van Schaik et al. 1999).

Finally, competition among hamadryas females, while well-documented in captivity, appears to occur to only a minimal degree in the wild and does not appear to correlate with differential access to resources or to confer reproductive benefits to some females at the expense of others. At both Filoha and Erer Gota, competition among females is seen mainly in the context of mutual attempts to groom the leader male, which appear to occur when two or more females seek protection or reassurance from their leader male simultaneously. To the extent that it occurs, female competition therefore appears to be mainly a by-product of each individual female's motivation to seek protection and reassurance from her leader male.

The Evolution of Female Behavior in Hamadryas Baboons

Hamadryas baboon social organization probably differentiated from that of other baboons as a response to the harsh habitat of the semideserts of the Horn of Africa and the Arabian peninsula, in which the temporary fissioning of groups into smaller parties likely resulted in greater foraging efficiency (Kummer 1968a, 1968b, 1971b). These foraging parties probably consisted of small kin groups of females, and males who were more aggressive and defended these small groups of females from other males probably sired more offspring than less aggressive or less competitive males. Eventually, selection probably also favored males that were able to take over individual females from other males and use force to keep those females nearby. Gradually, a social system evolved whereby all males had an inherent tendency to herd females and keep them nearby at all times, not just when the females were estrous. Along with this ritualized herding behavior (which, although it does occur in other baboon taxa, is not nearly so universal, stereotypical, and unresponsive to changes in environment as it is in hamadryas), hamadryas males also evolved specialized morphological traits such as their thick white manes and extensive red paracallosal skin. Both of these features may have evolved via sexual selection through male-male competition (they may be useful as signals to other males, as indicators of—or substitutes for—large body size and competitive abilities) and/or female choice (females may prefer males with larger manes, cf. Jolly 1963).

Hamadryas females, on the other hand, during the evolution of hamadryas social organization, were simply required to be able to be conditioned by neckbiting to follow a male. As no specialized behavioral or morphological traits of females need have been selected for during this process, female hamadryas would have essentially remained very similar to the ancestral female baboon. As a consequence, female hamadryas baboons retain the motivation to remain in their natal groups, form affiliative relationships with other females, and interact socially and sexually with multiple males. They are, however, usually prevented from doing these things because leader males forcibly transfer females between units, splitting up female kin groups in the process, and force females to limit their social interactions to within the OMU.

An adult female hamadryas baboon at the top of the Filoha sleeping cliff. *(Photo by the author)*

Ultimately, a female hamadryas baboon probably does not fully exercise her capability for choice—or simply chooses to associate with a protective male rather than remain with her female relatives—because maintaining a strong bond with a male that can protect her and her offspring is the main factor contributing to her reproductive success. While hamadryas females probably benefit proximately from grooming relationships with other females, they do not form alliances with other females in competition over food or other resources, so, unlike in other baboons, female-female relationships do not contribute much (if at all) to a female's fitness. Likewise, relationships with multiple males, while they are pursued by some hamadryas females and may contribute in some ways to a female's reproductive success, are clearly not as important as they are to females in other baboon subspecies. As a result of the evolution of hamadryas male herding behavior and the OMU social structure, therefore, a single protective leader male is probably the main contributor to a hamadryas female's reproductive success. Relationships with non-leader males and other females, while they appear to be important to at least some females, play a secondary role to the relationship between a hamadryas female and her leader male, and it is this relationship that defines hamadryas society.

10

Summary of Findings

The results of this research have, in many respects, supported those of previous field studies of hamadryas baboons. They have also described more fully the role of female behavior in hamadryas social organization and revealed that females do appear to have interests that do not always correspond to those of their leader males. While many of the results in this book are still preliminary, they are suggestive of a greater role of female behavior in hamadryas social organization than has previously been assumed. The major conclusions drawn from this research are outlined below and, where possible, briefly compared to results from previous studies of wild hamadryas baboons (e.g., Kummer 1968a; Sigg 1980; Sigg & Stolba 1981; Sigg et al., 1982; Abegglen 1984).

The two main ecological differences between the Filoha population and most other populations of wild hamadryas, as described in Chapter 4, are the substantially larger group sizes and the frequency with which Filoha baboons eat doum palm fruit. The year-round availability of doum palm fruits and subsequent lack of significant seasonal variation in food supply may be a key factor allowing large group sizes at Filoha compared to other populations. Interestingly, daily path lengths among the Filoha baboons are no shorter than other populations despite the apparent higher abundance of perennially-available food resources, suggesting that either there are certain critical resources that the baboons cannot obtain in the Filoha area or that hamadryas ranging patterns are to some degree constrained by their phylogenetic history. Ongoing research by Getenet Hailemeskel and Amy Schreier promises to further elucidate dietary patterns, seasonality, ranging patterns, and the relationship between food distribution and social structure in the hamadryas baboons at Filoha.

The high abundance of food resources and low abundance of natural predators in the Filoha area may explain the two main differences in social structure between the Filoha population and other populations of wild hamadryas: the larger group sizes and higher population growth rate at Filoha compared to elsewhere. While the broad patterns of social structure and social organization are the same at Filoha as in other wild hamadryas, social interactions within one-male units differ. Most notably, females at Filoha showed marked variation in their patterns of proximity to and interactions with their leader male and with other females. Much of this variation was attributable to the number of females in a one-male unit, in that females in larger units spent less time in social interactions with their leader male (and more time interacting with other females; see below) than did females in smaller units. Female reproductive condition also appeared to play a role: sexually cycling females remained, on average, closer to their leader male and engaged in more grooming interactions with him than did pregnant or lactating females, and females with sexual swellings remained closer to and received more grooming from their leader male than did non-swollen females.

Four takeovers occurred while the Filoha population was under observation. Of the thirteen females involved in these takeovers, seven were taken over by other leader males, three were taken over by solitary males, two were not seen again, and one returned to her previous leader two weeks after the takeover. This distribution of females contrasts with reports of takeovers at Erer Gota, which have indicated that most females are taken over by follower males rather than other leaders. Of the four infants involved in these takeovers, all either disappeared or died shortly afterwards, and one appears to have been deliberately killed by its mother's new leader male. Moreover, of the six females that were observed on days subsequent to their takeover, five came into estrus within two weeks of the takeover or, in the case of the female who returned to her previous leader, two weeks after returning to him. Reacquisition of a female by a defeated leader male has not been previously reported for hamadryas baboons, and, in this case, may be related to the fact that the female was pregnant at the time of the takeover. It is probably advantageous for a female to return to the male who fathered her unborn infant so as to ensure his contribution to the infant's protection and survival. The events surrounding this takeover—although not the others—suggest that female choice may play a role in takeovers in hamadryas baboons.

Thirty percent of one-male units at Filoha included the consistent presence of a follower male, and most females who interacted with non-leader males did so with the follower male associated with their unit. Neither the number of females in an OMU nor the number of females in estrus, however, appeared to be related to the presence of follower males in that unit. Rather, the most consistent factors associated with the presence of a follower male in an OMU were the presence of a pregnant female or a female infant or juvenile in that unit. Follower males probably associate with units that contain (or may soon contain) young females in order to establish social relationships with both the young female and her mother, which would presumably give the follower male a greater chance of eventually incorporating the young female into his own "initial unit."

The reproductive parameters and sexual interactions of the hamadryas females at Filoha, in general, did not differ qualitatively from those reported in previous studies. One notable difference, however, was the lack of reproductive synchrony at Filoha compared to high levels of synchrony reported for both the Erer Gota population and hamadryas in captivity. Similarly, females at Filoha showed no seasonal pattern of births, whereas seasonal birth peaks were observed at Erer Gota. Low levels of synchrony and seasonality among females at Filoha may reflect more consistently available food resources at Filoha compared to a more seasonally variable availability of food resources at Erer Gota.

With regard to sexual behavior, fifteen copulations with non-leader males were observed in this study. Nine of these were with males that may have been capable of producing viable sperm and four occurred when the female involved was sexually swollen. In addition to these copulations, various other observations of interactions between females and non-leader males suggested that females preferred some males over others and that they were occasionally able to exercise those preferences.

Also consistent with previous studies of wild hamadryas, the main form of female-female competition observed at Filoha was fights over grooming access to the leader male, which appeared to be a result of each female's apparent need for protection and reassurance from him. Other than in such contexts, females at Filoha did not appear to experience agonistic competition with one another, nor did they show any evidence of dominance hierarchies.

Although previous research on wild hamadryas has described hamadryas one-male units as having a star-shaped sociogram, wherein most social interactions occur between the leader male and each female and very few interactions occur amongst the females themselves, the results of this study do not support that characterization. At Filoha, females engaged in social interactions with other females to about the same degree, on average, as they did with their leader males, and a few females spent over twice as much of their social time with other females as they did with their leader male. The number of females in an OMU was positively correlated with the tendency of its females to interact with one another rather than with their leader male. Females varied widely, however, in their frequency of social interaction with other females, and those who did spend social time with other females did so at a relatively equal frequency whether or not their leader male was available for social interaction at the time. Social relationships among hamadryas females, possibly based on kinship, thus appear to play a larger role in hamadryas social organization than was suggested by early research on wild hamadryas. Hamadryas females may therefore be more similar to females of other baboon subspecies, who have strong, kinship-based, affiliative relationships with one another, than has previously been thought.

Social relationships among hamadryas females at Filoha, if they are based on kinship, imply a greater degree of female philopatry than has previously been assumed for this subspecies. Although hamadryas baboons have traditionally been considered to be characterized by male philopatry and female dispersal, neither of these notions may actually be true. Previous field studies and genetic data suggest that both male and female hamadryas tend to stay within their natal band, though neither always does so. The differentiated female social relationships found in this study, combined with genetic data, suggest that levels of relatedness among hamadryas females are higher than has previously been thought and that pairs of hamadryas females who interact the most may do so because they are closely related.

Finally, non-leader males at Filoha often attempted to kidnap infants from their mothers and sometimes succeeded in these attempts, most likely as a direct consequence of their interest in incorporating young females into their "initial units." Once a non-leader male had obtained a female's infant, she was usually unable to retrieve it unless aided by her leader male. Observations of kidnappings by follower males and protection of infants by leader males suggest that the behavior of non-leader males toward infants has the potential to lead to injury or death and that the protection of a female's leader male is critical to infant survival. Leader males also protect the females in their units, both from harassment by other baboons and from external threats, such as predators. It thus appears that, for a female hamadryas baboon, association with a protective leader male may be the most important factor affecting her reproductive success over the long term.

Epilogue

Since finishing my PhD in May 2000, I have returned to Filoha six times, both to collect additional behavioral data and to collect samples for DNA analysis. One of the main questions I have been interested in since finishing my PhD research has been whether social relationships among hamadryas females are based on kinship. As discussed in Chapter 7, this question is critical to an understanding of the function of hamadryas female social relationships, as well as to a better understanding of patterns of dispersal, philopatry, and social organization among hamadryas as a whole. The issue of female kinship can only be addressed by collecting samples from individual females and then comparing levels of relatedness between dyads characterized by varying degrees of social interaction. While live capture and release has proven to be a successful means of sample collection in the Awash hybrid zone, it was discovered in 1997 and 2000 (when the Filoha group was trapped as part of the ANPBRP) that not only are female hamadryas extremely trap-shy (of about 70 individuals trapped at Filoha over the two seasons, only 6 were females), but trapping disrupts the hamadryas social structure in that leader males typically lose their females to other males when either the male or his female is trapped.

After the year 2000, I avoided these problems by turning to noninvasive methods of sample collection. While fecal samples would be ideal in this respect, it has unfortunately proven quite difficult to collect fecal samples from identified individuals in this population due to the large group size, the typical visibility problems, and the fact that many defecations occur while on the sleeping cliff in the mornings, rendering the samples virtually unattainable. Fortunately, as the main study group becomes more habituated, fecal sample collection from identified individuals during the baboons' daily travel route is becoming increasingly feasible. As an alternative to fecal samples, my colleagues and I have been developing and testing two other noninvasive methods. The first is the duct tape method described by Valderrama et al. (1999), in which a small piece of duct tape is placed on the end of a dart and shot at the focal animal with an air pistol or blow gun. The second is the biopsy darting method of Karesh et al. (1987) and Di Fiore (2002), in which a dart consisting of a syringe fitted with a shortened 14 or 16 gauge needle is shot at the focal animal with an air pistol, piercing the skin and bouncing off with a small plug of tissue inside. These methods appear to work well, have yielded over 40 samples so far (thanks to Dave Gaynor and Julian Saunders), and promise to work even better when the females in Group 1 become more habituated to observers.

The Filoha Hamadryas Project, as it is now known, has expanded over the past several years to encompass more than just female social behavior and reproductive strategies. In 2001, Getenet Wondimu Hailemeskel of the Ethiopian Wildlife Conservation Organization joined my research team, and is currently conducting a study of activity patterns and diet of hamadryas males. As of the writing of this book, Getenet is a PhD student at the City University of New York and plans to focus on hamadryas feeding ecology for his dissertation research. Another CUNY student, Amy Schreier, is beginning her dissertation research at Filoha on hamadryas ranging behavior, and plans to map hamadryas travel routes more systematically than I did (see Chapter 4) and investigate the influence of resource abundance and distribution on hamadryas travel patterns and social structure. Both Getenet's and Amy's projects will provide critical links between hamadryas baboon feeding ecology and their unique multilevel social organization and male-dominated society.

In 2002, Julian Saunders of the University of Natal, South Africa, joined the Filoha Hamadryas Project, and has brought to it his expertise on primate vocal communication and acoustic analysis. Julian is currently focusing on hamadryas female copulation calls and comparing them to those of chacma baboons. He plans to incorporate other hamadryas vocalizations into his research program in the future, using playback experiments to elucidate their possible function. Finally, the most recent member of my research team is Teklu Tesfaye, my field assistant since August 2002, who has proven invaluable in continuing to habituate Group 1 and collecting key behavioral observations in my absence. Through collaboration with all of these individuals and others in the future, I hope that we will continue to gain a greater understanding of the evolution of behavior, social organization, and reproductive strategies of hamadryas baboons.

Appendix I

List of Behavioral Elements Recorded for This Study

Proximity-Related Behavior

approach A moves toward B, resulting in the two animals being within a meter of one another (an approach can end with either a "leave" or a "travel."

leave A moves away from B, from a position where the two animals were within a meter of one another to a position where they are farther than a meter from one another.

move toward A moves toward B but still stays within the same proximity category.

move away from A moves away from B but still stays within the same proximity category.

follow A adjusts its position in concordance with B as B is moving, so that the two animals remain within the same distance as they were before B moved.

pass A moves from a position farther than 1 meter away from B to another position farther than 1 meter away from B, passing B so that the two are temporarily within a meter of one another; B does not move and A does not stop moving (short pass = < 1 m).

avoid A moves away from B as B is approaching A, so that upon B's arrival, A is already gone; B and A remain farther than a meter from one another during this shift.

displace A moves toward B and takes the position where B was while B moves away; there may be bodily contact during this shift, and there is at least one moment when A and B are within a meter of one another.

Affiliative Behavior

look A looks at B briefly (< three seconds), without any specific accompanying facial gestures or head movements.

gaze A looks at B continuously for longer than three seconds.

infant inspect A shows interest in B's infant (while infant is on B's belly or within an adult's arm's length of B) by looking at it from a distance of less than an arm's length and touching it or coming close to it with the hand or face.

grunt Low-frequency vocalization emitted with the mouth closed or slightly open.

lipsmack While slightly puckering the lips, A moves the lips repeatedly apart and together, making a smacking sound.

sit close A changes position so that A and B are sitting or lying in contact or within 10 cm of one another; no interactive behavior is going on.

sit close end A changes position so that A and B are no longer in contact or within 10 cm of one another.

touch A touches any part of B with one of A's body parts, usually the hand; does not include grooming or any aggressive act of A toward B.

groom A uses its fingers to look through the hair of B, moving sections of hair to the side one by one, peering at the skin and often removing bits of dirt or insects.

groom end A stops grooming B.

groom solicit A moves a part of its body near B, in a position that it would not normally be in if A were alone; or A stands up directly in front of B, usually followed by B grooming A.

carry on back A carries B on back, that is, B sits or lies on A's back while A stands, walks, or runs.

carry on back invite A presents to B with bent knees and lowered tail and hindquarters; usually followed by B climbing onto A's back.

embrace A holds B against his underside and envelops B in his arms.

possession grip A puts one or both hands on the sides of B's torso; A may also stand over B, with one arm on each side of B, while B crouches.

huddle A sits in close proximity to all members of her OMU; that is, all members are touching or at least within arm's length of another unit member and most are within a meter of all other unit members.

Sexual Behavior

present   A moves so that her perineal region is pointed directly toward B, within 1 meter of B, with her tail raised; A might also bend her forelimbs and/or slightly bend her hindlimbs.

mount   A positions its body over B from the rear, so that A's genital region is just behind B's genital region; A's forelimbs are on B's torso and A's hindlimbs may be propped on the back of B's hindlimbs.

genital inspect   A looks closely at and/or touches B's genital region, bringing the nose and/or one or more hands close to it, smelling it, and/or touching it.

hip touch   Male A places one or both hands on the hips of female B; usually followed by a present and/or a mount.

intromit   While mounting B, A inserts his penis into B's vagina.

thrust   After mounting and intromitting B, A moves his penis in and out of B's vagina.

presumed ejaculation   After mounting and intromitting B and thrusting one or more times, A pauses (i.e., stops thrusting) for 1–3 seconds before withdrawing and dismounting.

confirmed ejaculation   After A mounts B, intromits, thrusts one or more times, and withdraws, ejaculate is visible on A's penis and/or B's vagina.

Agonistic Behavior

stare threat   A sharply turns its head so that it is facing B and looks at B intensely; A may also sharply move its head toward (in the direction of) B and/or eyebrow raise.

eyebrow raise   While looking at B, A raises eyebrows.

ground slap   While looking at B, A touches the ground on the side of A nearest to B.

head bob   While looking at B, A quickly moves its head down and then back up again.

lunge   While looking at B, A moves its upper body toward B by putting its forelimbs on the ground and bending its elbows while keeping its hindlimbs in the same place; usually accompanied by a facial threat.

short running attack   A, looking at B, runs toward B for a few seconds, as if intending to attack, then stops before reaching B.

chase   A runs behind B, following B, while B is running away from A.

bite A uses mouth to grab a piece of skin or body part of B, sometimes resulting in injury to B (not including neckbite).

neckbite Characteristic behavior of hamadryas in which A (usually an adult male) bites B (usually one of his females) on the nape of the neck or the upper back; usually B is crouching while this occurs.

grab at A uses hand to swipe at B, as if attempting to grab a piece of skin or body part of B, but no contact occurs because B moves away just enough.

grab A uses hand to grasp a piece of skin or body part of B, often pulling B's skin or hair slightly away from B's body.

hit A, with its hand, makes forceful physical contact with B.

fight A complex series of back-and-forth grabs, lunges, barks, and/or bites that happen too quickly to record individually.

counter charge A, after having received aggression from B, turns and lunges and/or runs toward B.

aid A joins an agonistic encounter between two or more other individuals; the individual(s) that A is not directing its aggression toward is that whom A is aiding.

grimace A pulls its lips back and shows at least part of its front teeth; mouth may be slightly open or fully open.

keck In response to aggression or threat of aggression from B, A emits a staccato-like vocalization with an open mouth (grimace), punctuated by silences between each "keck."

scream / screech In response to aggression or threat of aggression from B, A emits a loud vocalization that sounds like the scream of a human baby or the squawk of a bird (longer than a keck).

crouch In response to aggression or threat of aggression from B, A bends legs and arms so that her body is touching or almost touching the ground; usually accompanied by kecking or screaming.

backup A moves backward, away from an aggressor, while still facing the aggressor.

flee In response to aggression or threat of aggression from B, A runs quickly away from B.

run to A runs quickly toward B and approaches B, usually in response to aggression or threat of aggression from B or from a third individual.

Non-Social Behavior

sit alone While in either a sitting or lying position, no other individual is within 10 cm and no social interaction is going on.

scan Look around in a relaxed way, not at the ground or at any individual in particular, but at the group in general, another group, or other things in the environment.

look around Look around in a somewhat agitated or intense way, changing the direction of the gaze frequently as if looking for something or somebody; usually exhibited by males and seen in the context of one of his females not being in his presumed direct line of view.

stand up Positioned such that only the hind feet are touching the ground and the rest of the body is upright; usually associated with looking around.

self-groom A grooms one of its own body parts (see groom).

sleep While in either sitting or lying position, both eyes are closed.

travel Walk or run in coordination with (same direction and speed) as the other members of the OMU: if this functions to separate two individuals that were previously within a meter of one another, neither is considered to have "left" the other one.

forage Using the hands to manipulate parts of plants, turn over rocks, or dig in the ground, followed by putting food items (parts of plants, insects, etc.) into the mouth (either with the hands or with the mouth directly against the food source).

eat Chewing and swallowing food that is already in the mouth or in the cheek pouches.

explore ground Looking, digging, and/or poking at the ground, but not putting anything into the mouth.

scratch Using the hand to scratch a part of one's own body.

bark Loud vocalization that sounds somewhat like a dog's bark; usually directed towards an external threat (e.g., predator).

References Cited

Abbott, D. H. 1984. Behavioral and Physiological Suppression of Fertility in Subordinate Marmoset Monkeys. *American Journal of Primatology 6*: 169–186.

Abbott, D. H., L. M. George, J. Barrett, J. K. Hodges, K. T. O'Byrne, J. W. Sheffield, I. A. Sutherland, G. R. Chambers, S. F. Lunn, and M-C. Ruiz de Elvira. 1990. Social Control of Ovulation in Marmoset Monkeys: A Neuroendocrine Basis for the Study of Infertility. In *Socioendocrinology of Primate Reproduction*, ed. T. E. Ziegler and F. B. Bercovitch, 135–158. New York: Wiley-Liss.

Abbott, D. H., E. B. Keverne, G. F. Moore, and U. Yodyingyuad. 1986. Social Suppression of Reproduction in Subordinate Talapoin Monkeys, *Miopithecus talapoin*. In *Primate Ontogeny, Cognition and Social Behaviour*, vol. 3, ed. J. G. Else and P. C. Lee, 329–341. Cambridge: Cambridge University Press.

Abegglen, H. and J-J. Abegglen. 1976. Field Observation of a Birth in Hamadryas Baboons. *Folia Primatologica 26*: 54–56.

Abegglen, J-J. 1984. *On Socialization in Hamadryas Baboons*. London: Associated University Presses.

Alberts, S. C., and J. Altmann. 1995a. Balancing Costs and Opportunities: Dispersal in Male Baboons. *American Naturalist 145*: 279–306.

Alberts, S. C., and J. Altmann. 1995b. Preparation and Activation: Determinants of Age at Reproductive Maturity in Male Baboons. *Behavioral Ecology and Sociobiology 36*: 397–406.

Alberts, S. C., R. M. Sapolsky, and J. Altmann. 1992. Behavioral, Endocrine, and Immunological Correlates of Immigration by an Aggressive Male into a Natural Primate Group. *Hormones and Behavior 26*: 167–178.

Al-Safadi, M. M. 1994. The Hamadryas Baboon, *Papio hamadryas* (Linnaeus, 1758) in Yemen (Mammalia: Primates: Cercopithecidae). *Zoology in the Middle East 10*: 5–16.

Altmann, J. 1974. Observational Study of Behavior: Sampling Methods. *Behaviour 49*: 227–267.

Altmann, J. 1980. *Baboon Mothers and Infants*. Cambridge, MA: Harvard University Press.

Altmann, J., S. Altmann, and G. Hausfater. 1981. Physical Maturation and Age Estimates of Yellow Baboons, *Papio cynocephalus*, in Amboseli National Park, Kenya. *American Journal of Primatology 1*: 389–399.

Altmann, J., and S. A. Altmann. 1978. Primate Infant's Effects on Mother's Future Reproduction. *Science 201*: 1028–1029.

Altmann, J., S. A. Altmann, G. Hausfater, and S. A. McCuskey. 1977. Life History of Yellow Baboons: Physical Development, Reproductive Parameters, and Infant Mortality. *Primates 18*: 315–330.

Altmann, J., G. Hausfater, and S. A. Altmann. 1988. Determinants of Reproductive Success in Savannah Baboons, *Papio cynocephalus*. In *Reproductive Success: Studies of Individual Variation in Contrasting Breeding Systems*, ed. T. H. Clutton-Brock, 403–418. Chicago: University of Chicago Press.

Altmann, S. A. 1970. The Pregnancy Sign in Savannah Baboons. *Laboratory Animal Digest 6*: 7–10.

Andelman, S. J. 1987. Evolution of Concealed Ovulation in Vervet Monkeys (*Cercopithecus aethiops*). *American Naturalist 129*: 785–799.

Anderson, C. M. 1986. Female Age: Male Preference and Reproductive Success in Primates. *International Journal of Primatology 7*: 305–326.

Anderson, C. M. 1987. Female Transfer in Baboons. *American Journal of Physical Anthropology 73*: 241–250.

Anderson, C. M. 1990. Desert, Mountain and Savanna Baboons: A Comparison with Special Reference to the Suikerbosrand Population. In *Baboons: Behaviour and Ecology. Use and Care. Selected Proceedings of the XIIth Congress of the International Primatological Society*, ed. M. Thiago de Mello, A. Whiten, and R. W. Byrne, 89–103. Brasilia, Brasil.

Anderson, J. R., and W. C. McGrew. 1984. Guinea Baboons (*Papio papio*) at a Sleeping Site. *American Journal of Primatology 6*: 1–14.

Andersson, M. 1982. Female Choice Selects for Extreme Tail Length in a Widowbird. *Nature 299*: 818–820.

Andersson, M. 1994. *Sexual Selection*. Princeton, NJ: Princeton University Press.

Angst, W., and D. Thommen. 1977. New Data and a Discussion of Infant Killing in Old World Monkeys and Apes. *Folia Primatologica 27*: 198–229.

Asanov, S. S., and A. B. Mirvis. 1972. The Breeding of Hamadryas Baboons at the Sukhumi Primate Centre. *Acta Endocrinologica Supplementum 166*: 483–489.

Bachmann, C., and H. Kummer. 1980. Male Assessment of Female Choice in Hamadryas Baboons. *Behavioral Ecology and Sociobiology 6*: 315–321.

Barrett, L., S. P. Henzi, T. Weingrill, J. E. Lycett, and R. A. Hill. 1999. Market Forces Predict Grooming Reciprocity in Female Baboons. *Proceedings of the Royal Society of London B 266*: 665–670.

Bartlett, T. Q., R. W. Sussman, and J. M. Cheverud. 1993. Infant Killing in Primates: A Review of Observed Cases with Specific Reference to the Sexual Selection Hypothesis. *American Anthropologist 95*: 958–990.

Barton, R. 1985. Grooming Site Preferences in Primates and Their Functional Implications. *International Journal of Primatology 6*: 519–532.

Barton, R. 2000. Socioecology of Baboons: The Interaction of Male and Female Strategies. In *Primate Males: Causes and Consequences of Variation in Group Composition*, ed. P. M. Kappeler, 97–107. Cambridge: Cambridge University Press.

Barton, R. A. 1993. Sociospatial Mechanisms of Feeding Competition in Female Olive Baboons, *Papio anubis. Animal Behaviour 46*: 791–802.

Barton, R. A., R. W. Byrne, and A. Whiten. 1996. Ecology, Feeding Competition and Social Structure in Baboons. *Behavioral Ecology and Sociobiology 38*: 321–329.

Barton, R. A., and A. Whiten. 1993. Feeding Competition among Female Olive Baboons, *Papio anubis. Animal Behaviour 46*: 777–789.

Beach, F. A. 1976. Sexual Attractivity, Proceptivity, and Receptivity in Female Mammals. *Hormones & Behavior 7*: 105–138.

Beehner, J. 2003. Female Behavior and Reproductive Success in a Hybrid Baboon Group *(Papio hamadryas hamadryas* x *Papio hamadryas anubis).* PhD dissertation, Washington University.

Bentley-Condit, V. K., and E. O. Smith. 1997. Female Reproductive Parameters of Tana River Yellow Baboons. *International Journal of Primatology 18*: 581–596.

Berard, J. 1991. The Influence of Mating Success on Male Dispersal in Free-Ranging Rhesus Macaques. *American Journal of Primatology 24*: 89.

Berard, J. 1999. A Four-Year Study of the Association between Male Dominance Rank, Residency Status, and Reproductive Activity in Rhesus Macaques (*Macaca mulatta*). *Primates 40*: 159–175.

Berard, J. D. 1993. Male Rank, Mating Success, and Dispersal: A Four-Year Study of Mating Patterns in Free-Ranging Rhesus Macaques. *American Journal of Primatology 30*: 298.

Bercovitch, F. B. 1987. Female Weight and Reproductive Condition in a Population of Olive Baboons (*Papio anubis*). *American Journal of Primatology 12*: 189–195.

Bercovitch, F. B. 1989. Body Size, Sperm Competition, and Determinants of Reproductive Success in Male Savanna Baboons. *Evolution 43*: 1507–1521.

Bercovitch, F. B. 1991a. Mate Selection, Consortship Formation, and Reproductive Tactics in Adult Female Savanna Baboons. *Primates 32*: 437–452.

Bercovitch, F. B. 1991b. Social Stratification, Social Strategies, and Reproductive Success in Primates. *Ethology and Sociobiology 12*: 315–333.

Bercovitch, F. B. 1992. Sperm Competition, Reproductive Tactics, and Paternity in Savanna Baboons and Rhesus Macaques. In *Paternity in Primates: Genetic Tests and Theories*, ed. R. D. Martin, A. F. Dixson, and E. J. Wickings, 225–227. Basel: Karger.

Bercovitch, F. B. 1995. Female Cooperation, Consortship Maintenance, and Male Mating Success in Savanna Baboons. *Animal Behaviour 50*: 137–149.

Bercovitch, F. B., and J. D. Berard. 1993. Life History Costs and Consequences of Rapid Reproductive Maturation in Female Rhesus Macaques. *Behavioral Ecology and Sociobiology 32*: 103–109.

Bercovitch, F. B., and R. S. O. Harding. 1993. Annual Birth Patterns of Savanna Baboons (*Papio cynocephalus anubis*) over a Ten-Year Period at Gilgil, Kenya. *Folia Primatologica 61*: 115–122.

Bercovitch, F. B., and S. C. Strum. 1993. Dominance Rank, Resource Availability, and Reproductive Maturation in Female Savanna Baboons. *Behavioral Ecology and Sociobiology 33*: 313–318.

Berenstain, L., and T. D. Wade. 1983. Intrasexual Selection and Male Mating Strategies in Baboons and Macaques. *International Journal of Primatology 4*: 201–235.

Berger, J. 1983. Induced Abortion and Social Factors in Wild Horses. *Nature 303*: 59–61.

Bergman, T. J. 1999. Mating Behavior and Success of Hybrid Male Baboons (*Papio hamadryas hamadryas x Papio hamadryas anubis*) in Ethiopia's Awash National Park. *American Journal of Primatology 49*: 34–35.

Beyene, S. 1993. Group-Fusion and Hybridization between Anubis and Hamadryas Baboons at Gola, Ethiopia. *SINET: Ethiopian Journal of Science 16*: 61–70.

Beyene, S. 1998. The Role of Female Mating Behavior in Hybridization between Anubis and Hamadryas Baboons in Awash, Ethiopia. PhD dissertation, Washington University.

Biquand, S., V. Biquand-Guyot, A. Boug, and J-P. Gautier. 1992a. The Distribution of *Papio hamadryas* in Saudi Arabia: Ecological Correlates and Human Influence. *International Journal of Primatology 13*: 223–243.

Biquand, S., V. Biquand-Guyot, A. Boug, and J-P. Gautier. 1992b. Group Composition in Wild and Commensal Hamadryas Baboons: A Comparative Study in Saudi Arabia. *International Journal of Primatology 13*: 533–543.

Biquand, S., V. Biquand-Guyot, and A. Boug. 1994a. Vasectomy of Free-Ranging *Papio hamadryas* in Saudi Arabia, Effects on Social Structure and Demography. *Congress of the International Primatological Society 15*: 251.

Biquand, S., A. Boug, V. Biquand-Guyot, and J-P. Gautier. 1994b. Management of Commensal Baboons in Saudi Arabia. *Revue d'Ecologie (La Terre et la Vie) 49*: 213–222.

Blumstein, D. T. 2000. The Evolution of Infanticide in Rodents: A Comparative Analysis. In *Infanticide by Males and Its Implications*, ed. C. P. van Shaik and C. H. Janson, 178–197. Cambridge: Cambridge University Press.

Boese, G. K. 1975. Social Behavior and Ecological Considerations of West African Baboons (*Papio papio*). In *Socioecology and Psychology of Primates*, ed. R. H. Tuttle, 205–230. The Hague: Mouton.

Boggess, J. 1984. Infant Killing and Male Reproductive Strategies in Langurs. In *Infanticide: Comparative and Evolutionary Perspectives*, ed. G. Hausfater and S. B. Hrdy, 283–310. New York: Aldine.

Boinski, S. 1987. Birth Synchrony in Squirrel Monkeys. *Behavioral Ecology and Sociobiology 21*: 393–400.

Borries, C., and A. Koenig. 2000. Infanticide in Hanuman Langurs: Social Organization, Male Migration, and Weaning Age. In *Infanticide by Males and Its Implications*, ed. C. P. van Shaik and C. H. Janson, 99–122. Cambridge: Cambridge University Press.

Borries, C., K. Launhardt, C. Epplen, J. T. Epplen, and P. Winkler. 1999. DNA Analyses Support the Hypothesis That Infanticide Is Adaptive in Langur Monkeys. *Proceedings of the Royal Society of London B 266*: 901–904.

Boug, A., S. Biquand, V. Biquand-Guyot, and K. Kamal. 1994a. Home Range and Daily March of Commensal *Papio hamadryas* in the Alhada Mountain of Saudi Arabia. *Congress of the International Primatological Society 15*: 148.

Boug, A., S. Biquand, V. Biquand-Guyot, and K. Kamal. 1994b. The Response of Commensal Hamadryas Baboons to Seasonal Reduction in Food Provisioning. *Revue d'Ecologie (La Terre et la Vie) 49*: 307–319.

Brereton, A. R. 1992. Alternative Reproductive Tactics in Stumptail Macaques *(Macaca arctoides)*. *Folia Primatologica 59*: 208–212.

Brereton, A. R. 1995. Coercion-Defence Hypothesis: The Evolution of Primate Sociality. *Folia Primatologica 64*: 207–214.

Brett, F. L., C. J. Jolly, W. Socha, and A. S. Wiener. 1977. Human-Like ABO Blood Groups in Wild Ethiopian Baboons. *Yearbook of Physical Anthropology 20*: 276–289.

Brett, F. L., T. R. Turner, C. J. Jolly, and R. G. Cauble. 1982. Trapping Baboons and Vervet Monkeys from Wild, Free-Ranging Populations. *Journal of Wildlife Management 46*: 164–174.

Brooks, R. J. 1984. Causes and Consequences on Infanticide in Populations of Rodents. In *Infanticide: Comparative and Evolutionary Perspectives*, ed. G. Hausfater and S. B. Hrdy, 331–348. New York: Aldine.

Buchan, J. C., Alberts, S. C., Silk, J.B., & Altmann, J. 2003. True Paternal Care in a Multi-Male Primate Society. *Nature 425: 179-181.*

Butynski, T. M. 1982. Harem-Male Replacement and Infanticide in the Blue Monkey (*Cercopithecus mitus stuhlmanni*) in the Kibale Forest, Uganda. *American Journal of Primatology 3*: 1–22.

Byrne, R. 1981. Distance Vocalisations of Guinea Baboons (*Papio papio*) in Senegal: An Analysis of Function. *Behaviour 78*: 283–313.

Byrne, R. W., A. Whiten, and S. P. Henzi. 1989. Social Relationships of Mountain Baboons: Leadership and Affiliation in a Non-Female-Bonded Monkey. *American Journal of Primatology 18*: 191–207.

Caljan, V. G., N. V. Meisvili, and M. A. Vancatova. 1987. Sexual Behaviour of Hamadryas Baboons. *Anthropologie 25*: 183–187.

Chalyan, V. G., B. A. Lapin, and N. V. Meishvili. 1994a. Kinship and Troop Structure Formation in Baboons in Gumista Reserve. *Congress of the International Primatological Society 15*: 238.

Chalyan, V. G., B. A. Lapin, N. V. Meishvili, and M. A. Vancatova. 1994b. Reproductive Aspects of Free-Ranging Groups of Hamadryas Baboons. In *Current Primatology: Volume III: Behavioural Neuroscience, Physiology and Reproduction*, ed. J. J. Roeder, B. Thierry, J. R. Anderson, and N. Herrenschmidt, 237–244. Strasbourg: Université Louis Pasteur Press.

Chalyan, V. G., and N. V. Meishvili. 1990. Infanticide in Hamadryas Baboons. *Biologischeskie Nauki 3*: 99–106.

Chalyan, V. G., N. V. Meishvili, and R. Dathe. 1991. Dominance Rank and Reproduction in Female Hamadryas Baboons. *Primate Report 29*: 35–40.

Chism, J., D. K. Olson, and T. E. Rowell. 1983. Diurnal Births and Perinatal Behavior among Wild Patas Monkeys; Evidence of an Adaptive Pattern. *International Journal of Primatology* 4: 167–184.

Clarke, M. R. 1983. Infant-Killing and Infant Disappearance Following Male Takeovers in a Group of Free-Ranging Howling Monkeys (*Allouatta palliata*) in Costa Rica. *American Journal of Primatology* 5: 241–247.

Clarke, M. R., and K. E. Glander. 1984. Female Reproductive Success in a Group of Free-Ranging Howling Monkeys (*Alouatta palliata*) in Costa Rica. In *Female Primates: Studies by Women Primatologists*, ed. M. F. Small, 111–126. New York: Liss.

Clutton-Brock, T. H. 1984. Size, Sexual Dimorphism, and Polygyny in Primates. In *Size and Scaling in Primate Biology*, ed. W. L. Jungers, 51–60. New York: Plenum.

Clutton-Brock, T. H., and G. A. Parker. 1995. Sexual Coercion in Animal Societies. *Animal Behaviour 49*: 1345–1365.

Coelho, A. M., Jr., S. A. Turner, and C. A. Bramblett. 1983. Allogrooming and Social Status: An Assessment of the Contributions of Female Behavior to the Social Organization of Hamadryas Baboons (*Papio hamadryas*). *Primates 24*: 184–197.

Collins, D. A., C. D. Busse, and J. Goodall. 1984. Infanticide in Two Populations of Savanna Baboons. In *Infanticide: Comparative and Evolutionary Perspectives*, G. Hausfater and S. B. Hrdy, 193–215. New York: Aldine.

Colmenares, F. 1990. Greeting Behaviour in Male Baboons, I: Communication, Reciprocity and Symmetry. *Behaviour 113*: 81–116.

Colmenares, F. 1992. Social Relationships between Adult Males and Females in a Multiharem Colony of Baboons: The Currency of Their Reciprocity. *Congress of the International Primatological Society 14*: 159–160.

Colmenares, F. 1997. Grooming for Protection in Baboons: Two Tests of the Hypothesis. *Advances in Ethology 32*: 269.

Colmenares, F., and M. Gomendio. 1988. Changes in Female Reproductive Condition Following Male Take-Overs in a Colony of Hamadryas and Hybrid Baboons. *Folia Primatologica 50*: 157–174.

Colmenares, F., M. G. Lozano, and P. Torres. 1994. Harem Social Structure in a Multiharem Colony of Baboons (*Papio* spp.): A Test of the Hypothesis of the "Star-Shaped" Sociogram. In *Current Primatology, Volume II: Social Development, Learning & Behavior*, ed. J. J. Roeder, 93–101. Strasbourg: Université Louis Pasteur.

Conaway, C. H., and C. B. Koford. 1964. Estrous Cycles and Mating Behavior in a Free-Ranging Band of Rhesus Monkeys. *Journal of Mammalogy* 45: 577–588.

Cords, M. 1984. Mating Patterns and Social Structure in Redtail Monkeys (*Cercopithecus ascanius*). *Zeitschrift für Tierpsychologie 64*: 313–329.

Cords, M. 1987. Forest Guenons and Patas Monkeys: Male-Male Competition in One-Male Groups. In *Primate Societies*, ed. B. B. Smuts, D. L. Cheney, R. M. Seyfarth, R. W. Wrangham, and T. T. Struhsaker, 98–111. Chicago: University of Chicago Press.

Cords, M. 1988. Mating Systems of Forest Guenons: A Preliminary Review. In *A Primate Radiation: Evolutionary Biology of the African Guenons*, ed. A. Gautier-Hion, F. Bourliere, J-P. Gautier, and J-P. Kingdon, 323–339. Cambridge: Cambridge University Press.

Cords, M. 1993. On Operationally Defining Reconciliation. *American Journal of Primatology 29*:255–267.

Cords, M. 1997. Friendships, Alliances, Reciprocity, and Repair. In *Machiavellian Intelligence II: Extensions and Evaluations*, ed. A. Whiten, and R. W. Byrne, 24–49. Cambridge: Cambridge University Press.

Cords, M., B. J. Mitchell, H. M. Tsingalia, and T. E. Rowell. 1986. Promiscuous Mating among Blue Monkeys in the Kakamega Forest, Kenya. *Ethology 72*: 214–226.

Cords, M. & Thurnheer, S. 1993. Reconciling with Valuable Partners by Long-Tailed Macaques. *Ethology 93*: 315–325.

Cox, C. R., and B. J. Le Boeuf. 1977. Female Incitation of Male Competition: A Mechanism in Sexual Selection. *American Naturalist 111*: 317–335.

Crockett, C. M. 1984. Emigration by Female Red Howler Monkeys and the Case for Female Competition. In *Female Primates: Studies by Women Primatologists*, ed. M. F. Small, 159–173. New York: Liss.

Crockett, C. M., and C. H. Janson. 2000. Infanticide in Red Howlers: Female Group Size, Male Membership, and a Possible Link to Folivory. In *Infanticide by Males and Its Implications*, ed. C. P. van Shaik and C. H. Janson, 75–98. Cambridge: Cambridge University Press.

Crockett, C. M., and R. Sekulic. 1984. Infanticide in Red Howler Monkeys. In *Infanticide: Comparative and Evolutionary Perspectives*, ed. G. Hausfater and S. B. Hrdy, 173–191. New York: Aldine.

Darwin, C. R. 1871. *The Descent of Man and Selection in Relation to Sex*. London: John Murray.

de Waal, F. 1982. *Chimpanzee Politics: Power and Sex Among Apes*. New York: Harper & Row.

Disotell, T. R. 2000. Molecular Systematics of the Cercopithecidae. In *Old World Monkeys*, ed. P. F. Whitehead and C. J. Jolly, 29–56. Cambridge: Cambridge University Press.

Di Fiore, A. 2002. Molecular Perspectives on Dispersal in Lowland Woolly Monkeys (*Lagothrix lagotricha poeppigii*). *American Journal of Physical Anthropology Supplement 34.*

Dixson, A. F. 1992. Observations on Postpartum Changes in Hormones and Sexual Behavior in Callitrichid Primates: Do Females Exhibit Postpartum "Estrus"? In *Topics in Primatology, Vol. 2: Behavior, Ecology, and Conservation*, ed. N. Itoigawa, Y. Sugiyama, G. P. Hacket, and R. K. R. Thompson, 141–149. Tokyo: University of Tokyo Press.

Dixson, A. F. 1993. Sexual Selection, Sperm Competition and the Evolution of Sperm Length. *Folia Primatologica 61*: 221–227.

Dixson, A. F. 1998. *Primate Sexuality: Comparative Studies of the Prosimians, Monkeys, Apes, and Human Beings.* Oxford: Oxford University Press.

Dolhinow, P. 1999. Understanding Behavior: A Langur Monkey Case Study. In *The Nonhuman Primates*, ed. P. Dolhinow and A. Fuentes, 189–195. Mountain View, CA: Mayfield.

Domb, L. G., and M. Pagel. 2001. Sexual Swellings Advertise Female Quality in Wild Baboons. *Nature 410*: 204–206.

Drickamer, L. C., and S. H. Vessey. 1973. Group Changing in Free-Ranging Male Rhesus Monkeys. *Primates 14*: 359–368.

Dunbar, R. I. M. 1980. Determinants and Evolutionary Consequences of Dominance Among Female Gelada Baboons. *Behavioral Ecology and Sociobiology 7*: 253–265.

Dunbar, R. I. M. 1983. Relationships and Social Structure in Gelada and Hamadryas Baboons. In *Primate Social Relationships: An Integrated Approach*, ed. R. A. Hinde, 299–307. Sunderland, MA: Sinauer Associates.

Dunbar, R. I. M. 1984a. Infant-Use by Male Gelada in Agonistic Contexts: Agonistic Buffering, Progeny Protection or Soliciting Support? *Primates 25*: 28–35.

Dunbar, R. I. M. 1984b. *Reproductive Decisions.* Princeton, NJ: Princeton University Press.

Dunbar, R. I. M. 1988. *Primate Social Systems.* Ithaca, NY: Cornell University Press.

Dunbar, R. I. M., and E. P. Dunbar. 1977. Dominance and Reproductive Success among Female Gelada Baboons. *Nature 266*: 351–352.

Dunbar, R. I. M., and M. F. Nathan. 1972. Social Organization of the Guinea Baboon, *Papio papio. Folia Primatologica 17*: 321–334.

Dunbar, R. I. M., and M. Sharman. 1984. Is Social Grooming Altruistic? *Zeitschrift für Tierpsychologie 64*: 163–173.

Emlen, S. T., and L. W. Oring. 1977. Ecology, Sexual Selection, and the Evolution of Mating Systems. *Science 197*: 215–223.

Epple, G., and Y. Katz. 1980. Social Influences on First Reproductive Success and Related Behaviors in the Saddle-Back Tamarin. *International Journal of Primatology 1*: 171–183.

Epple, G., and Y. Katz. 1984. Social Influences on Estrogen Excretion and Ovarian Cyclicity in Saddle Back Tamarins (*Saguinus fuscicollis*). *American Journal of Primatology 6*: 215–227.

Fairbanks, L. A., and M. T. McGuire. 1984. Determinants of Fecundity and Reproductive Success in Captive Vervet Monkeys. *American Journal of Primatology 7*: 27–38.

Fairgrieve, C. 1995. Infanticide and Infant Eating in the Blue Monkey (*Cercopithecus mitis stuhlmanni*) in the Budongo Forest Reserve, Uganda. *Folia Primatologica 64*: 69–72.

Fedigan, L. M. 1982. *Primate Paradigms: Sex Roles and Social Bonds*. Chicago: University of Chicago Press.

Fedigan, L. M. 1983. Dominance and Reproductive Success in Primates. *Yearbook of Physical Anthropology 26*: 91–129.

Fossey, D. 1984. Infanticide in Mountain Gorillas (*Gorilla gorilla beringei*); With Comparative Notes on Chimpanzees. In *Infanticide: Comparative and Evolutionary Perspectives*, ed. G. Hausfater and S. B. Hrdy, 217–235. New York: Aldine.

Galdikas, B. M. F. 1985a. Adult Male Sociality and Reproductive Tactics among Orangutans at Tanjung Puting. *Folia Primatologica 45*: 9–24.

Galdikas, B. M. F. 1985b. Subadult Male Orangutan Sociality and Reproductive Behavior at Tanjung Puting. *American Journal of Primatology 8*: 87–99.

Gauthier, C-A. 1999. Reproductive Parameters and Paracallosal Skin Color Changes in Captive Female Guinea Baboons, *Papio papio*. *American Journal of Primatology 47*: 67–74.

Germond, P., and J. Livet. 2001. *An Egyptian Bestiary: Animals in Life and Religion in the Land of the Pharaohs*. London: Thames & Hudson.

Getachew, K. N. 2001. *Among the Pastoral Afar in Ethiopia: Tradition, Continuity, and Socio-Economic Change*. Utrecht: International Books.

Gil-Burmann C., and F. Peláez. 1997. Spatial Cohesion of Baboon OMUs in Captivity: "Interest" of Females to Follow as a Function of the Competitive Ability of Males. *Primate Report Special Issue 48–2*: 19–20.

Glander, K. E. 1980. Reproduction and Population Growth in Free-Ranging Mantled Howling Monkeys. *American Journal of Physical Anthropology 53*: 25–36.

Glander, K. E. 1992. Dispersal Patterns in Costa Rican Mantled Howling Monkeys. *International Journal of Primatology 13*: 415–436.

Glick, B. B. 1980. Ontogenetic and Psychobiological Aspects of the Mating Activities of Male *Macaca radiata*. In *The Macaques: Studies in Ecology, Behavior and Evolution*, ed. D. G. Lindburg, 345–369. New York: van Nostrand Reinhold.

Goldberg, T. L., and R. W. Wrangham. 1997. Genetic Correlates of Social Behaviour in Wild Chimpanzees: Evidence from Mitochondrial DNA. *Animal Behaviour 54*: 559–570.

Gomendio, M., and F. Colmenares. 1989. Infant Killing and Infant Adoption Following the Introduction of New Males to an All-Female Colony of Baboons. *Ethology 80*: 223–244.

Goodall, J. 1977. Infant Killing and Cannibalism in Free-Living Chimpanzees. *Folia Primatologica 28*: 259–282.

Goodall, J. 1986. *The Chimpanzees of Gombe: Patterns of Behavior*. Cambridge: Belknap Press of Harvard Univ.

Gore, M. A. 1991. A Comparative Study of the Relationships and Behaviours in a Female and a Non-Female Bonded Social System. In *Primatology Today: Proceedings of the XIIIth Congress of the International Primatological Society (Nagoya & Kyoto 1990)*, ed. A. Ehara, T. Kimura, O. Takenaka, and M. Iwamoto, 189–192. Amsterdam: Elsevier.

Gore, M. A. 1993. Effects of Food Distribution on Foraging Competition in Rhesus Monkeys, *Macaca mulatta*, and Hamadryas Baboons, *Papio hamadryas*. *Animal Behaviour 45*: 773–786.

Gore, M. A. 1994. Dyadic and Triadic Aggression and Assertiveness in Adult Female Rhesus Monkeys, *Macaca mulatta*, and Hamadryas Baboons, *Papio hamadryas*. *Animal Behaviour 48*: 385–392.

Gouzoules, S., and H. Gouzoules. 1987. Kinship. In *Primate Societies*, ed. B. B. Smuts, D. L. Cheney, R. M. Seyfarth, R. W. Wrangham, and T. T. Struhsaker, 299–305. Chicago: University of Chicago Press.

Groves, C. P. 1993. Order Primates. In *Mammal Species of the World: A Taxonomic and Geographic Reference*, ed. D. E. Wilson and D. M. Reeder, 243–277. Washington, DC: Smithsonian Institution Press.

Gygax, L. 1995. Hiding Behaviour of Liontailed Macaques (*Macaca fascicularis*). I. Theoretical Background and Data on Mating. *Ethology 101*: 10–24.

Haig, D., and C. T. Bergstrom. 1995. Multiple Mating, Sperm Competition and Meiotic Drive. *Journal of Evolutionary Biology 8*: 265–282.

Halliday, T. R. 1983. The Study of Mate Choice, IN *Mate Choice* (ed. by P. Bateson), pp. 3–32. Cambridge: Cambridge University Press.

Hamilton, W. J., III, and J. Bulger. 1992. Facultative Expression of Behavioral Differences Between One-Male and Multimale Savanna Baboon Groups. *American Journal of Primatology 28*: 61–71.

Hapke, A., D. Zinner, and H. Zischler. 2001. Mitochondrial DNA Variation in Eritrean Hamadryas Baboons (*Papio hamadryas hamadryas*): Life History Influences Population Genetic Structure. *Behavioral Ecology and Sociobiology 50*: 483–492.

Harcourt, A. H. 1978. Strategies of Emigration and Transfer by Primates, with Particular Reference to Gorillas. *Zeitschrift für Tierpsychologie 48*: 401–420.

Harcourt, A. H. 1987. Dominance and Fertility among Female Primates. *Journal of Zoology, London 213*: 471–487.

Harcourt, A. H., P. H. Harvey, S. G. Larson, and R. V. Short. 1981. Testis Weight, Body Weight, and Breeding System in Primates. *Nature 293*: 55–57.

Harding, R. S. O. 1975. Meat-Eating and Hunting in Baboons. In *Socioecology and Psychology of Primates*, ed. R. H. Tuttle, 245–257. The Hague: Mouton.

Hausfater, G. 1975. Estrous Females: Their Effects on the Social Organization of the Baboon Group. *Proceedings from the Symposia of the Fifth Congress of the International Primatological Society (Nagoya, Japan, August 1974)*: 117–127.

Hausfater, G. 1984. Infanticide in Langurs: Strategies, Counterstrategies, and Parameter Values. In *Infanticide: Comparative and Evolutionary Perspectives*, ed. G. Hausfater and S. B. Hrdy, 257–281. New York: Aldine.

Hausfater, G., and S. B. Hrdy. 1984. *Infanticide: Comparative and Evolutionary Perspectives*. New York: Aldine.

Hayes, V. J., L. Freedman, and C. E. Oxnard. 1990. The Taxonomy of Savannah Baboons: An Odontomorphometric Analysis. *American Journal of Primatology 22*: 171–190.

Heape, W. 1900. The "Sexual Season" on Mammals and the Relation of the "Pro-estrum" to Menstruation. *Quarterly Journal of Microscopical Science 44*: 1–70.

Hearn, J. P. 1978. The Endocrinology of Reproduction in the Common Marmoset. In *The Biology and Conservation of the Callitrichidae*, ed. D. G. Kleiman, 163–171. Washington, DC: Smithsonian Institution Press.

Heisler, L., M. B. Andersson, S. J. Arnold, C. R. Boake, G. Borgia, G. Hausfater, M. Kirkpatrick, R. Lande, J. Maynard Smith, P. O'Donald, A. R. Thornhill, and F. J. Weissing. 1987. The Evolution of Mating Preferences and Sexually Selected Traits: Group Report. In *Sexual Selection: Testing the Alternatives*, ed. J. W. Bradbury and M. B. Andersson, 96–118. New York: John Wiley.

Hendrickx, A. G., and D. C. Kraemer. 1969. Observations on the Menstrual Cycle, Optimal Mating Time and Pre-Implantation Embryos of the Baboon, *Papio anubis* and *Papio cynocephalus*. *Journal of Reproduction and Fertility*: 119–128.

Henzi, S. P., and L. Barrett. 1999. The Value of Grooming to Female Primates. *Primates 40*: 47–59.

Henzi, S. P., J. E. Lycett, A. Weingrill, and S. E. Piper. 2000. Social Bonds and the Coherence of Mountain Baboon Troops. *Behaviour 137*: 663–680.

Henzi, S. P., J. E. Lycett, and T. Weingrill. 1997. Cohort Size and the Allocation of Social Effort by Female Mountain Baboons. *Animal Behaviour 54*: 1235–1243.

Hill, R. A. 1999. Size-Dependent Tortoise Predation by Baboons at De Hoop Nature Reserve, South Africa. *South African Journal of Science 95*: 123–124.

Hill, W. C. O. 1967. Taxonomy of the Baboon. In *The Baboon in Medical Research, Volume 2*, ed. H. Vagtborg, 4–11. Austin: University of Texas Press.

Hiraiwa, M. 1981. Maternal and Alloparental Care in a Troop of Free-Ranging Japanese Monkeys. *Primates 22*: 309–329.

Hogg, J. T. 1984. Mating in Bighorn Sheep: Multiple Creative Male Strategies. *Science 225*: 526–529.

Hrdy, S. B. 1974. Male-Male Competition and Infanticide among the Langurs (*Presbytis entellus*) of Abu, Rajasthan. *Folia Primatologica 22*: 19–58.

Hrdy, S. B. 1977. *The Langurs of Abu: Female and Male Strategies of Reproduction*. Cambridge, MA: Harvard University Press.

Hrdy, S. B. 1979. Infanticide Among Animals: A Review, Classification, and Examination of the Implications for the Reproductive Strategies of Females. *Ethology and Sociobiology 1*: 13–40.

Hrdy, S. B. 1981. *The Woman That Never Evolved*. Cambridge, MA: Harvard University Press.

Hrdy, S. B. 1984. Assumptions and Evidence Regarding the Sexual Selection Hypothesis: A Reply to Boggess. In *Infanticide: Comparative and Evolutionary Perspectives*, ed. G. Hausfater and S. B. Hrdy, 315–319. New York: Aldine.

Hrdy, S. B. 1986. Sources of Variance in the Reproductive Success of Female Primates. *Problemi Attuali de Scienza e di Cultura 259*: 191–203.

Hrdy, S. B., C. Janson, and C. van Schaik. 1995. Infanticide: Let's Not Throw Out the Baby with the Bathwater. *Evolutionary Anthropology 3*: 151–154.

Huck, U. W. 1984. Infanticide and the Evolution of Pregnancy Block in Rodents. In *Infanticide: Comparative and Evolutionary Perspectives*, ed. G. Hausfater and S. B. Hrdy, 349–365. New York: Aldine.

Huffman, M. A. 1987. Consort Intrusion and Female Mate Choice in Japanese Macaques. *Ethology 75*: 221–234.

Huffman, M. A. 1992. Influences of Female Partner Preference on Potential Reproductive Outcome in Japanese Macaques. *Folia Primatologica 59*: 77–88.

Hutchins, M., and D. P. Barash. 1976. Grooming in Primates: Implications for Its Utilitarian Function. *Primates 17*: 145–150.

Imanishi, K. 1957. Social Behaviour in Japanese Monkeys, *Macaca fuscata. Psychologia: An International Journal of Psychology in the Orient 1*: 47–54.

Ions, V. 1982. *Egyptian Mythology*. New York: Peter Bedrick Books.

Isbell, L. A. 1991. Contest and Scramble Competition: Patterns of Female Aggression and Ranging Behavior among Primates. *Behavioral Ecology 2*: 143–155.

Izard, M. K. 1990. Social Influences on the Reproductive Success and Reproductive Endocrinology of Prosimian Primates. In *Socioendocrinology of Primate Reproduction*, ed. T. E. Ziegler and F. B. Bercovitch, 159–186. New York: Wiley-Liss.

Janson, C. H. 1984. Female Choice and Mating System of the Brown Capuchin Monkey *Cebus apella* (Primates: Cebidae). *Zeitschrift für Tierpsychologie 65*: 177–200.

Jolly, A., S. Caless, S. Cavigelli, L. Gould, M. E. Pereira, A. Pitts, R. E. Pride, H. D. Rabenandrasana, J. D. Walker, and T. Zafison. 2000. Infant Killing, Wounding and Predation in *Eulemur* and *Lemur. International Journal of Primatology 21*: 21–40.

Jolly, C. J. 1963. A Suggested Case of Evolution by Sexual Selection in Primates. *Man 222*: 177–178.

Jolly, C. J. 1993. Species, Subspecies, and Baboon Systematics. In *Species, Species Concepts, and Primate Evolution*, ed. W. H. Kimbel and L. B. Martin, 67–107. New York: Plenum.

Jolly, C. J., and F. L. Brett. 1973. Genetic Markers and Baboon Biology. *Journal of Medical Primatology 2*: 85–99.

Jolly, C. J., and J. E. Phillips-Conroy. 1998. Taxon-Specific Reactions to Trapping among Ethiopian Baboons. *American Journal of Physical Anthropology Supplement 26*: 129.

Jolly, C. J., and J. E. Phillips-Conroy. 1999. Towards a Proximate Model of Baboon Speciation. *American Journal of Primatology 49*: 66–67.

Jolly, C. J., and J. E. Phillips-Conroy. 2003. Testicular Size, Mating System, and Maturation Schedules in Wild Anubis and Hamadryas Baboons. *International Journal of Primatology 24*: 125–142.

Kamal, K. B., A. M. Ghandour, and P. F. Brain. 1994. Studies on New Geographical Distribution of Hamadryas Baboons *Papio hamadryas* in the Wester Region of Saudi Arabia. *Journal of the Egyptian Veterinary Medical Association 54*: 81–89.

Karesh, W. B., F. Smith, and H. Frazier-Taylor. 1987. A Remote Method for Obtaining Skin Biopsy Samples. *Conservation Biology 1*: 261–262.

Kaumanns, W., T. Olfenbüttel, V. Pudel, G. Schwibbe, M. Schwibbe, and A. Wolf. 1987. Determinants of Feeding Behaviour of Hamadryas Baboons (*Papio hamadryas*) in Captivity. *Primate Report 17*: 33–43.

Kaumanns, W., B. Rohrhuber, and D. Zinner. 1989. Reproductive Parameters in a Newly Established Colony of Hamadryas Baboons *(Papio hamadryas)*. *Primate Report 24*: 25–33.

Keddy, A. C. 1986. Female Mate Choice in Vervet Monkeys *(Cercopithecus aethiops sabaeus)*. *American Journal of Primatology 10*: 125–134.

Keller, L., and H. K. Reeve. 1995. Why Do Females Mate with Multiple Males? The Sexually Selected Sperm Hypothesis. *Advances in the Study of Behavior 24*: 291–315.

Keverne, E. B. 1979. Sexual and Aggressive Behavior in Social Groups of Talapoin Monkeys. In *Sex, Hormones, and Behavior: Ciba Foundation Symposium 62 (new series)*, 271–286. New York: Elsevier.

Keverne, E. B., N. D. Martensz, and B. Tuite. 1989. Beta-Endorphin Concentrations in Cerebrospinal Fluid of Monkeys are Influenced by Grooming Relationships. *Psychoneuroendocrinology 14*: 155–161.

Kingdon, J. 1974. *East African Mammals: An Atlas of Evolution in Africa*. Chicago: University of Chicago Pres.

Kirkpatrick, M. 1987. Sexual Selection by Female Choice in Polygynous Animals. *Annual Review of Ecology and Systematics 18*: 43–70.

Knowlton, N. 1979. Reproductive Synchrony, Parental Investment, and the Evolutionary Dynamics of Sexual Selection. *Animal Behaviour 27*: 1022–1033.

Kuester, J., A. Paul, and J. Arnemann. 1994. Kinship, Familiarity and Mating Avoidance in Barbary Macaques. *Animal Behaviour 48*: 1183–1194.

Kummer, H. 1967. Tripartite Relations in Hamadryas Baboons. In *Social Communication among Primates*, ed. S. A. Altmann, 63–71. Chicago: University of Chicago Press.

Kummer, H. 1968a. *Social Organization of Hamadryas Baboons: A Field Study*. Chicago: University of Chicago Press.

Kummer, H. 1968b. Two Variations in the Social Organization of Baboons. In *Primates: Studies in Adaptation and Variability*, ed. P. C. Jay, 293–312. New York: Holt, Rinehart Winston, Inc.,

Kummer, H. 1971a. Immediate Causes of Primate Social Structures. In *Proceedings of the 3rd International Congress in Primatology, Zurich 1970*, vol 3, 1–11.

Kummer, H. 1971b. *Primate Societies: Group Techniques of Ecological Adaptation*. Chicago: Aldine.

Kummer, H. 1990. The Social System of Hamadryas Baboons and Its Presumable Evolution. In *Baboons: Behaviour and Ecology. Use and Care. Selected Proceedings of the XIIth Congress of the International Primatological Society*, ed. M. Thiagode Mello, A. Whiten, and R. W. Byrne, 43–60. Brasilia, Brasil.

Kummer, H. 1992. Potential Causes and Effects of the Dependency Syndrome of Female Hamadryas Baboons. *Congress of the International Primatological Society* 14: 246.

Kummer, H. 1995. *In Quest of the Sacred Baboon*. Princeton, NJ: Princeton University Press.

Kummer, H., J. J. Abegglen, C. Bachmann, J. Falett, and H. Sigg. 1978. Grooming Relationship and Object Competition among Hamadryas Baboons. In *Recent Advances in Primatology, Volume One: Behaviour*, ed. D. J. Chivers and J. Herbert, 31–38. New York: Academic Press.

Kummer, H., A. A. Banaja, A. N. Abo-Khatwa, and A. M. Ghandour. 1981. Mammals of Saudi Arabia: Primates: A Survey of Hamadryas Baboons in Saudi Arabia. *Fauna of Saudi Arabia* 3: 441–471.

Kummer, H., A. A. Banaja, A. N. Abo-Khatwa, and A. M. Ghandour. 1985. Differences in Social Behavior between Ethiopian and Arabian Hamadryas Baboons. *Folia Primatologica* 45: 1–8.

Kummer, H., W. Goetz, and W. Angst. 1970. Cross-Species Modifications of Social Behavior in Baboons. In *Old World Monkeys: Evolution, Systematics, and Behavior*, ed. J. R. Napier and P. H. Napier, 351–363. New York: Academic Press.

Kummer, H., W. Götz, and W. Angst. 1974. Triadic Differentiation: An Inhibitory Process Protecting Pair Bonds in Baboons. *Behaviour 49*: 62–87.

Kummer, H., and F. Kurt. 1963. Social Units of a Free-Living Population of Hamadryas Baboons. *Folia Primatologica 1*: 4–19.

Kummer, H., and F. Kurt. 1965. A Comparison of Social Behavior in Captive and Wild Hamadryas Baboons. In *The Baboon in Medical Research: Proceedings of the First International Symposium on the Baboon and Its Use as an Experimental Animal*, ed. H. Vagtborg, 65–80. Austin: University of Texas Press.

Labov, J. B. 1981. Pregnancy Blocking in Rodents: Adaptive Advantages for Females. *American Naturalist 118*: 361–371.

Lackman-Ancrenaz, I. 1994. Effects of Commensalism on Population Structure and Behaviour in a Troop of Hamadryas Baboons in Saudi Arabia. *Congress of the International Primatological Society 15*: 81.

Le Boeuf, B. J., and S. L. Mesnick. 1991. Sexual Behavior of Male Northern Elephant Seals: I. Lethal Injuries to Adult Females. *Behaviour 116*: 143–162.

Lee, P. C. 1996. The Meanings of Weaning: Growth, Lactation, and Life History. *Evolutionary Anthropology 5*: 87–96.

Leinfelder, I., H. de Vries, R. Deleu, and M. Nelissen. 2001. Rank and Grooming Reciprocity among Females in a Mixed-Sex Group of Captive Hamadryas Baboons. *American Journal of Primatology 55*: 25–42.

Leland, L., T. T. Struhsaker, and T. M. Butynski. 1984. Infanticide by Adult Males in Three Primate Species of Kibale Forest, Uganda: A Test of Hypotheses. In *Infanticide: Comparative and Evolutionary Perspectives*, ed. G. Hausfater and S. B. Hrdy, 151–172. New York: Aldine.

Lindburg, D. G. 1969. Rhesus Monkeys: Mating Season Mobility of Adult Males. *Science 166*: 1176–1178.

Lindburg, D. G. 1983. Mating Behavior and Estrus in the Indian Rhesus Monkey. In *Perspectives in Primate Biology*, ed. P. K. Seth, 45–61. New Delhi: Today & Tomorrow's Printers and Publishers.

Lindburg, D. G. 1987. Seasonality of Reproduction in Primates. In *Comparative Primate Biology, Volume 2B: Behavior, Cognition, and Motivation*, vol. 2B. ed. G. Mitchell and J. Erwin, 167–218. New York: Liss.

Linn, G. S., D. Mase, D. LaFrancois, R. T. O'Keeffe, and K. Lifshitz. 1991. Social Behavior of Group-Housed *Cebus apella* over the Menstrual Cycle. *American Journal of Primatology 24*: 116.

Maestripieri, D. 1994a. Infant Abuse Associated with Psychosocial Stress in a Group-Living Pigtail Macaque (*Macaca nemestrina*) Mother. *American Journal of Primatology 32*: 41–49.

Maestripieri, D. 1994b. Influence of Infants on Female Social Relationships in Monkeys. *Folia Primatologica 63*: 192–202.

Manson, J. H. 1991. Female Mate Choice in Cayo Santiago Rhesus Macaques. PhD dissertation, University of Michigan.

Manson, J. H. 1993. Rhesus Macaques Don't Choose Their Friends as Mates. *American Journal of Primatology 30*: 332.

Manson, J. H. 1994. Male Aggression: A Cost of Female Mate Choice in Cayo Santiago Rhesus Macaques. *Animal Behaviour 48*: 473–475.

Manson, J. H. 1995a. Do Female Rhesus Macaques Choose Novel Males? *American Journal of Primatology 37*: 285–296.

Manson, J. H. 1995b. Female Mate Choice in Primates. *Evolutionary Anthropology 3*: 192–195.

Manson, J. H., S. Perry, and A. R. Parish. 1997. Nonconceptive Sexual Behavior in Bonobos and Capuchins. *International Journal of Primatology 18*: 767–786.

Manson, J. H., and S. E. Perry. 1993. Inbreeding Avoidance in Rhesus Macaques: Whose Choice? *American Journal of Physical Anthropology 90*: 335–344.

McCann, C. M. 1995. Social Factors Affecting Reproductive Success in Female Gelada Baboons (*Theropithecus gelada*). PhD dissertation, City University of New York.

McNeilly, A. S., P. W. Howie, and A. Glasier. 1988. Lactation and the Return of Ovulation. In *Natural Human Fertility: Social and Biological Determinants*, ed. P. Diggory, M. Potts, and S. Teper, 102–117. London: Macmillan.

Melnick, D. J., and M. C. Pearl. 1987. Cercopithecines in Multimale Groups: Genetic Diversity and Population Structure. In *Primate Societies*, ed. B. B. Smuts, D. L. Cheney, R. M. Seyfarth, R. W. Wrangham, and T. T. Struhsaker, 121–134. Chicago: University of Chicago Press.

Mesnick, S. L., and B. J. Le Boeuf. 1991. Sexual Behavior of Male Northern Elephant Seals: II. Female Response to Potentially Injurious Encounters. *Behaviour 117*: 262–280.

Miller, P. S., and P. W. Hedrick. 1993. Inbreeding and Fitness in Captive Populations: Lessons From *Drosophila*. *Zoo Biology 12*: 333–351.

Missakian, E. A. 1973. Genealogical Mating Activity in Free-Ranging Groups of Rhesus Monkeys (*Macaca mulatta*) on Cayo Santiago. *Behaviour 45*: 224–241.

Mitani, J. C. 1985. Mating Behaviour of Male Orangutans in the Kutai Game Reserve, Indonesia. *Animal Behaviour 33*: 392–402.

Møller, A. P. 1988. Female Choice Selects for Male Sexual Tail Ornaments in the Monogamous Swallow. *Nature 332*: 640–642.

Moore, J. 1984. Female Transfer in Primates. *International Journal of Primatology 5*: 537–589.

Moore, J. 1993. Inbreeding and Outbreeding in Primates: What's Wrong with "The Dispersing Sex"? In *The Natural History of Inbreeding and Outbreeding*, ed. N. W. Thornhill, 392–426. Chicago: University of Chicago Press.

Moore, J., and R. Ali. 1984. Are Dispersal and Inbreeding Avoidance Related? *Animal Behaviour 32*: 94–112.

Mori, U. 1979a. Individual Relationships Within a Unit. In *Ecological and Sociological Studies of Gelada Baboons*, vol. 16, ed. M. Kawai, 93–124. Basel: Karger.

Mori, U. 1979b. Reproductive Behaviour. In *Ecological and Sociological Studies of Gelada Baboons*, vol. 16, ed. M. Kawai, 183–197. Basel: Karger.

Mori, U., and R. I. M. Dunbar. 1985. Changes in the Reproductive Condition of Female Gelada Baboons Following the Takeover of One-Male Units. *Zeitschrift für Tierpsychologie 67*: 215–224.

Morin, P. A. 1993. Reproductive Strategies in Chimpanzees. *Yearbook of Physical Anthropology 36*: 179–212.

Müller, H. U. 1980. Variations of Social Behavior in a Baboon Hybrid Zone. PhD dissertation, University of Zurich.

Nadler, R. D. 1988. Sexual Aggression in the Great Apes. In *Human Sexual Aggression: Current Perspectives*, ed. R. A. Prentky and V. L. Quinsey, 154–162. New York: New York Academy of Science.

Nadler, R. D., and L. C. Miller. 1982. Influence of Male Aggression on Mating of Gorillas in the Laboratory. *Folia Primatologica 38*: 233–239.

Nagel, U. 1971. Social Organization in a Baboon Hybrid Zone. In *Proceedings of the Third International Congress of Primatology*, vol. 3, 48–57. Zurich: Karger.

Nagel, U. 1973. A Comparison of Anubis Baboons, Hamadryas Baboons and Their Hybrids at a Species Border in Ethiopia. *Folia Primatologica 19*: 104–165.

Nakatsuru, K., and D. L. Kramer. 1982. Is Sperm Cheap? Limited Male Fertility and Female Choice in the Lemon Tetra (Pisces, Characidae). *Science 216*: 753–755.

Napier, J. R., and P. H. Napier. 1967. *A Handbook of Living Primates*. London: Academic Press.

Napier, J. R., and P. H. Napier. 1985. *The Natural History of the Primates*. Cambridge, MA: MIT Press.

Newton, P. N. 1986. Infanticide in an Undisturbed Forest Population of Hanuman Langurs (*Presbytis entellus*). *Animal Behaviour 34*: 785–789.

Newton, P. N., and R. I. M. Dunbar. 1994. Colobine Monkey Society. In *Colobine Monkeys: Their Ecology, Behaviour, and Evolution*, ed. A. G. Davies and J. F. Oates, 311–346. Cambridge: Cambridge University Press

Nystrom, P. D. A. 1992. Mating Success of Hamadryas, Anubis and Hybrid Male Baboons in a "Mixed" Social Group in the Awash National Park, Ethiopia. PhD dissertation, Washington University.

O'Connell, S. M., and G. Cowlishaw. 1994. Infanticide Avoidance, Sperm Competition, and Mate Choice: The Function of Copulation Calls in Female Baboons. *Animal Behaviour 48*: 687–694.

O'Donald, P. 1983. Sexual Selection by Female Choice. In *Mate Choice*, ed. P. Bateson, 53–66. Cambridge: Cambridge University Press.

Oda, R., and N. Masataka. 1992. Functional Significance of Female Japanese Macaque Copulatory Calls. *Folia Primatologica 58*: 146–149.

Olson, D. K. 1985. The Importance of Female Choice in the Mating System of Wild Patas Monkeys. *American Journal of Physical Anthropology 66*: 211.

Onderdonk, D. 2000. Infanticide of a Newborn Black-and-White Colobus Monkey in Kibale National Park, Uganda. *Primates 41*: 209–212.

Packer, C. 1979. Inter-Troop Transfer and Inbreeding Avoidance in *Papio anubis. Animal Behaviour 27*: 1–36.

Packer, C. 1985. Dispersal and Inbreeding Avoidance. *Animal Behaviour 33*: 676–678.

Packer, C., and A. E. Pusey. 1983. Adaptations of Female Lions to Infanticide by Incoming Males. *The American Naturalist 121*: 716–728.

Packer, C., and A. E. Pusey. 1984. Infanticide in Carnivores. In *Infanticide: Comparative and Evolutionary Perspectives*, ed. G. Hausfater and S. B. Hrdy, 31–42. New York: Aldine.

Palombit, R. A. 1994. Extra-Pair Copulations in a Monogamous Ape. *Animal Behaviour 47*: 721–723.

Palombit, R. A. 1999. Infanticide and the Evolution of Pair Bonds in Nonhuman Primates. *Evolutionary Anthropology 7*: 117–129.

Palombit, R. A., D. L. Cheney, J. Fischer, S. Johnson, D. Rendall, R. M. Seyfarth, and J. B. Silk. 2000. Male Infanticide and Defense of Infants in Chacma Baboons. In *Infanticide by Males and Its Implications*, ed. C. P. van Schaik and C. H. Janson, 123–152. Cambridge: Cambridge University Press.

Palombit, R. A., R. M. Seyfarth, and D. L. Cheney. 1997. The Adaptive Value of "Friendships" to Female Baboons: Experimental and Observational Evidence. *Animal Behaviour 54*: 599–614.

Paul, A., and J. Kuester. 1985. Intergroup Transfer and Incest Avoidance in Semifree-Ranging Barbary Macaques (*Macaca sylvanus*) at Salem (FRG). *American Journal of Primatology 8*: 317–322.

Pereira, M. E. 1983. Abortion Following the Immigration of an Adult Male Baboon (*Papio cynocephalus*). *American Journal of Primatology 4*: 93–98.

Pereira, M. E., and M. L. Weiss. 1991. Female Mate Choice, Male Migration, and the Threat of Infanticide in Ringtailed Lemurs. *Behavioral Ecology and Sociobiology 28*: 141–152.

Peters, R., and L. D. Mech. 1975. Behavioral and Intellectual Adaptations of Selected Mammalian Predators to the Problem of Hunting Large Animals. In *Socioecology and Psychology of Primates*, ed. R. H. Tuttle, 279–300. The Hague: Mouton.

Petrie, M., and T. R. Halliday. 1994. Experimental and Natural Changes in the Peacock's (*Pavo cristatus*) Train Can Affect Mating Success. *Behavioral Ecology and Sociobiology 35*: 213–217.

Pfeiffer, G., W. Kaumanns, and M. Schwibbe. 1985. A Female "Defeated Leader" in Hamadryas Baboons. A Case Study. *Primate Report 12*: 18–26.

Phillips-Conroy, J. E., T. Bergman, and C. J. Jolly. 2000. Quantitative Assessment of Occlusal Wear and Age Estimation in Ethiopian and Tanzanian Baboons. In *Old World Monkeys*, ed. P. F. Whitehead and C. J. Jolly, 321–340. Cambridge: Cambridge University Press.

Phillips-Conroy, J. E., C. F. Hildebolt, J. Altmann, C. J. Jolly, and P. Muruthi. 1993. Periodontal Health in Free-Ranging Baboons of Ethiopia and Kenya. *American Journal of Physical Anthropology 90*: 359–371.

Phillips-Conroy, J. E., and C. J. Jolly. 1981. Sexual Dimorphism in Two Subspecies of Ethiopian Baboons (*Papio hamadryas*) and Their Hybrids. *American Journal of Physical Anthropology 56*: 115–129.

Phillips-Conroy, J. E., and C. J. Jolly. 1986. Changes in the Structure of the Baboon Hybrid Zone in the Awash National Park, Ethiopia. *American Journal of Physical Anthropology 71*: 337–350.

Phillips-Conroy, J. E., and C. J. Jolly. 1988. Dental Eruption Schedules of Wild and Captive Baboons. *American Journal of Primatology 15*: 17–29.

Philips-Conroy, J. & Jolly, C. J. 2004. Male Dispersal and Philopatry in the Awash Baboon Hybrid Zone, *Primate Report 68*:27–52.

Phillips-Conroy, J. E., C. J. Jolly, and F. L. Brett. 1991. Characteristics of Hamadryas-Like Male Baboons Living in Anubis Troops in the Awash Hybrid Zone, Ethiopia. *American Journal of Physical Anthropology 86*: 353–368.

Phillips-Conroy, J. E., C. J. Jolly, and P. Nystrom. 1986. Palmar Dermatoglyphics as a Means of Identifying Individuals in a Baboon Population. *International Journal of Primatology 7*: 435–447.

Phillips-Conroy, J. E., C. J. Jolly, P. Nystrom, and H. A. Hemmalin. 1992. Migration of Male Hamadryas Baboons into Anubis Groups in the Awash National Park, Ethiopia. *International Journal of Primatology 13*: 455–476.

Plavcan, J. M., and C. P. van Schaik. 1992. Intrasexual Competition and Canine Dimorphism in Anthropoid Primates. *American Journal of Physical Anthropology 87*: 461–477.

Popp, J. L. 1983. Ecological Determinism in the Life Histories of Baboons. *Primates 24*: 198–210.

Price, E. C. 1990. Infant Carrying as a Courtship Strategy of Breeding Male Cotton-Top Tamarins. *Animal Behaviour 40*: 784–786.

Pusey, A. E. 1980. Inbreeding Avoidance in Chimpanzees. *Animal Behaviour 28*: 543–552.

Pusey, A. E., and C. Packer. 1987. Dispersal and Philopatry. In *Primate Societies*, ed. B. B. Smuts, D. L. Cheney, R. M. Seyfarth, R. W. Wrangham, and T. T. Struhsaker, 250–266. Chicago: University of Chicago Press.

Ralls, K., and J. Ballou. 1982. Effects of Inbreeding on Infant Mortality in Captive Primates. *International Journal of Primatology 3*: 491–505.

Ralls, K., P. H. Harvey, and A. M. Lyles. 1986. Inbreeding in Natural Populations of Birds and Mammals. In *Conservation Biology*, ed. M. E. Soulé, 35–56. Sunderland, MA: Sinauer Associates.

Rasoloharijaona, S., B. Rakotosamimanana, and E. Zimmermann. 2000. Infanticide by a Male Milne-Edwards' Sportive Lemur (*Lepilemur edwardsi*) in Ampijoroa, NW-Madagascar. *International Journal of Primatology 21*: 41–45.

Reichard, U. 1995. Extra-Pair Copulations in a Monogamous Gibbon (*Hylobates lar*). *Ethology 100*: 99–112.

Richard, A. F. 1985. Social Boundaries in a Malagasy Prosimian, the Sifaka (*Propithecus verreauxi*). *International Journal of Primatology 6*: 553–568.

Rijksen, H. D. 1981. Infant Killing: A Possible Consequence of a Disputed Leader Role. *Behaviour 78*: 138–168.

Robbins, M. M. 1995. A Demographic Analysis of Male Life History and Social Structure of Mountain Gorillas. *Behaviour 132*: 21–47.

Robinson, J. G. 1982. Intrasexual Competition and Mate Choice in Primates. *American Journal of Primatology Supplement 1*: 131–144.

Rowell, T. E. 1966. Forest Living Baboons in Uganda. *Journal of Zoology, London 149*: 344–364.

Rowell, T. E. 1988. Beyond the One-Male Group. *Behaviour 104*: 189–201.

Rudran, R. 1973. Adult Male Replacement in One-Male Troops of Purple-Faced Langurs (*Presbytis senex senex*) and its Effect on Population Structure. *Folia Primatologica 19*: 166–192

Sade, D. S. 1968. Inhibition of Son-Mother Mating among Free-Ranging Rhesus Monkeys. *Science & Psychoanalysis 12*: 18–38.

Samuels, A., J. B. Silk, and P. S. Rodman. 1984. Changes in the Dominance Rank and Reproductive Behaviour of Male Bonnet Macaques *(Macaca radiata). Animal Behaviour 32*: 994–1003.

Sapolsky, R. M. 1983. Endocrine Aspects of Social Instability in the Olive Baboon (*Papio anubis*). *American Journal of Primatology 5*: 365–379.

Sapolsky, R. M. 1996. Why Should an Aged Male Baboon Ever Transfer Troops? *American Journal of Primatology 30*: 149–157.

Saunders, C. D. 1988. Ecological, Social and Evolutionary Aspects of Baboon (*Papio cynocephalus*) Grooming Behavior. PhD dissertation, Cornell University.

Schino, G., S. Scucchi, D. Maestripieri, and P. G. Turillazzi. 1988. Allogrooming as a Tension-Reduction Mechanism: A Behavioral Approach. *American Journal of Primatology 16*: 43–50.

Schwibbe, M., D. Zinner, and H. Klensang. 1992. Factors and Effects of the Synchronisation of the Reproductive Cycle of Hamadryas Baboons (*Papio hamadryas*). *Congress of the International Primatological Society 14*: 315.

Searcy, W. A. 1982. The Evolutionary Effects of Mate Selection. *Annual Review of Ecology and Systematics 13*: 57–85.

Sekulic, R. 1982. Behavior and Ranging Patterns of a Solitary Female Red Howler (*Alouatta seniculus*). *Folia Primatologica 38*: 217–232.

Sekulic, R. 1983. Male Relationships and Infant Deaths in Red Howler Monkeys (*Alouatta seniculus*). *Zeitschrift für Tierpsychologie 61*: 185–202.

Seyfarth, R. M. 1976. Social Relationships among Adult Female Baboons. *Animal Behaviour 24*: 917–938.

Seyfarth, R. M. 1977. A Model of Social Grooming among Adult Female Monkeys. *Journal of Theoretical Biology 65*: 671–698.

Seyfarth, R. M. 1978. Social Relationships among Adult Male and Female Baboons. II. Behaviour Throughout the Female Reproductive Cycle. *Behaviour 64*: 227–247.

Seyfarth, R. M., and D. L. Cheney. 1984. Grooming, Alliances and Reciprocal Altruism in Vervet Monkeys. *Nature 308*: 541–543.

Shaikh, A. A., C. L. Celaya, I. Gomez, and S. A. Shaikh. 1982. Temporal Relationship of Hormonal Peaks to Ovulation and Sex Skin Deturgescence in the Baboon. *Primates 23*: 444–452.

Shields, W. M. 1982. *Philopatry, Inbreeding, and the Evolution of Sex*. Albany: State University of New York Press.

Shopland, J. M. 1982. An Intergroup Encounter with Fatal Consequences in Yellow Baboons (*Papio cynocephalus*). *American Journal of Primatology* 3: 263–266.

Short, R. V. 1979. Sexual Selection and Its Component Parts, Somatic and Genital Selection, as Illustrated by Man and the Great Apes. In *Advances in the Study of Behavior*, vol. 9, 131–158. New York: Academic Press.

Sicotte, P. 1993. Inter-Group Encounters and Female Transfer in Mountain Gorillas: Influence of Group Composition on Male Behavior. *American Journal of Primatology 30*: 21–36.

Siegel, S., and N. J. Castellan. 1988. *Nonparametric Statistics for the Behavioral Sciences*, 2nd ed. New York: McGraw-Hill.

Sigg, H. 1980. Differentiation of Female Positions in Hamadryas One-Male-Units. *Zeitschrift für Tierpsychologie 53*: 265–302.

Sigg, H. 1986. Ranging Patterns in Hamadryas Baboons: Evidence for a Mental Map. In *Primate Ontogeny, Cognition and Social Behaviour*, vol. 3, ed. J. G. Else and P. C. Lee, 87–91. Cambridge: Cambridge University Press.

Sigg, H., and J. Falett. 1985. Experiments on Respect of Possession and Property in Hamadryas Baboons (*Papio hamadryas*). *Animal Behaviour 33*: 978–984.

Sigg, H., and A. Stolba. 1981. Home Range and Daily March in a Hamadryas Baboon Troop. *Folia Primatologica 36*: 40–75.

Sigg, H., A. Stolba, J-J. Abegglen, and V. Dasser. 1982. Life History of Hamadryas Baboons: Physical Development, Infant Mortality, Reproductive Parameters and Family Relationships. *Primates 23*: 473–487.

Silk, J. B. 1980. Kidnapping and Female Competition among Captive Bonnet Macaques. *Primates 21*: 100–110.

Silk, J. B., Alberts, S. C., & Altmann, J. 2003. Social Bonds of Female Baboons Enhance Infant Survival. *Science 302*: 1231–1234.

Silk, J. B., C. B. Clark-Wheatley, P. S. Rodman, and A. Samuels. 1981. Differential Reproductive Success and Facultative Adjustment of Sex Ratios among Captive Female Bonnet Macaques. *Animal Behaviour 29*: 1106–1120.

Silk, J. B., A. Samuels, and P. S. Rodman. 1980. Rank, Reproductive Success, and Skewed Sex Ratio in *Macaca radiata*. *American Journal of Physical Anthropology 52*: 279.

Silk, J. B., R. M. Seyfarth, and D. L. Cheney. 1999. The Structure of Social Relationships Among Female Savanna Baboons in Moremi Reserve, Botswana. *Behaviour 136*: 679–703.

Small, M. F. 1981. Body Fat, Rank, and Nutritional Status in a Captive Group of Rhesus Macaques. *International Journal of Primatology 2*: 91–96.

Small, M. F. 1983. Females without Infants: Mating Strategies in Two Species of Captive Macaques. *Folia Primatologica 40*: 125–133.

Small, M. F. 1984. *Female Primates: Studies by Women Primatologists*. New York: Liss.

Small, M. F. 1988. Female Primate Sexual Behavior and Conception: Are There Really Sperm to Spare? *Current Anthropology 29*: 81–100.

Small, M. F. 1989. Female Choice in Nonhuman Primates. *Yearbook of Physical Anthropology 32*: 103–127.

Small, M. F. 1990. Promiscuity in Barbary Macaques (*Macaca sylvanus*). *American Journal of Primatology 20*: 267–282.

Small, M. F. 1993. *Female Choices: Sexual Behavior of Female Primates*. Ithaca, NY: Cornell University Press.

Smith, D. G. 1986. Incidence and Consequences of Inbreeding in Three Captive Groups of Rhesus Macaques. In *Primates: The Road to Self-Sustaining Populations*, ed. K. Benirschke, 857–874. New York: Springer-Verlag.

Smuts, B., and N. Nicolson. 1989. Reproduction in Wild Female Olive Baboons. *American Journal of Primatology 19*: 229–246.

Smuts, B. B. 1985. *Sex and Friendship in Baboons*. New York: Aldine.

Smuts, B. B., D. L. Cheney, R. M. Seyfarth, R. W. Wrangham, and T. T. Struhsaker. 1987. *Primate Societies*. Chicago: University of Chicago Press.

Smuts, B. B., and R. W. Smuts. 1993. Male Aggression and Sexual Coercion of Females in Nonhuman Primates and Other Mammals: Evidence and Theoretical Implications. *Advances in the Study of Behavior 22*: 1–63.

Soltis, J. 2002. Do Primate Females Gain Nonrocreative Benefits by Mating With Multiple Males? Theoretical and Empirical Considerations. *Evolutionary Anthropology 11*: 185–197.

Sommer, V. 1989a. Infant Mistreatment in Langur Monkeys—Sociobiology Tackled from the Wrong End? In *The Sociobiology of Sexual and Reproductive Strategies*, ed. A. E. Rasa, C. Vogel, and E. Voland, 110–127. New York: Chapman & Hall.

Sommer, V. 1989b. Sexual Harassment in Langur Monkeys (*Presbytis entellus*): Competition for Ova, Sperm, and Nurture? *Ethology 80*: 205–217.

Sommer, V. 1994. Infanticide among the Langurs of Jodhpur: Testing the Sexual Selection Hypothesis with A Long-Term Record. In *Infanticide and Parental Care*, ed. S. Parmigiani and F. S. vom Saal, 155–187. New York: Harwood Academic.

Sommer, V., A. Srivastava, and C. Borries. 1992. Contest for Conception in Hanuman Langur Harems. *Congress of the International Primatological Society 14*: 266.

Sprague, D. S. 1991. Mating by Nontroop Males among the Japanese Macaques of Yakushima Island. *Folia Primatologica 57*: 156–158.

Stammbach, E. 1978. On Social Differentiation in Groups of Captive Female Hamadryas Baboons. *Behaviour 67*: 322–338.

Stammbach, E. 1987. Desert, Forest and Montane Baboons: Multilevel-Societies. In *Primate Societies*, ed. B. B. Smuts, D. L. Cheney, R. M. Seyfarth, R. W. Wrangham, and T. T. Struhsaker, 112–120. Chicago: University of Chicago Press.

Stammbach, E., and H. Kummer. 1982. Individual Contributions to a Dyadic Interaction: An Analysis of Baboon Grooming. *Animal Behaviour 30*: 964–971.

Steenbeek, R. 2000. Infanticide by Males and Female Choice in Wild Thomas's Langurs. In *Infanticide by Males and Its Implications*, ed. C. P. van Schaik and C. H. Janson, 153–177. Cambridge: Cambridge University Press.

Steenbeek, R., R. C. Piek, M. van Buul, JARAM van Hooff. 1999. Vigilance in Wild Thomas's Langurs (*Presbytis thomasi*): The Importance of Infanticide Risk. *Behavioral Ecology and Sociobiology 45*: 137–150.

Sterck, E. H. M. 1997. Determinants of Female Dispersal in Thomas Langurs. *American Journal of Primatology 42*: 179–198.

Sterck, E. H. M., D. P. Watts, and C. P. van Schaik. 1997. The Evolution of Female Social Relationships in Nonhuman Primates. *Behavioral Ecology and Sociobiology 41*: 291–309.

Stewart, K. J., and A. H. Harcourt. 1987. Gorillas: Variation in Female Relationships. In *Primate Societies*, ed. B. B. Smuts, D. L. Cheney, R. M. Seyfarth, R. W. Wrangham, and T. T. Struhsater, 155–164. Chicago: University of Chicago Press.

Stolba, A. 1979. Entscheidungsfindung in Verbänden von *Papio hamadryas*. PhD dissertation, University of Zurich.

Strier, K. B. 1999a. The Atelines. In *The Nonhuman Primates*, ed. P. Dolhinov and A. Fuentes, 109–114. Mountain View, CA: Mayfield Publishing Company.

Strier, K. B. 1999b. Why is Female Kin Bonding so Rare? Comparative Sociality of Neotropical Primates. In *Comparative Primate Socioecology*, ed. P. C. Lee, 300–319. Cambridge: Cambridge University Press.

Struhsaker, T. T. 1975. *The Red Colobus Monkey*. Chicago: University of Chicago Press.

Struhsaker, T. T., and L. Leland. 1987. Colobines: Infanticide by Adult Males. In *Primate Societies*, ed. B. B. Smuts, D. L. Cheney, R. M. Seyfarth, R. W. Wrangham, and T. T. Struhsaker, 83–97. Chicago: University of Chicago Press.

Strum, S. C. 1981. Processes and Products of Change: Baboon Predatory Behavior at Gilgil, Kenya. In *Omnivorous Primates: Gathering and Hunting in Human Evolution*, ed. R. S. O. Harding and G. Teleki, 255–302. New York: Columbia University Press.

Strum, S. C., and W. Mitchell. 1987. Baboon Models and Muddles. In *The Evolution of Human Behavior: Primate Models*, ed. W. G. Kinzey, 87–104. Albany: State University of New York Press.

Strum, S. C., and J. D. Western. 1982. Variations in Fecundity with Age and Environment in Olive Baboons (*Papio anubis*). *American Journal of Primatology 3*: 61–76.

Sugawara, K. 1979. Sociological Study of a Wild Group of Hybrid Baboons Between *Papio anubis* and *P. hamadryas* in the Awash Valley, Ethiopia. *Primates 20*: 21–56.

Sugawara, K. 1982. Sociological Comparison between Two Wild Groups of Anubis-Hamadryas Hybrid Baboons. *African Study Monographs 2*: 73–131.

Sugawara, K. 1988. Ethological Study of the Social Behavior of Hybrid Baboons Between *Papio anubis* and *P. hamadryas* in Free-Ranging Groups. *Primates 29*: 429–448.

Sussman, R. W., J. M. Cheverud, and T. Q. Bartlett. 1995. Infant Killing as an Evolutionary Strategy: Reality or Myth? *Evolutionary Anthropology 3*: 149–151.

Swedell, L. 2000. Two Takeovers in Wild Hamadryas Baboons. *Folia Primatologica 71*: 169–172.

Swedell, L., and T. Tesfaye. 2003. Infant Mortality After Takeovers in Wild Ethiopian Hamadryas Baboons. *American Journal of Primatology 60*: 113–118.

Szalay, F. S., and E. Delson. 1979. *Evolutionary History of the Primates*. New York: Academic Press.

Taub, D. M. 1980. Female Choice and Mating Strategies among Wild Barbary Macaques (*Macaca sylvanus* L.). In *The Macaques: Studies in Ecology,*

Behavior and Evolution, ed. D. G. Lindburg, 287–344. New York: van Nostrand Reinhold.

Terry, R. L. 1970. Primate Grooming as a Tension Reduction Mechanism. *Journal of Psychology 76*: 129–136.

Thorington, R. W., Jr., and C. P. Groves. 1970. An Annotated Classification of the Cercopithecoidea. In *Old World Monkeys: Evolution, Systematics, and Behavior,* ed. J. R. Napier and P. H. Napier, 629–647. New York: Academic Press.

Treves, A. 1998. Primate Social Systems: Conspecific Threat and Coercion-Defense Hypotheses. *Folia Primatologica 69*: 81–88.

Trivers, R. L. 1972. Parental Investment and Sexual Selection. In *Sexual Selection and the Descent of Man,* ed. B. Campbell, 136–179. Chicago: Aldine.

Tutin, C. E. G. 1979. Mating Patterns and Reproductive Strategies in a Community of Wild Chimpanzees (*Pan troglodytes schweinfurthii*). *Behavioral Ecology and Sociobiology 6*: 29–38.

Valderrama, X., W. B. Karesh, D. E. Wildman, and D. J. Melnick. 1999. Noninvasive Methods for Collecting Fresh Hair Tissue. *Molecular Ecology 8*: 1749–1750.

Valderrama, X., S. Srikosamatara, and J. G. Robinson. 1990. Infanticide in Wedge-Capped Capuchin Monkeys, *Cebus olivaceus. Folia Primatologica 54*: 171–176.

van Schaik, C. P. 1989. The Ecology of Social Relationships amongst Female Primates. In *Comparative Socioecology: The Behavioural Ecology of Humans and Other Mammals,* Special Publication Number 8 of the British Ecological Society, ed. V. Standen and R. A. Foley, 195–218. Oxford: Blackwell Scientific Publications.

van Schaik, C. P. 2000a. Infanticide by Male Primates: The Sexual Selection Hypothesis Revisited. In *Infanticide by Males and Its Implications,* ed. C. P. van Schaik and C. H. Janson, 27–60. Cambridge: Cambridge University Press.

van Schaik, C. P. 2000b. Vulnerability to Infanticide by Males: Patterns among Mammals. In *Infanticide by Males and Its Implications,* ed. van Schaik and C. H. Janson, 61–71. Cambridge: Cambridge University Press.

van Schaik, C. P., and R. I. M. Dunbar. 1990. The Evolution of Monogamy in Large Primates: A New Hypothesis and Some Crucial Tests. *Behaviour 115*: 30–62.

van Schaik, C. P., J. K. Hodges, and C. L. Nunn. 2000. Paternity Confusion and the Ovarian Cycles of Female Primates. In *Infanticide by Males and Its*

Implications, ed. C. P. van Schaik and C. H. Janson, 361–387. Cambridge: Cambridge University Press.

van Schaik, C. P., and C. H. Janson. 2000. *Infanticide by Males and Its Implications*. Cambridge: Cambridge University Press.

van Schaik, C. P., and A. Paul. 1996. Male Care in Primates: Does It Ever Reflect Paternity? *Evolutionary Anthropology 5*: 152–156.

van Schaik, C. P., M. A. van Noordwijk, and C. L. Nunn. 1999. Sex and Social Evolution in Primates. In *Comparative Primate Socioecology*, ed. P. C. Lee, 204–231. Cambridge: Cambridge University Press.

Verrell, P. A. 1992. Primate Penile Morphologies and Social Systems: Further Evidence for an Association. *Folia Primatologica 59*: 114–120.

Vervaecke, H., R. Dunbar, L. van Elsacker, and R. Verheyen. 1992. Interactions with and Spatial Proximity to the Males in Relation to Rank of Captive Female Adult Hamadryas Baboons (*Papio hamadryas*). *Acta Zoologica et Pathologica Antverpiensia 82*: 61–77.

Vogel, C., and H. Loch. 1984. Reproductive Parameters, Adult-Male Replacements, and Infanticide among Free-Ranging Langurs (*Presbytis entellus*) at Jodhpur (Rajasthan), India. In *Infanticide: Comparative and Evolutionary Perspectives*, ed. G. Hausfater and S. B. Hrdy, 237–255. New York: Aldine.

Wallen, K. 1990. Desire and Ability: Hormones and the Regulation of Female Sexual Behavior. *Neuroscience & Biobehavioral Reviews 14*: 233–241.

Wallen, K., and L. A. Winston. 1984. Social Complexity and Hormonal Influences on Sexual Behavior in Rhesus Monkeys *(Macaca mulatta)*. *Physiology & Behavior 32*: 629–637.

Wallis, J. 1982. Sexual Behavior of Captive Chimpanzees (*Pan troglodytes*): Pregnant versus Cycling Females. *American Journal of Primatology 3*: 77–88.

Walters, J. 1981. Inferring Kinship from Behaviour: Maternity Determinations in Yellow Baboons. *Animal Behaviour 29*: 126–136.

Walters, J. R. 1987. Transition to Adulthood. In *Primate Societies*, ed. B. B. Smuts, D. L. Cheney, R. M. Seyfarth, R. W. Wrangham, and T. T. Struhsaker, 358–369. Chicago: University of Chicago Press.

Wasser, S. K. 1983a. Reproductive Competition and Cooperation Among Female Yellow Baboons. In *Social Behavior of Female Vertebrates*, ed. S. K. Wasser, 349–390. New York: Academic Press.

Wasser, S. K. 1983b. *Social Behavior of Female Vertebrates*. New York: Academic Press.

Watts, D. P. 1989. Infanticide in Mountain Gorillas: New Cases and a Reconsideration of the Evidence. *Ethology 81*: 1–18.

Watts, D. P. 1990. Ecology of Gorillas and Its Relation to Female Transfer in Mountain Gorillas. *International Journal of Primatology 11*: 21–45.

Watts, D. P. 1994a. Agonistic Relationships Between Female Mountain Gorillas (*Gorilla gorilla beringei*). *Behavioral Ecology and Sociobiology 34*: 347–358.

Watts, D. P. 1994b. Social Relationships of Immigrant and Resident Female Mountain Gorillas, II: Relatedness, Residence, and Relationships between Females. *American Journal of Primatology 32*: 13–30.

Watts, D. P. 1996. Comparative Socio-Ecology of Gorillas. In *Great Ape Societies*, ed. W. C. McGrew, I. F. Marchant, and T. Nishida, 16–28. Cambridge: Cambridge University Press.

Weingrill, T. 2000. Infanticide and the Value of Male-Female Relationships in Mountain Chacma Baboons. *Behaviour 137*: 337–359.

White, F. J. 1996. Comparative Socio-Ecology of *Pan paniscus*. In *Great Ape Societies*, ed. W. C. McGrew, I. F. Marchant, and T. Nishida, 29–41. Cambridge: Cambridge University Press.

Whitten, P. L. 1982. Do Female Primates Compete? *International Journal of Primatology 3*: 347.

Whitten, P. L. 1983a. Diet and Dominance Among Female Vervet Monkeys (*Cercopithecus aethiops*). *American Journal of Primatology 5*: 139–159.

Whitten, P. L. 1983b. Flowers, Fertility and Females. *American Journal of Physical Anthropology 60*: 269–270.

Whitten, P. L. 1984. Competition among Female Vervet Monkeys. In *Female Primates: Studies by Women Primatologists*, ed. M. F. Small, 127–140. New York: Liss.

Williams-Blangero, S., J. L. Vanderberg, J. Blangero, L. Konigsberg, and B. Dyke. 1990. Genetic Differentiation between Baboon Subspecies: Relevance for Biomedical Research. *American Journal of Primatology 20*: 67–81.

Wilson, M. E., T. P. Gordon, and D. Chikazawa. 1982. Female Mating Relationships in Rhesus Monkeys. *American Journal of Primatology 2*: 21–27.

Wolfe, L. D. 1984. Japanese Macaque Female Sexual Behavior: A Comparison of Arashiyama East and West. In *Female Primates: Studies by Women Primatologists*, ed. M. F. Small, 141–157. New York: Liss.

Wolfe, L. D. 1986. Sexual Strategies of Female Japanese Macaques (*Macaca fuscata*). *Human Evolution 1*: 267–275.

Wolfheim, J. H. 1983. *Primates of the World: Distribution, Abundance, and Conservation.* Seattle: University of Washington Press.

Woolley-Barker, T. 1998. Genetic Structure Reflects Social Organization in Hybrid Hamadryas and Anubis Baboons. *American Journal of Physical Anthropology Supplement 26*: 235.

Woolley-Barker, T. 1999. Social Organization and Genetic Structure in a Baboon Hybrid Zone. PhD dissertation, New York University.

Wrangham, R. W. 1979a. On the Evolution of Ape Social Systems. *Social Science Information 18*: 335–368.

Wrangham, R. W. 1979b. Sex Differences in Chimpanzee Dispersion. In *The Great Apes*, ed. D. A. Hamburg and E. R. McCown, 481–489. Menlo Park; CA: Benjamin/Cummings.

Wrangham, R. W. 1980. An Ecological Model of Female-Bonded Primate Groups. *Behaviour 75*: 262–300.

Wrangham, R. W. 1982. Mutualism, Kinship and Social Evolution. In *Current Problems in Sociobiology*, ed. K. C. S. Group, 269–289. Cambridge: Cambridge University Press.

Wrangham, R. W. 1987. The Significance of African Apes for Reconstructing Human Social Evolution. In *The Evolution of Human Behavior: Primate Models*, ed. W. G. Kinzey, 51–71. Albany: State University of New York Press.

Yalden, D. W., M. J. Largen, D. Kock, and J. C. Hillman. 1996. Catalogue of the Mammals of Ethiopia and Eritrea. 7. Revised Checklist, Zoogeography and Conservation. *Tropical Zoology 9*: 73–164.

Zaragoza, F., and F. Colmenares. 1997. Reconciliation and Consolation in Hamadryas Baboons, *Papio hamadryas. Advances in Ethology 32*: 158.

Zaragoza, F., F. Colmenares, M. V. Hernández-Lloreda, and C. Lamarque. 1996. Grooming, Aggression, Cohesion, and Time Budgets in Harems of Hamadryas Baboons in Captivity. In *XVIth Congress of the International Primatological Society & XIXth Conference of the American Society of Primatologists*, Madison, WI.

Ziegler, T. E., A. Savage, G. Scheffler, and C. T. Snowdon. 1987. The Endocrinology of Puberty and Reproductive Functioning in Female Cotton-Top Tamarins *(Saguinus oedipus)* under Varying Social Conditions. *Biology of Reproduction 37*: 618–627.

Zinner, D. 1997. Male Take-overs and Sexual Swellings in Hamadryas Baboons (*Papio hamadryas*). *Primate Report Special Issue 48–2*: 41.

Zinner, D. 1998. Male Take-overs and Sexual Swellings in Hamadryas Baboons (*Papio hamadryas*). *Folia Primatologica 69*: 240.

Zinner, D., and T. Deschner. 2000. Sexual Swellings in Female Hamadryas Baboons after Male Take-Overs: "Deceptive" Swellings as a Possible Female Counter-Strategy Against Infanticide. *American Journal of Primatology 52*: 157–168.

Zinner, D., W. Kaumanns, and B. Rohrhuber. 1993. Infant Mortality in Captive Hamadryas Baboons (*Papio hamadryas*). *Primate Report 36*: 97–113.

Zinner, D., and F. Peláez. 1999. Verreaux's Eagles (*Aquila verreauxi*) as Potential Predators of Hamadryas Baboons (*Papio hamadryas hamadryas*) in Eritrea. *American Journal of Primatology 47*: 61–66.

Zinner, D., F. Peláez, and F. Torkler. 2001a. Distribution and Habitat Associations of Baboons (*Papio hamadryas*) in Central Eritrea. *International Journal of Primatology 22*: 397–413.

Zinner, D., F. Peláez, and F. Torkler. 2001b. Group Composition and Adult Sex-Ratio of Hamadryas Baboons (*Papio hamadryas hamadryas*) in Central Eritrea. *International Journal of Primatology 22*: 415–430.

Zinner, D., M. H. Schwibbe, and W. Kaumanns. 1994. Cycle Synchrony and Probability of Conception in Female Hamadryas Baboons *Papio hamadryas. Behavioral Ecology and Sociobiology 35*: 175–183.

Zuckerman, S. 1932. *The Social Life of Monkeys and Apes.* London: Routledge & Kegan Paul.

Zuckerman, S., and A. S. Parkes. 1930. The Oestrous Cycle of the Hamadryas Baboon. *Journal of Physiology 69*: xxxi.

Zuckerman, S., and A. S. Parkes. 1939. Observations on Secondary Sexual Characters in Monkeys. *Journal of Endocrinology 1*: 430–439.

Index